COACHING & CONTROL

Controlling Your Program, Your Team, and Your Opponents

William E. Warren

D0209838

PRENTICE HALL
Englewood Cliffs, New Jersey 07632

Library of Congress Cataloging-in-Publication Data

Warren, William E.
    Coaching & control : controlling your program, your team, and your
    opponents / William Warren.
        p.   cm.
    Includes bibliographical references and index.
    ISBN 0–13–576232–4 (case). — ISBN 0–13–576224–3 (paper)
    1. Coaching (Athletics)   I. Title.
    GV711.W335   1997
    796'.07'7—dc21   96–45361
                                                                                              CIP

Printed in the United States of America

10 9 8 7 6 5 4 3 2 1

ISBN 0-13-576232-4 (c)   ISBN 0-13-576224-3 (p)

ATTENTION: CORPORATIONS AND SCHOOLS

Prentice Hall books are available at quantity discounts with bulk purchase for educational, business, or sales promotional use. For information, please write to: Prentice Hall Career & Personal Development Special Sales, 113 Sylvan Avenue, Englewood Cliffs, NJ 07632. Please supply: title of book, ISBN number, quantity, how the book will be used, date needed.

PRENTICE HALL
Career & Personal Development
Englewood Cliffs, NJ 07632
A Simon & Schuster Company

On the World Wide Web at http://www.phdirect.com

Prentice Hall International (UK) Limited, *London*
Prentice Hall of Australia Pty. Limited, *Sydney*
Prentice Hall Canada, Inc., *Toronto*
Prentice Hall Hispanoamericana, S.A., *Mexico*
Prentice Hall of India Private Limited, *New Delhi*
Prentice Hall of Japan, Inc., *Tokyo*
Simon & Schuster Asia Pte. Ltd., *Singapore*
Editora Prentice Hall do Brasil, Ltda., *Rio de Janeiro*

DEDICATION

For Kristen Bell, whose dedication, commitment, and hard work in the classroom as well as on the court and playing field epitomize what the term *student-athlete* is supposed to mean;

and

For Beckie Bell, the newest member of the family.

ACKNOWLEDGMENTS

As a young coach entering the profession, I learned by trial-and-error, by watching the way other coaches handled their teams, by attending coaching clinics, and by reading what other coaches have written about the sports I was coaching. I've never stopped reading, listening, or observing. In that respect I have stood, as Sir Isaac Newton put it, "on the shoulders of giants," other coaches who, in ways large and small, showed me how it's done.

Mike Koehler is one such coach. I've reviewed Mike's books for Simon & Schuster and he's reviewed mine; his notion of "the Tyranny of Talent," cited in Chapter 3, is but one of the many valuable and thought-provoking insights I've gleaned from his comments over the years.

As for the players I've coached—well, the memories will last a lifetime, but what I appreciate most is that they allowed me to love them. And I have, and always will, even if time tends to blur some of the names along the periphery. Every roller-coaster season has been unforgettable in its own way; I hope they—my players—have enjoyed the rides as much as I have.

Two people at Simon & Schuster merit a special thanks: Win Huppuch, whose support and assistance have gone far beyond the requirements of his position as Vice President/Publisher; and Connie Kallback, Editor, from whom I learned that you don't have to dread calls from your editor. If winning games were as easy as working with those two wonderful people has been, I'd be the winningest coach on the planet. As it is, I must content myself with having been the most fortunate.

Of course, there is my wife Louise, who, for 25 years now, has made it possible for me to pursue my dual goals of coaching and writing. Her loving influence on the players I've coached has been powerful, positive, and lasting, reaching far beyond the boundaries of the court, playing field, and locker room. Every married coach should be as lucky as I have been.

I love you, babe.

Finally: no writer can be successful without readers. I feel very deeply my sense of responsibility to you, the reader, to make my writing informative, entertaining, and easy to read and understand. None of us has time to waste. In each of the ten coaching books I've written, I've tried to tell the reader, *this* is what you need to know about this subject to be successful in your coaching—the sort of things I needed to know but couldn't always find when I was young and my coaching experience was a book of blank pages.

At any rate, I want to express my heartfelt gratitude to everyone who has purchased this book or any of the others I've written. Your interest in my book(s) means more to me than I can possibly express. I hope this book helps you in your coaching, and that you enjoy good health, happiness, and success in your own roller-coaster rides along the way.

—Bill Warren
July 19, 1996

ABOUT THE AUTHOR

Dr. William Warren has written or co-authored ten coaching books, including two basketball books with Jerry Tarkanian and one with Bob Cousy and Frank Power. His other books include *Coaching and Motivation* (1983), *Coaching and Winning* (1988), and *Basketball Coach's Survival Guide* (1994), the latter co-authored with Larry Chapman.

Although the bulk of his coaching experience over more than two decades has been in basketball, Dr. Warren has also coached football, baseball, tennis, golf, and track and field at levels ranging from junior high school through college. In 1977, he was named Georgia's High School Coach of the Year in girls' track. He presently lives in Griffin, Georgia, with his wife Louise.

I claim not to have controlled events,
but confess plainly that events have controlled me.

—Abraham Lincoln,
referring in a letter (April 4, 1864)
to his role in the Civil War

The controlling intelligence understands its own nature,
and what it does, and whereon it works.

—Marcus Aurelius,
Meditations VI, 5

CONTENTS

3 "SPECIAL" EFFECTS: MAKING YOUR TEAM ALL THAT IT CAN AND SHOULD BE / 33

4 Effective Teaching and Practicing / 61

Part Two
THE NATURE OF CONTROL / 89

5 Competitiveness and Control / 91

6 INDIVIDUAL MODES OF CONTROL / 105

PART THREE
CONTROLLING OPPONENTS / 125

7 BLENDING PHILOSOPHY AND STYLE / 127

8 UNDERSTANDING STYLES OF PLAY / 147

10 THE UNCONTROLLABLES / 205

INTRODUCTION

During his presidency, Richard Nixon once was asked by a reporter why anyone would possibly want to become President of the United States. It is, after all, the second most difficult, demanding and pressure-filled job in the world (behind coaching football at Notre Dame).

"It's power," Mr. Nixon replied in a rare moment of candor with the press. It's the power to make decisions at the highest level—decisions that affect billions of lives around the globe. Other jobs pay more, he explained, but none carries the awesome responsibilities and power of the presidency. Then, almost as an afterthought, he added: "People who don't understand power will never have it."

Coaches don't want power; at least, the ones who care about the players they coach aren't power-hungry. What coaches want is *control*—control over the many variables that affect their on-the-job performance.

To paraphrase the late Mr. Nixon, *Coaches who don't understand control seldom have it—or if they* do *have it, they seldom use it effectively.* That's what this book is all about: understanding control and using it to achieve your goals in coaching.

Part One, "The Four Phases of Program Building," considers ways to promote the healthy growth and development of your program.

Chapter 1 explores ways of building a strong feeder system that prepares young athletes for the next level of competition they will face. In this chapter, we'll take a look at possibly the finest high school football feeder system ever devised, and also at a variety of approaches that have worked in other situations and other sports. Some of them relate to the coach's working within (or building on) an existing framework; others describe the process of starting from scratch where no feeder system currently exists. All of them emphasize the importance of getting youngsters involved in your sport early and striving to ensure that they are taught what they need to know by the time they get to you.

You may or may not have to do most of the work yourself (and let's hope that you don't), depending on your situation and the backing you get from the school board and community. Either way, though, one fact is inescapable: Without a viable feeder program to continually restock your teams with young athletes, your program will always be in flux and you'll always be more or less in a state of rebuilding from one year to the next.

Chapter 2 deals with recruiting—not from the standpoint of dealing with college coaches, but as a far more basic concern: identifying prospects for your athletic teams and persuading them to attend your team tryouts.

What used to be a simple, cut-and-dried process—putting up a sign or two announcing the tryout dates and waiting for the eager hordes of candidates to show up on the first day of preseason practice—is, alas, a thing of the past in many (if not most) situations. With an almost infinite variety of influences (and some of them highly negative) vying for young people's time and attention nowadays, we coaches cannot afford to sit back idly and wait for kids to come to us. That may be the macho way to do it, but the fact is, *we're not the only ones recruiting our schools' young athletes.* Drug dealers and street gangs are doing it, too, and in many cases they're doing a better job of it than we are.

We have a wonderful product to sell to our youngsters, but we should not assume that they understand the benefits of being a part of our team without being told. Unless we sell them on the idea that team membership will make a significant—and positive—difference in their lives, we may lose the battle to other capable salespeople who contend that happiness and fulfillment are to be found in the point of a needle or the barrel of a gun.

Chapter 2 offers suggestions on how to find, approach, and attract into your program the young people in your school who possess athletic potential but are not currently involved in your sport. It also offers an analysis of the desirable physical and mental qualities to look for in the youngsters who come out for your team.

Chapter 3 is concerned with finding ways to establish and maintain a team environment in which players and coaches feel a deep sense of commitment and responsibility to each other. Such an environment will tend to attract—and keep—young people who need the discipline, direction, security, sense of purpose, and shared commitment to something higher than themselves that team membership affords.

Once upon a time, coaches could get away with treating their players impersonally, but society has changed (and is continuing to change rapidly) in ways that directly affect our coaching. Today, the coach who does not relate to, and communicate with, his or her players on a personal as well as a professional level is at a severe handicap in attracting and retaining young athletes.

I've always believed that the surest path to success in coaching is to meet the needs of the players we coach. To do so, it is important not only to understand the nature of those needs within the context of today's society, but also to build a family-like atmosphere that will fill whatever voids exist in our players' lives.

An environment of shared concern for one another and team goals doesn't arise by itself, however. It must be fostered and nurtured on a daily basis with the care a gardener lavishes upon the flowering plants in a greenhouse. In coaching or gardening, the results are likely to exceed our fondest hopes and greatest expectations.

Teaching is the heart and soul of effective coaching. Because practice time is both limited and valuable, it must be used wisely if the team's needs are to be met. The keys to effective time management are *planning* and *preparation*: knowing what you hope to accomplish and having a plan to do it. Chapter 4 deals with the nuts and bolts of daily coaching, namely, teaching and practice organization. Besides offering hints for effective teaching and suggesting that prioritizing your needs can help to streamline your practice organization, Chapter 4 deals with such topics as: preparing daily and weekly practice schedules; using breakdown drills to simplify your teaching of team patterns and plays; finding a proper balance between drills and scrimmaging; using self-motivating drills and controlled scrimmaging; and keeping daily practices fresh. Considerable space is also devoted to the all-important goal of teaching players to concentrate.

In Part Two, "The Nature of Control," team quality and individual skills are examined relative to what a given team may or may not be able to do in terms of controlling opponents.

Chapter 5 defines *competitiveness* in terms of a team's relative willingness to work hard at any given stage of a game—or a season, for that matter—and *control* as the team's ability to find ways to minimize the effects of opponents' strengths. It also describes five levels of team quality that will be used throughout Parts Two and Three of this book as a basis for comparing teams. Such a guide may prove useful in three ways: (a) in evaluating your team's present developmental level, (b) in determining what it will take for your team to move up to the next level of competition, and (c) in considering ways in which opponents are likely to try to control your team and what you may or may not be able to do to stop them.

Chapter 6 examines the individual qualities and team characteristics that affect the selection of offensive and defensive playing styles: speed and quickness, size (height and weight), athleticism, fundamental soundness, experienced or veteran players, and depth. Each trait is analyzed in terms of its relative merits as a contributing factor in controlling opponents.

Part Three, "Controlling Opponents," analyzes the effective use of playing styles, strategies, and tactics in controlling opponents.

Chapter 7 pursues a theme from my earlier book *Coaching and Winning*[1], namely, that *every coach must develop a plan for success based on his or her vision of how the game should be played and coached*. That plan—your coaching philosophy—provides consistency in your efforts to blend what you know about the game with what your players can do, in building a team offense or defense. The brief, self-administered quiz in Chapter 7 will help to identify your basic philosophy regarding playing styles.

Chapter 8 explores the styles of play common to all team sports: *aggressive* styles that force the action, and *conservative* styles that bide their time and wait for favorable opportunities to develop. Two other contrasting playing styles noted in Chapter 8 apply to some sports more than to others: power vs. finesse. Power is the most direct route to controlling opponents. In offensive football, for example, power is based on the notion that *my* blockers can beat *your* defenders, whether by blowing them off the line of scrimmage or by outexecuting them. Finesse approaches, on the other hand, rely on misdirection, spread formations, traps, option plays, or other tactics designed to transform opponents' strengths into weaknesses.

In game situations, the ultimate goals of control are for coaches to control their players' performances, and for their players to

---

[1] Englewood Cliffs, N.J.: Prentice Hall, 1988.

control the opponents, whether individually or as a team and whether throughout entire games or during those portions of games in which victory and defeat are on the line. The coach's role in that process is threefold: to develop in the players the individual and team skills that are necessary to win games; to motivate players toward optimal performances in every phase of the game; and to provide offensive and defensive styles of play, patterns, and strategies that maximize the team's chances of winning or remaining competitive.

Chapter 9 examines strategies relating to the effective use of playing styles that teams of varying ability might employ to control their opponents. The five levels of team quality described in Chapter 5 serve as the basis for comparisons.

The more variables that coaches can control, the greater their chances of winning games. The precise nature of those variables depends largely on what the coach is able to control, and to a lesser extent on what he or she wants to control. Some coaches are so control-oriented that, if they could find a way to do so, they would monitor and control their players' heartbeats and respiration rates. Chapter 10 focuses on the "uncontrollables" of coaching—luck, the weather, playing conditions and surfaces, the fans, and referees—and describes ways in which coaches attempt to control, influence, or at least cope with those factors in a rational manner. As one south Georgia football coach put it, "Maybe I cain't control 'em (the referees), but that don't mean I ain't gonna try!"

> *In running the bases, it's always wise to touch*
> *first base before heading for second.*

> —Fred Rossi, Griffin, GA
> (veteran tee league baseball coach)

MR. MURPHY AND HIS LAW[2]

Having been associated with sports, you undoubtedly are familiar with Murphy's Law: *"Whatever* can *go wrong,* will *go wrong."* Sooner or

---

[2] Although Murphy's gender has never been established beyond a reasonable doubt, women readers will readily agree that only a man could produce the sort of universal misery that Murphy's unscheduled visits bring.

later, Murphy's Law catches up with each of us—usually when we least expect it. Is there a rational explanation for why things go wrong so often for so many of us? And if so, is there anything we can do to minimize the damages incurred by Murphy's Law? The answer to both questions is *yes*—within limits, of course, since Murphy is the only player who always comes to the game ready to play.

THE 85 PERCENT THEORY

Part of the reason things go wrong is attributable to downright bad luck, but luck is, I think, grossly overrated as a factor in winning or losing games.

Like you, I've experienced my share of good luck and bad over the years. While I might prefer to attribute the bad luck my teams have suffered to the aforementioned Mr. Murphy and the good luck to my splendid coaching, I know that's not the case. Teams win games by doing things right or outplaying their opponents; they lose games by doing things wrong or being outplayed. Probably no more than 15 percent of the games played at any level, and in any sport, are decided by luck, fate, bad karma, or whatever you prefer to call it. Realization of this "fact"—which, if it's wrong, isn't far off the mark—led me to formulate what I call "The 85 Percent Theory," namely, that *85 percent of practically everything is b.s.* Think about it.

In almost any human endeavor you care to name, the vast majority of people involved aren't doing nearly as good a job as they could be doing (or think they're doing). Most of the movies we watch and the books we read aren't worth the time and money we invest in them. (With television, the true figure is closer to 100 percent.) Most of the products we buy with lifetime guarantees fall apart within a year or so, and most of those guarantees aren't worth the recycled paper they're written on.

In any corporation or business you want to name (and in most committee projects or group endeavors), at least 85 percent of the work is done by about 15 percent of the workers. Most of the coaches you know probably could be doing more than they currently are doing to improve their teams, and most of their players are underachievers in one respect or another.

If you accept my ballpark 85 percent b.s. figure as accurate—and you should, since it's probably a lot closer to the truth than the

1990 U.S. Census was—several notable points begin to emerge regarding winning and program building:

■ If only 15 percent of all coaches and teams are working to their full potential, your goal should be for you and your players to be part of that 15 percent.

■ If a given school produces better teams and has a better feeder system than yours, catching them will be a full-time, long-term process that will tax your coaching skills to the limit.

■ If a team has better players than yours, you won't outplay them at what they do best. Your only real hope of defeating them is to be better prepared than they are. From a coaching standpoint, this means proper attention to conditioning, carefully defining roles, and motivating players to meet the challenge that lies ahead.

CONTROL THROUGH PREPARATION

What The 85 Percent Theory really says is that, in any profession, group, or organization, most of the participants are underachievers. They underachieve, not because they are unlucky or because they lack the potential to succeed, but because they are unwilling to pay the price for success.

Some underachieving coaches are lazy; they prefer to avoid such time-consuming tasks as studying their sport, teaching skills, scouting opponents, and preparing daily practice schedules or game plans. Sometimes they regard themselves as helpless victims of cruel fate when their teams are mediocre or weak. Like fickle fans, they prefer to be associated with Good, Very Good, or Great teams; they find it difficult to relate to players who lack the skills to compete on a par with other, better teams and players. Some underachievers jealously guard their "free" time away from daily practice and games, reserving it for outside interests such as hunting, fishing, or golf; such coaches tend to regard coaching as a pastime that brings in extra income.

In contrast to the above, consider the coaching of "The General," Indiana's Bobby Knight. Although Knight's intensity, style, and outspoken manner have made him an easy target for his detractors, he is regarded among his peers as one of the finest basketball coaches ever to toss a chair. With three NCAA titles and an Olympic gold medal to his credit, there isn't much that he hasn't accomplished in his coaching career.

Coach Knight's game preparations are legendary; if I had to choose a coach to come in cold and prepare a basketball team for one game, I'd take Bobby Knight, give you whoever you want from the rest of the field, and neither of us would lose sleep over whether the job was being done right by either coach. He's that good.

Knight is an avid hunter and fisherman, too, but not to the extent of allowing those activities to detract from his professional preparations. His teams come out *ready to play* in every sense of the phrase; if you were to look up *overcoaching* in a sports dictionary, you'd probably find a photo of Bobby Knight beside the definition. He believes, as do all of the very best coaches in every sport, that *control* is the key to winning games: controlling your team, controlling your individual players, controlling opponents. The more you can control, the less likely you are to be controlled by others.

If all this reads like homage to Coach Knight—well, no, it isn't. It is, rather, an acknowledgment of his coaching skills and the thoroughness with which he approaches his job. You don't have to be—and shouldn't try to be—a Bobby Knight clone in your coaching; I'm sure that Knight would be the first to tell you that. (The second person to tell you not to coach like Knight probably would be your principal or athletic director.) What you *must* do is pay strict attention to detail in every facet of your coaching.

No amount of control or preparation is going to win every game every time, but undercoaching your team can and will lose games that should not have been lost.

THE ROOTS OF CONTROL: FIRST STEPS

It all starts with *you*, and with your dream of what you, your team, and your program can become through hard work, sacrifice, dedication, and determination. If you remain faithful to that dream, it will sustain you through hard times and lean years. It is the beacon that lights your way; you are its caretaker.

Eventually, your vision will be adopted and embraced by those around you. Until that point is reached, however, *you* are the team and the program. You don't say it that way to your players, of course, but it's *your* vision, and *your* short- and long-range goals, that shape and mold the destiny of your team and your program. Thus, it is important to take charge at the earliest possible moment. "Taking charge" means assuming full responsibility for everything that affects your team and your program.

Nominally, at least, the head coach is in charge of the team and the program; in reality, that's not always the case. In some cases, booster clubs wield far more influence on a program's direction or a head coach's longevity than their position merits. I also recall an instance in which a high school principal—an ex-football coach— ran off four head football coaches in four years because he was jealous of them. He was afraid that somewhere down the line they might be regarded as better coaches than he had been. He in effect sabotaged his school's football program so people would listen when he bragged about how good his teams were back when he was coaching.

That's why I think it's important to find out during pre-employment interviews exactly how much control you're likely to be granted regarding your team and your program. There are at least three areas where a coach needs control: (a) in building and maintaining a strong feeder program at lower levels to supply the varsity team with experienced athletes; (b) in monitoring players' academic status, behavior, and personal problems on a daily basis; and (c) in handling disciplinary problems. If those topics don't arise naturally during the interview, they should be brought up and discussed by you when the inevitable question arises, "Do you have any questions for *us*?"

Regarding point (a), a high level of program continuity is impossible without an effective feeder system. Building a strong feeder program where none existed previously requires commitment and support at the highest levels in the school system and community. If that commitment and support are missing, then maybe the job isn't quite as desirable as it might otherwise appear to be.

I've had it both ways, with good feeder programs and with none at all when I arrived at the school. I can tell you from personal experience that you don't want to spend the bulk of your professional life wondering where your next athlete who exhibits a detectable pulse is coming from. You *don't* want the school's physical education classes to be your only (or even main) source of players.

Regarding points (b) and (c), I think it's important to teach at the same school where you coach. It's not always possible, of course, but it *is* always desirable. I've talked with a number of coaches who teach at one school and coach at another; all of them feel strongly that the coach's presence is, or can be, a deterrent to player misconduct. As a baseball coach explained somewhat ruefully, "Just seeing me in the halls or on campus every day would be a constant reminder to the players that I was watching them."

A tennis coach said that being at another school all day prevented him from interceding in disciplinary problems involving his athletes. He cited an example in which the principal suspended three of his players for ten days before he even knew they had done anything wrong.

A basketball coach said that, in interviews for coaching vacancies, she always makes a point of discussing the school's disciplinary process.

> First, I carefully outline the behavioral expectations I set for my players. In the same way that I want my teams to outperform our opponents on the basketball court, I expect my players' conduct to be superior to that of other students in the school. If it's a principal or athletic director interviewing me, and it usually is, I tell them that, if I'm permitted to handle disciplinary problems involving my players, there won't *be* any problems as long as they're on my team. For my girls, it's a matter of will power and priorities; if they want to stay on the team, they'll stay out of trouble and make good grades. If they get into trouble, they'll take my punishment or they can quit the team.
>
> *Anyone* can discipline an unruly student; but if what we're after is *changed behavior, my* way is better than anyone else's for my players. It's severe enough to make them think twice before bending or breaking school rules, but it also carries the reward of continued team membership for taking the punishment and improving their conduct to the level I expect of them.
>
> Principals generally respect my desire to control my team in the manner I express. They should; if I can control my little corner of the world, it's one area within the school that they don't have

to worry about. And that should mean a lot, considering that the average high school principal is almost as overworked as the average coach is.

Of course, a few of them have expressed reservations about it. One principal said he'd like to do it my way, but if he did, he'd have to let the other coaches handle their own discipline, too, and he didn't trust some of his coaches. An athletic director told me that his hands were tied because his school system had written disciplinary guidelines to follow and a student-faculty disciplinary board to conduct hearings.

I have nothing against written policies and review boards; I just think *I* can do a better job than they can because my players and I have more to lose than they do.

At any rate, the coach said, she had turned down a couple of promising jobs because they didn't allow her the kind of freedom she felt she needed to conduct her program. "The pay was better, and both jobs were a step up in classification, bigger schools than where I was coaching at the time. But bigger isn't necessarily better, not when they expect you to conduct the orchestra with your hands tied behind your back."

In our age of easy and instant litigation, you're liable to stir up a hornet's nest of angry parents seeking lawyers if you attempt to supplant school authorities in handling your players' nonathletic disciplinary problems. You probably can't do it anyway in most cases, since, as the coach noted, many school and school systems have written guidelines and a specified chain of command for handling disciplinary problems. Still, that doesn't mean you cannot or should not be a part of the disciplinary process in situations involving your athletes. You, your program, and your athletes deserve that much, at least.

No two coaches are alike. Personal goals and coaching philosophies differ markedly from one coach to the next. One goal that shouldn't differ, however, is that of building the kind of program that every participant can be proud to be a part of. And *that* goal, at least, is within reach of each and every one of us, no matter where we're coaching or how formidable the task might appear to be. In team sports, pride comes from teaching players to do their best, and to accept their best as sufficient under the circumstances, whatever those circumstances might be.

PART ONE

THE FOUR PHASES
of
PROGRAM BUILDING

1

Building and Maintaining a Strong Feeder Program

There are two ways to build a team. Either you get better players,
or you get the players you've got to be better.

—Bum Phillips (Houston Oilers)

If there has ever been a "perfect" feeder program at the prep level, it might have been the one developed by Wright Bazemore at Valdosta (GA) High School during the 1950s. Coach Bazemore's Wildcat football teams won more than 300 games (including 7 of the school's 16 state championships), averaging an incredible 11 wins per season in the process, before he hung up his whistle in the late 1970s.

Bazemore's extraordinary success was due to many factors: the almost religious significance Valdostans attached to their sons' playing football for the Wildcats; the fact that VHS was the only high school in the county (in his early years at the school, anyway), and thus had a monopoly on the young athletes who came up through the county's massive recreation program; a military base nearby that provided tax monies to support the recreation program and a steady stream of young athletes for his football program; an annual influx of families moving to Valdosta from north Florida in order for their sons to play in the Wildcats' widely heralded football program; and, of course, Bazemore's coaching skills, which have long since become legendary in south Georgia.

It was not at all uncommon for Bazemore to suit out 125 players for home games. His domination of prep football in Georgia was

3

such that, during the mid-1960s, one of his teams had fifteen players named to the South squad for the annual Georgia North-South
All-Star high school football game.

At any rate, Bazemore's control of football in Lowndes County
was virtually absolute during that period. Not only the junior high
football teams, but *all of the football teams in the local rec leagues as well*,
ran the Wildcats' offenses and defenses. By the time a Valdosta
youngster was ready for varsity football, he was thoroughly familiar
with Bazemore's system, having played it since peewee league rec
football.

BUILDING FROM THE TOP DOWN

The Bible tells us, "All things work together for the good of them
that love the Lord"; in a similar fashion, all things worked together
for the good of them that loved Valdosta Wildcat football, Wright
Bazemore style. He built a feeder system the likes of which probably
have not been seen before or since, and certainly not in Georgia.

Not everyone can build such a system, or else coaches every-
where would already be doing so. Coach Bazemore's situation was,
as we've noted, unique in several respects. Most notably, the town
wanted a football powerhouse and was willing to back his efforts to
give them one. But if such a system were to be duplicated, the steps
in its formation most likely would be predictable.

It would start at the top, at the varsity level, with the head coach
assuming total control of his or her program. Ideally, that control
would extend downward to include having a say in the hiring and fir-
ing of coaches at all levels, from varsity through junior high or middle school. It would also include coordinating those programs to
ensure continuity at the various levels to produce athletes who are
ready for varsity ball when they reach that level. Realistically, however, it's not likely to happen until you've experienced the sort of success that gives you leverage that you can use to negotiate greater
overall athletic control within your school system. If you win enough
games, you can ask for the moon and they'll give it to you. (And if
they won't, you shouldn't have much trouble finding another coaching job where they *want* to support a winner.) At the very least,
though, you should try to extend your control downward to ensure
the highest possible quality within your feeder program.

WORKING WITHIN AN EXISTING FRAMEWORK

Even if you *don't* have control over what goes on at the lower levels of play, you may be able to strongly influence the coaches to adopt methods and techniques that are compatible with your program goals. The most obvious way is to develop positive personal and professional ties with the coaches in your feeder system.

Here are a few of the things you might do:

■ Host periodic informal get-togethers (e.g., backyard cookouts, meals at a local steak house or pizzeria) where coaches can discuss their problems, exchange ideas, and just get to know one another better. Include spouses whenever possible.

■ Send cards to coaches, their spouses, and their children on holidays, birthdays, illnesses, or other occasions.

■ Attend their home games and drop by their practices whenever possible. When you can't attend a game, call later and chat with the coach. Support is a two-way street. Your continuing interest in all of the teams in your feeder system shows players and coaches alike that what they're doing is important to you.

■ Get the coaches involved in your program. If you want their loyalty, ask for their help—and *use* it. Invite them to go scouting with you or an assistant coach, or even by themselves as the situation warrants. You can also ask them to scout your varsity team in preseason or early in the season, in order to get an idea of how opponents might regard your team. (Three *don'ts* here: 1. Don't expect them to pay their own expenses. 2. Don't ask them to do anything you wouldn't want to do [e.g., help you refinish your gym floor]. 3. Don't forget to thank them for what they do for you, *every time* they do it.)

■ If you operate a summer camp in your sport, use them as instructors (paid, of course). It's an excellent way to indoctrinate them in your methods and philosophy.

■ Invite them to be guests on your radio show, if you have one. Encourage local media to broaden coverage of teams and coaches in your feeder program.

■ Look for opportunities to compliment them for the fine job they're doing. Recognize them as honored guests at Booster Club meetings. Speak at their postseason award dinners, and invite them to your own. If they're important to you—and they *are,* unquestionably so—they should be made to *feel* important. Another way of doing this is to ask their advice, whether tactical or regarding a player of yours who came up through their program. Since by virtue of your position as varsity head coach you're the resident expert, your asking advice will reveal your high regard for their opinions or expertise.

■ Offer them full access to your personal coaching library and resources.

■ Hold a one-day, off-season clinic in your sport for all of the coaches in your feeder program. You can either conduct the entire affair yourself or invite the coaches to speak on topics of your or their choosing. At any rate, encourage them to share new ideas, techniques, and information with other coaches in the program.

STARTING FROM SCRATCH

In 1972, I took the job as varsity girls basketball coach at a small rural K–12 school that had no feeder program at all, unless you want to count B-team boys basketball. There were no junior high teams, and most of the parents in the area were farmers who weren't inclined to drive their children twelve miles to participate in the county's rec league basketball program. Some of the parents felt they were doing the school and their children a favor by letting them play varsity basketball. The school had no organized physical education classes at the elementary level; for many of the children, their first exposure to any sort of organized sports program came in seventh-grade p. e. class.

The school had only two coaches, the boys basketball coach and me. Both of us were beginning our first year at the school. There was no athletic director, and neither of us volunteered to serve in that capacity on an unpaid basis. It was our first—and biggest—mistake, since the position carries greater decision-making authority than head coaching does. Our varsity basketball coaching supplement was $750. Our athletic program consisted of varsity basketball and whatever else we wanted to coach on an unpaid basis, except football. (The school had no football field or equipment.)

During the first week of school, we had the high school students fill out questionnaires indicating what interscholastic sports they might want to participate in. Aside from basketball, baseball, football, and softball there wasn't sufficient interest in anything to warrant expanding the athletic program immediately, even if funds had been available. (None of the schools in our area played girls softball.) Three years later, when interest in girls basketball had grown somewhat, we added a girls track team.

For now, though, our main concern was creating a feeder program for the basketball teams. We established junior high and B-teams, and coached all of the teams ourselves. With only eight varsity players and eleven junior high players, players from both squads were on the B-team. All three teams used the same game plan, which made us the easiest teams in the world to scout. When you saw one of my teams play, you knew what all of them were going to do.

During the season, the junior high teams practiced one or two nights a week, on an alternating-week basis with the boys. My wife Louise, who had been a far more productive high school player than I ever was, served as my assistant coach, chief statistician, and team chaperon as well. Eight of my junior high players were sixth-graders. None of them knew the first thing about basketball; still, they were good kids and I reasoned that, if I could keep them in the program and add a few more recruits along the way, I'd have at least six more years' worth of players to fill the team rosters. At least 90 percent of our practice time was devoted to conditioning, and to teaching them the rules of the game and how to pass, shoot layups, pivot, play defense, and dribble without looking at the ball or bouncing it off their feet.

We also practiced all summer (you could do that sort of thing back then), the varsity teams on two nights a week and the junior high teams on two others. We opened the gym on weekends to anyone who wanted to come by and shoot around or play for an hour or two. We tried to organize an intramural basketball league on Saturday mornings, but there just weren't enough kids interested or able to come. In farming communities, daylight hours are for working, not for playing games.

Our varsity girls won 7 games that year, losing 14. It wasn't a season to brag about, except in comparison with the previous three years, when the varsity girls won 12 games and lost 57. At least we didn't have any players quit the team.

The junior high girls lost their first four games, and the B-team four of its first five games, before I got my first real break: I finally persuaded a seventh-grader, the sister of a freshman on our girls varsity, to come out for my junior high team. Her name was Clara Harden, and she was the kind of athlete every coach dreams of coaching. Clara was only 5′2″, but her vertical jump was 26″ and her quickness was unbelievable; two years later, as a freshman, Clara won the 100- and 220-yard dashes in the region and state track meets. Three years after that, as a captain of the girls basketball team, she averaged 27.3 ppg. with a single-game high of 63 points.

With Clara in the lineup, the junior high girls won their last three games to finish at 3–4. The B-team won six of its last nine games and wound up at 7–7, our only nonlosing team.

The boys varsity won five games that year; compared with their previous three-year total of six wins, however, it was a landmark season for them.

The following season was remarkable for both varsity teams. Partly as a result of judicious scheduling of weak nonregion opponents, the varsity girls went 25–2 (including a 22-game winning streak) and the boys posted a highly respectable 15–9 mark. Neither team was as good as its record indicated, but we didn't tell the kids that. We knew that, in order to build a winning attitude, you have to win more often than occasionally. A winning program would build confidence and attract new player candidates for our respective programs in ways that losing could never accomplish. More challenging schedules could be arranged later, after our players developed the sort of confidence that winning breeds.

I can't recall how the boys' B-team and junior high squad did that year, but on the girls' side Clara & Co. went 10–2 and 9–0, respectively. Our junior high girls held their opponents to 13 points a game defensively.

The boys' coach left after that year, and that program quickly slid downhill, with a revolving door of new coaches coming and going every year. Admittedly, it's neither easy nor fun to coach three teams at once; you have to be dedicated, desperate, or downright daffy to try it. But it's also true that *you have to do what's best for your program.* If there's no one to do it but you, your choices are to do it, ignore it, or go somewhere else, where the coaching is less demanding of your time, energy, and talents.

OVERCOMING THE HARDSHIPS

I've always believed that encountering and overcoming hardships is an important step in the education of every young coach. It teaches you that there are no superstars in coaching—just ordinary people who have committed themselves to the pursuit of excellence. It is that commitment—or the lack of it—that determines how successful a person will be in life's undertakings.

Unless you're a glutton for punishment, however, you don't want to spend your entire coaching career juggling three teams at a time. I coached at the school for six years, during which time our girls varsity basketball team won 100 games and lost 41, playing mostly larger schools that previously had used us as a breather between tougher opponents. Our girls track team won two region titles and one state championship, and they were runnerup in the state once. They were satisfying years in many respects, but when they were over, none of us had anything left to give to the team.

As difficult as turning around a losing program always is, it was easy in my case compared with the task of keeping the three team rosters filled. The school's small enrollment—ninety-eight students in grades 10–12—was an important factor, of course; still, the biggest problem we faced was its location twelve miles from the nearest town. We simply had no way of involving the elementary students in rec league play, or of introducing them to basketball before they reached the sixth grade. We taught p. e. six periods a day to students in grades 7–12, with no planning periods.

A varsity boys and girls coach in a neighboring county used roughly the same procedure as ours in extending his feeder system, although he coached only the two varsity teams. His assistant coaches handled the B-teams; the junior high teams were coached by two other coaches. All of the schools in his county were located within the city limits, and more than half of the students lived within walking distance of their school. As assistant principal at the high school, he asked and received permission from the board of education to let the county recreation department use the gym for basketball on Saturdays, and he persuaded the county commissioners to fund the program.

At the elementary level, he initiated a noncompetitive basketball skills program similar to the Tiger Tots program Dale Brown developed in Louisiana as LSU head coach, and the kids staged Globetrotter-like ballhandling demonstrations at halftimes of varsity games. He also staged peewee league minigames at other halftimes—in both cases, bringing not only the children *but their parents as well* to his varsity games.

In six years, my varsity girls beat every other girls basketball team in our region at least once—except his. (I hated him with a purple passion.) At the time, I could recite a thousand reasons why his teams were going to the state tournament every year while mine were staying at home: His school was twice as large as ours; he had inherited winning varsity programs in girls and boys basketball while mine had been a perennial doormat; his recreation program versus our inability to get one started; his comparatively smaller coaching load and reduced teaching load as assistant principal; and so forth. But beyond all the excuses, the truth was that he was doing the job he was hired to do—and he was doing it so well that, try as we might, we couldn't catch up with him. We made it to the state tournament in basketball exactly once in my six years at the school; his teams made it *four* times, three of them by beating us to get there.

(There was a payback of sorts for us, however: In girls track, one of his basketball players saw us at the region track meet one year and said, "We're gonna beat y'all like we beat you in basketball!" Later, she probably regretted having said it: we won every running event, finished second in two events and third in another, and scored 126 points; they were on the bus and heading home before the meet was over.)

DEVELOPING PROGRAM CONTINUITY

An athletic director said that he'd rather have a mediocre head coach for four years than four different good head coaches in the same time span. I asked him why he felt that way.

"Consistency breeds confidence," he said, "and change breeds confusion. The mediocre coach might not teach his kids as much, but at least he'll have them pointed in the same direction for four years. If they're decent athletes, they'll continue to develop because they know what's expected of them; and if they're good enough, they'll win in spite of the coach."

I knew what he meant. His county produced so many good athletes that, if you shook a tree, five or six gifted athletes would fall out. The varsity girls basketball team won eighteen or more games every year, despite the fact that its coach—who was also the head football coach—knew practically nothing about basketball and cared even less. The girls basketball job was part of the coaching supplement package offered to lure top prospects for the head coaching position in football.

I watched the coach in action on several occasions while I was scouting other basketball teams. He usually sat with his arms folded across his chest, seldom stirred except to signal timeouts, said little to the girls during timeouts—just busied himself with passing out towels and water. Sometimes they switched from 2-3 zone defense to man-to-man or vice versa, which indicated that he probably had said *something* during the timeouts. They didn't always win by blowouts, but they seldom lost games they should have won. I guess that means they were well coached, but you couldn't have proven it by me—or by their athletic director, either.

To return to the a.d.'s statement: *Consistency breeds confidence; change breeds confusion.* In my case, while coaching three teams at once had some rather obvious drawbacks, it also afforded me one major advantage—namely, that *every player on every level was learning what I wanted my players to learn.* Transition from one level to the next was smooth because all of the teams were focused in the same direction. They used the same drills in practice and, with minor modifications, the same offensive and defensive playing styles. The continuity afforded by such a unified approach reduced wasted time and speeded up the learning process. A seventh-grader watching a varsity game could see older and more accomplished players doing the same things that she was learning to do.

In its present context, *continuity* refers to consistency in what players are taught from one level to the next. Most coaches regard continuity as a major factor in determining a team's rate of progress. In football, even minor changes such as the different ways that coaches number the line gaps can create confusion. In diagramming basketball plays, some coaches use Os to denote offensive players and Xs for defensive players; other coaches reverse the procedure. While neither of those problems is insurmountable, they interrupt the learning process at least momentarily. When added to the other, larger problems that arise when players change coaches (e.g., differences in philosophy, work ethic, expectations, playing styles, etc.), they underscore the importance of making players' transitions from one level to another—and from one coach to another—as smooth as possible.

Coaching two teams (e.g., the varsity and B-team or jayvees) is a common practice, especially in basketball and in small schools. Four-year continuity is thus assured as long as the coach stays at the school.

Many schools, however, use different head coaches at each level; in such cases, continuity rests on the varsity head coach's ability to extend his or her program downward to lower levels of play. Mine was the hard way, by doing it by myself because there was no one else to do it; Valdosta High's Wright Bazemore did it by requiring all of the coaches in his feeder program to teach football the Wright way.

Not every coach can or must do it by himself or herself, and not every coach wields the kind of control that Coach Bazemore had over his feeder program—but there *is* a third way to do it, if the situation is right and your powers of persuasion are sufficient. It treads the middle ground between extending yourself too far (as I did), and failing to acquire absolute control over what is being taught or learned down the line in your feeder system; it is a multilevel approach.

A MULTILEVEL APPROACH TO PROGRAM BUILDING

A few years ago, a friend of mine was named varsity boys basketball coach at a Class AA high school in southeast Georgia. His report follows:

> It was a strange situation. Deep in the heart of football country, here was this school that never won more than two or three games a season in football. The only industry in the county was logging, and the area's per capita income ranked near the bottom of the state. Ninety-three percent of the students at the high school received free lunches. Maybe that's why the county recreation department offered basketball but not football; it cost less.

Whatever the reason, I felt that the situation was ideally suited for me. The people were dirt-poor, but every house you passed had a rickety old basketball goal somewhere in the yard. The area wasn't exactly a hotbed of basketball talent, but the varsity boys had made it to the region semifinals two years before I arrived. Usually, though, they won 10–12 games a year, and that seemed to satisfy everybody.

It wouldn't have satisfied me, though. My goal was to raise expectations beyond breaking even, and to take the program to the next level. I believed that I could do it because, first, there were no dominating basketball schools in our region, and second, I thought I could unify the boys basketball program at least from the junior high level up.

One of the first things I did after accepting the job was arrange a meeting in the spring with my new assistant varsity-jayvee coach and the junior high boys coach. At that meeting, I began by outlining my goals for our basketball program. A large part of my job, I explained, was to make their jobs as easy as possible.

"Why would you want to help me?" the junior high coach asked. "Do you think I need your help?" He had been at his school for five years. The jayvee-assistant coach was, like me, new to the job.

"Coaches always need help, and *I do* most of all," I told them. "Both of you are very important to me. I need your help, and I think I can help you, too. I want to build the best basketball program in the state. If I can help you, I'll actually be helping myself, since eventually I'll inherit the kids you're coaching now." That seemed to satisfy him.

To that end, I went on, I wanted to discuss the possibility of the three of us working cooperatively as a team to solve each other's problems. I asked if they were interested in talking about it, since it meant they would be doing *less* work, and not more, than they had been doing previously.

"Sounds good to me," the jayvee coach said. The junior high coach nodded. "Go on," he said. I hadn't won him over yet, but at least he was willing to listen.

"By working together," I told them, "I think we can streamline the planning process and save time and work for all of us." I proceeded to outline my plan. If they would adopt the same offensive and defensive styles of play that my varsity boys would be using next year, they could use my basketball playbook and daily practice schedules.

"You'll never have to prepare another practice schedule," I explained. "You'll have a detailed, minute-by-minute breakdown of all of the individual and team drills and activities you'll need, including teaching tips and troubleshooting hints, for every practice session from the beginning of preseason tryouts to the last day of the season. That alone should save you an enormous amount of time and energy over the course of the season.

"Best of all, though, because all of us will be doing the same things, we'll be familiar with the sorts of problems and concerns that each of the others will be facing. We'll be able to share resources and help one another in ways that we couldn't do as easily if we were all going our separate ways." We would get together during the summer to familiarize them with my system and the drills and activities associated with it—and to incorporate their own ideas and drills as well, where applicable. During the season, we would meet on weekends to discuss the upcoming week's activities and resolve any problems we were having.

They agreed to do it my way for a season on a trial basis, and it worked splendidly. We maintained close communicative ties throughout the season, even to the extent of occasionally swapping teams for daily practices and subbing for one another during bouts of illness. It gave the jayvee coach and me a chance to get to know the young athletes we would be coaching later, and vice versa.

The junior high coach, whose school was on the other side of town from the high school, seemed to enjoy the experience immensely. He scouted two or three varsity opponents for me, and I helped him to raise money for summer camp for his players. The three of us put on a half-day clinic for the rec league coaches one Saturday. At our awards banquet, I presented both coaches with handsome engraved plaques for their outstanding contributions to our varsity basketball program. Later, the junior high coach told the jayvee coach that it was the first time he had ever been made to feel that what he was doing was important to anyone besides himself and his players.

Unity makes strength, and since we must be strong, we must also be one.
—Friedrich von Baden

The key to the success of such an undertaking lies, first and foremost, in its presentation. In the previous example, the coach might have simply called the other coaches in, tossed a couple of playbooks on the desk, and said, "Here's what I want you to do this season." If he had done that, they probably would have rejected his proposal—and *him,* as well—before he ever got around to explaining it in detail. By emphasizing *teamwork, helping one another,* and *working together,* he was using the same approach with them that all coaches use with their teams and players—and for the very same reasons. Acknowledging the importance of the coaches' contributions and treating them as equals made it easy for him to ask for their help, not as a personal favor or obligation on their part but as a way of making all of their jobs easier and less time-consuming.

The words "I need your help" are powerfully attractive; they tell the listener that what he or she is capable of contributing is important; they also imply that, by working together, we can accomplish more than either of us could accomplish by working separately.

While "I want to help you" is attractive, it may be met with suspicion or hostility from coaches who either think they don't need help or question the value of the kind of help you can give them. In either case, your salesmanship must include solid evidence that your assistance will in fact make things easier for them, and your assurances that it will be there when they need it.

MAKING YOUR APPROACH WORK FOR YOU

A multilevel approach to program building requires planning, preparation, and cooperation. As Joe Namath sagely observed, "Nobody wants to follow somebody who doesn't know where he's going." You must believe that your particular playing style is superior to that of others in terms of your own coaching philosophy, and you must understand it well enough to teach it to the coaches who will be using it. Your style of play must be flexible enough to permit such adaptations as might be necessary to accommodate various team compositions, or else you'll have to change playing styles every time you lose key players to graduation, injury, and so forth. That won't do when other coaches and teams are following your lead and using your system.

It isn't absolutely necessary to provide playbooks or practice schedules for coaches at other levels in your program. In fact, most coaches probably would consider it unwise to do so, at least, in the case of playbooks that might eventually turn up in the hands of opposing coaches. (There's a trade-off here, though: When your program reaches a certain level of success based in part on a given playing style, opponents will know what you're going to do most of the time anyway, but most of them won't be able to stop it. When Vince Lombardi was coaching football at Green Bay, his famous sweep play was so predictable that an opposing linebacker once began shouting "Sweep! Sweep!" as the Packers lined up to run the play. "Yeah, it's a sweep," Bart Starr told him with a grin and a wink, "but you don't know which *way* we're gonna run it!")

What *is* necessary is your willingness to offer your full support for the coaches in your feeder program, including whatever assistance is necessary for them to master your system. If you want their trust, the best way to earn it is to keep your promises by working long and hard to make their jobs as easy as possible. If you want their loyalty, let the world know that *they* are the ones responsible for whatever success your program achieves. According to Gene Stallings (University of Alabama), "One of the greatest things Coach Bryant used to do was *pass along the credit.*"

Beyond that, in your dealings with other coaches at your school and others in your feeder system, you should constantly promote the development of multisport athletes. Just as a well-rounded education produces well-rounded individuals, multisport athletes gain a broader and more realistic perspective of their role in the scheme of things than those whose vision is limited to one sport. More important, year-round participation in a variety of sports keeps young athletes under constant coaching supervision—helping to steer them away from the many negative influences around them.

Not every one-sport athlete turns to drugs, gangs, or crime during the off-season, of course, and not every multisport athlete is immune to those same temptations. It is far easier, however, for athletes to avoid such temptations—and easier for their coaches to monitor and influence their behavior away from the court or playing field in a positive, ongoing manner—when they are involved in team practices and activities throughout the school year.

2

RECRUITING: GETTING THE PLAYERS YOU NEED

No athletic program can ever be better than its recruiting.

—Frank Broyles (Univ. of Arkansas)

While recruiting usually is associated with collegiate athletics, it is also true that every coach functions at one time or another as a recruiter.

It wasn't always that way, though. In 1965, I announced the date for basketball practice to begin, put up a few signs in the halls, and fifty boys showed up for the first day of tryouts. One year, eighty-five boys tried out for my basketball team.

Times have changed; even in successful athletic programs where winning traditions exist, the day is largely past when coaches can afford to sit back and wait for athletes to come to them. If you don't actively recruit the kids in your school who possess athletic potential, you're likely to find your teams dwindling in size year by year, especially in sports like football, where you need a lot of players. To recruit effectively nowadays, it's important to understand how the times have changed, and how those changes have affected the young people we coach.

The first major societal factor to affect sports participation negatively was television. Whereas formerly children went outside to play, starting in the late 1950s television quickly became the nation's babysitter (with emphasis on the *sitting*). As early as 1959, president-elect John Kennedy warned us that we were becoming lazy Americans, a nation of spectators rather than doers. Nowadays, it's computerized video games as well as television, but the effect is the same: youngsters finding enjoyment sitting in front of a screen for hours at a time.

Then, in the 1960s, a second and even more far-reaching, negative influence arose: the advent of the drug revolution–free love era,[1] both of whose advocates urged young people, "*Do whatever makes you feel good.*" Apart from the all-too-familiar horrors associated with drug abuse, the attitude that one is responsible only to oneself for one's actions is diametrically opposed to what team sport is all about. Drug abuse is essentially a selfish act, since the user isn't taking drugs to make someone else feel good. For teens who are into the drug scene, the choice between sitting around stoned or working to the brink of physical exhaustion at daily practice isn't really a choice at all.

Those wonderful sixties also ushered in three other negative influences on young people, namely, the decline of religion, patriotism, and the traditional family. Although religion and patriotism emphasize values that are common to team sports, such as dedication, sacrifice, and commitment to higher values than oneself, it is the changes in the traditional family that have had the most immediate negative impact on team sports. Latchkey children in families in which both parents work simply don't get the supervision they need while growing up; often, they don't get the kind of quality time with their parents that they need. And with single-parent families becoming the rule rather than the exception, youngsters are often deprived of the kind of role models, guidance, and sense of family that could provide structure and security in their lives. In many cases, they turn to the streets and gangs to fill the void.

The previous paragraphs illustrate a curious paradox; *coaching is both easier and more difficult than it has ever been before.* It's more difficult because, as we've seen, there are a vast number of influences vying for the time and attention of young people today, and many of those influences are negative. It's easier because now, more than ever before, the values we as coaches believe in and stand for are precisely the values that young people need. We are ideally suited to meet those needs; in many cases, we spend far more quality time with our players than their parent(s) do.

---

[1] A national survey recently found that high school girls who participate in team sports are less likely to use drugs or get pregnant than girls who do not participate in team sports. But there's not a girls *or* boys coach between here and Bangkok who didn't know that—perhaps because these youngsters are *already* more committed to hard work and their own well-being.

Sports are among the few remaining strongholds where such traditional values as dedication, sacrifice, and commitment to excellence and team goals are upheld with any real vigor. Youngsters, however, don't always know that when they come to us. We are making a grave mistake any time we automatically assume that today's young people respect those values or associate them with athletic participation. Even those we are coaching now must be reminded constantly that individual excellence and commitment to team goals are worth pursuing.

RECRUITING PRINCIPLES

1. BE YOURSELF

Recruiting is salesmanship. As University of Georgia men's basketball coach Tubby Smith has pointed out, the first thing a recruiter is selling is *himself* or *herself*[2]. Program is important, of course—it's the most important thing, in fact—but it's also important to remember that *the coach is the most vocal and visible link to the team and the program.* While it's true that, in Tommy Prothro's words, "The coach is the team and the team is the coach. You reflect each other," it's also true that, in the prospect's eyes, the coach *is* the team. If a coach falls short in the prospect's estimation, neither the program nor anything else is likely to save the day.

Since initially, at least, you're promoting yourself and the values you support, it follows that the only person you're capable of portraying convincingly is yourself. As Charlie McLendon put it, "The worst mistake a coach can make is not being himself." Young people have what horror writer Stephen King has described as a "built-in b.s. detector" that sees through falseness and pretense with unerring accuracy. You may worship the water that Joe Paterno or Pat Summitt walks on, but if you try to emulate them in your coaching or your recruiting you'll wind up resembling neither him, her, nor yourself. That's why Darrell Royal urged coaches never to try to fool a player: "You can't kid a kid."

---

[2] "The coach is the focal point . . . If there's no tradition, he has to build some. If there's no interest, he has to create it." Mark Bradley, "Upbeat debut by Tubby Smith." *Atlanta Journal-Constitution* (December 22, 1995), p. E-1.

2. USE EVERY POSSIBLE SOURCE IN YOUR SEARCH FOR POTENTIAL ATHLETES FOR YOUR TEAM

If you're new to the school, a good starting point in looking for players is last season's scorebook, eligibility forms, stat sheets, team roster, or school yearbook. If you move into the school area during the summer, you can use that time to contact the returning players regarding such things as: whether they intend to play next season; what you might want them to do to get ready for next season; summer activities such as your weight training program or camp; and scheduled dates such as the beginning of fall practice. Ask them also to recommend candidates for the team who didn't play last year but might be persuaded to play next year. You could call or write the players regarding these sorts of things, of course, but for your first year, at least, a personal visit will tell both of you more about each other than a phone call or a letter would ever do. Additionally, personal visits may allow you to meet their parent(s) or guardian(s) and possibly enlist their assistance or support for your program (e.g., as concession workers or members of your booster club). If you *do* visit the players, a follow-up letter expressing your optimism and expectation of a challenging and rewarding season is a nice touch.

A second source for the names of potential candidates for your team is other coaches and physical education teachers. (If you're a high school coach, this includes the junior high coaches and physical education teachers.) Physical education teachers have all of the students in the school in class at least once—in Georgia, at least—so they generally have a good idea of who ought to be playing but isn't. That can be especially important to a coach who is a classroom teacher.

A warning, however: You can—and should—listen to everyone who may have suggestions, but don't prejudge anyone on the basis of what someone else says about him or her. I once warned an incoming basketball coach that a boy, a senior, had made the varsity squad three years in a row and quit the team all three times (under three different coaches). The coach allowed the boy to try out, he made the team—and promptly quit again two weeks later. In another instance, the same coach persuaded a boy to come out for his team, even though everyone in the school said the boy would never play for anyone. The boy ended up starting and averaging six points and eight rebounds per game. In both cases, the coach was right to find out for himself whether the recruitment was worth the effort. Sometimes it's just a matter of personality or timing.

Sometimes help comes from unexpected sources. A shop teacher once steered me to two candidates for my basketball team; only one of them was willing to try out, but he made the B-team as a sophomore and played two years of varsity ball. On another occasion, I tried my best—and failed—to persuade a girl to come out for basketball as a freshman. The following year, the principal, who was a close friend of her family, talked her into playing. She ended up being one of the most productive players I've ever coached. Sometimes it's a matter of finding the right key to unlock the door.

3. Don't Wait Until Just Before Tryouts Begin to Start Recruiting

The sooner you begin, the more opportunities you'll have to reach the people you need to reach.

4. Advertise Your Tryouts at Least Two Weeks in Advance

Local newspapers or other media may be willing to make spot announcements of upcoming tryout dates and other pertinent information. At school, preseason tryouts can be announced over the school's intercom and listed in the school newspaper. If you're not particularly artistic—or if you prefer to get other people involved in your program—you can ask the cheerleaders or the art department to prepare signs for display in the gym, lunchroom, and other prominent locations in the school.

Where there is no vision, the people perish.

—Proverbs 29:18

5. Share Your Dream

What do you say to the young person you're trying to recruit for your team? If introductions are necessary you start there, of course. The second step consists of asking if the youngster might be interested in coming out for the team. Anything but a definite "no" allows you to advance to the third stage, namely, describing the goals you have in mind for the team and expressing your desire for him or her to be a part of it.

The long-range aspect of your dream or vision need not be realistic, and it certainly should not be specific. It should be lofty enough to make participation seem inviting and worthwhile, but it should not tie you to specific accomplishments within a specific time frame. For example, there's nothing wrong with saying you want to build the best program in the state, as long as you don't overstate your case and promise to do it by the end of this season or next.

Your short-term vision—what you hope to accomplish this season—is the one you'll be held accountable for. Although no one but a fool would promise to win X number of games, you can, even with the weakest program, promise to have a team that the prospect will be proud to be a part of. You can promise that the team will accomplish great things, and that being a part of the team will have a lasting, positive effect on everyone involved. You can promise those things because, even in a losing situation, you can make team membership a source of pride for every player. You can, by promoting team unity, harmony, and respect, build a family atmosphere that will have a greater positive effect on your players than they could ever have imagined.

Another area where sharing your dream is important is that of persuading one-sport athletes to expand their athletic horizons by playing for your team. The gymnast who is absorbed in high-level competition; the golfer or tennis player who, like the gymnast, may be privately coached and prefers to specialize in that sport to the exclusion of others; and the basketball player who fears that a football injury will jeopardize his chances of earning a college basketball scholarship—all of these and other one-sport athletes with broad athletic potential may be difficult to sell on the idea of joining your team and playing your sport.

However slim your chances might be in such cases, your best bet is to describe, in very personal terms, your vision of what they and the team can become by working together. In the case of the basketball player, you'll have to convince him that the potential rewards are worth the risk involved; in other instances, you'll have to convince prospects that the time spent practicing your sport will justify the time spent away from their other, preferred sport.

Your success rate is likely to be low in all cases, but that's the nature of the selling process: persuading people to buy a product that they don't know they need until you remind them of it. As any successful real estate agent will tell you, you don't have to persuade every prospect to buy; all you need to join real estate's elite "Million Dollar Club" is sell *one* house a year for $1 million, not 50 houses at $20 thousand apiece.

6. BE POSITIVE, UPBEAT

One of Jesus' first acts in His ministry was to select twelve disciples. They were His first recruits. He told them, "Go into all the world and preach the gospel." That gospel message was, *There's a better day coming that will enrich your life if you're willing to become a part of it.* To me, *that's* the essence of recruiting: spreading the word that being a part of our team will make a huge, positive difference in the life of every player. If we don't believe that, we probably shouldn't have become coaches (or teachers, for that matter) in the first place. If we *do* believe it, we should avail ourselves of every opportunity to tell youngsters how special membership on our team really is (or will be)—not necessarily in terms of winning and losing games but rather in building strong relationships and bonds based on loyalty, respect, and commitment to common goals.

For many people—adults, teens, or children—life tends to be more or less true to the "one damned thing after another" description of it offered by one humorist. It doesn't have to be that way, though; participating in team sports is the ideal antidote to the sorts of problems that lead young people to experiment with drugs or join gangs.

Most superior teams exhibit a deep sense of shared obligation, responsibility, and commitment among the players, and that sense makes the team feel like a second family. You may not always be able to control your team's ability to win games, but you *can* control the way your players relate to one another. The process begins by finding players who will be loyal to you and their teammates, and players who want to be a part of something bigger than themselves.

7. THE FIRST YEAR IS ALWAYS THE HARDEST

After your first year at a school, your best recruiting will be done, not by you, but by the players you coach. The players who believe in you and appreciate what you're trying to accomplish will spread the word that there's something special about playing for your team.

They'll encourage their friends to try out for the team, and their younger brothers and sisters will form positive opinions of you that will make your recruiting even easier down the line.

Regarding the malcontents you may have inherited: The bad news is that you're pretty much stuck with them and their negativity, at least, for the present year, since you can't very well dismiss players from the team just because they don't like you. You probably won't change bad attitudes that were forged long before you arrived on the scene. That's why coaches far wiser than you or I devised the old coaching adage, *You graduate your problems.*[3] And that's why most coaches will tell you that it takes three to four years to turn around a losing program.

The good news is that the grumblers, gripers, backbiters, and ne'er-do-wells that you might have inherited won't be able to persuade their equally negative, bad-apple friends to come out for the team next year, because you're a source of discomfort and misery that their friends don't need or want. They'd rather gripe about you from the comfort of the stands.

If you're starting your first year in a school and sport where losing is expected and taken for granted, you're in for an extremely rough year.[4] Although coaching is always difficult, it is infinitely more so in losing situations in which the previous coach didn't lay a proper groundwork for changing negative attitudes and teaching the players how to win. Under such circumstances, all you can do is start at Ground Zero and work your way up in small steps, teaching basic skills and searching every day for ways to show the players that their hard work is paying off. Focus on the *good* kids in your program, the ones who give the proverbial 110 percent in practice and in games, day in and day out, win or lose, because they believe in you and the goals you set for them and the team. *Those* are your disciples, the true believers; it is *their* dedication, commitment, and loyalty that will sustain you through the darkest hours in that first season, if you only let them.

---

[3] "Doctors bury their mistakes; we still have ours on scholarship." —Abe Lemons, University of Texas

[4] "Coaching a first-year team is a religious experience. You do a lot of praying, but most of the time the answer is 'No.'" —Bill Fitch, NBA coach

In terms of recruiting, however, your goal should be to get every available able-bodied potential athlete to attend your preseason tryouts. You can use those tryouts to begin separating the wheat from the chaff, the athletes from the pretenders, and the team players from the prima donnas whose first and only real loyalty is to themselves. The more players you have trying out, the more selective you can be in choosing your team.

The selection process is hardly scientific, and there is always considerable room for error;[5] still, you may improve your chances of making choices that you can live with comfortably during your first season at a school by taking time to sit down and list the qualities you'd like your players to have, and then to prioritize that list from *most* to *least* important. Your priorities are likely to be different from mine or anyone else's, which is precisely why you should take the time to list them. It serves as a reminder of what you're looking for in candidates for your team.

The next section offers a sample listing of the qualities a coach might look for in prospective players.

AN ANNOTATED SAMPLE PLAYER QUALITY PRIORITY LIST

Lest the imposing title suggest deeper significance than intended, I hasten to point out that this section represents my own priorities, and no one else's, regarding the qualities I look for in the young people who try out for my teams. I offer it simply as a guide in weighing the various physical attributes and psychological traits that can help or hinder a team's development.

---

[5] During the late 1960s, Drs. Tom Tutko and Bruce Ogilvie of San Jose State College developed a psychological motivation test, the Athletic Motivation Inventory, that measured individual personality traits such as self-confidence, aggressiveness, coachability, leadership ability, and mental toughness. The test was used by a number of professional teams, and by college and high school coaches as well, and generally with favorable results as a predictor of psychological readiness for competitive athletics. (Joe Jares, "We have a neurotic in the backfield, Doctor." *Sports Illustrated*, Vol. 34 [January 18, 1971], pp. 30–34.

Another notable article on psychological testing for athletes is "Test of champions" by William P. Morgan. In the July, 1980, issue of *Psychology Today* (pp. 93–99+), the author discusses such tests as the Minnesota Multiphasic Personality Inventory (MMPI), which predates Tutko and Ogilvie's AMI, and the Profile of Mood States (POMS), which the author describes as the most predictive test of athletic success he has found.

1. LOYALTY

Over the years, two slogans more than any others have come to represent my personal coaching philosophy. They are: *You can do more than you think you can* and *The Team Above All.* Like all coaches, I prefer to coach highly talented, skilled athletes; still, I've found that, regardless of player quality, I suffer fewer sleepless nights when my team is composed of players who share my belief that good things happen when everyone gives a total effort for the sake of the Team. (I capitalize the word *Team* to emphasize its importance above and beyond the needs of any individual player or coach; after all, if the Team is to be truly special, it absolutely *must* be more important than any of its component parts.)

Since, as we have seen, the coach is the team in the initial stages of its development, loyalty must initially be directed toward the coach(es). Only when players make the squad do they become part of the larger Team; until that point is reached at the end of the first year's tryouts, players need merely treat each other with the sort of respect that is due anyone who cares enough to try out for the team.

Unfortunately, such positive traits as loyalty, leadership ability, and compatibility are seldom revealed in the compressed time frame of preseason tryouts. Thus, in monitoring tryouts I also look for such signs of *disloyalty* as complaining, arguing with or talking back to coaches, pouting, missing practices, or showing up late for no good reason. Violations do not automatically disqualify a player from making the team—but they *do* earn a stern warning that future infractions will be dealt with as harshly as necessary to preserve the integrity of the Team.

I recall reading about an incident a number of years ago in which a college basketball coach got into a shouting match in the team's dressing room with his freshman point guard after a game. Two questions came to mind as I read the article: (a) Can you imagine such a thing happening to, say, Dean Smith or John Thompson? and (b) Why not? The answers, of course, are (a) no, and (b) because such a complete loss of control by either party would be unthinkable for either of those gentlemen—and their players know it!

I believe that every coach should take time to verbally draw a line in the sand for his or her players, saying, "*This* is what I believe in, and what I stand for; *this* is why I believe it; and *this* is what you, your teammates, and I can expect from each other. *Don't cross that line unless you're prepared to accept the consequences.*" In my particular case, that line in the sand involves loyalty to one another and the program.

Phil Maloney, coach of the NHL Vancouver Canucks, expressed his opinion on the subject of character versus ability thus: "I try for good players and I try for good character (in my players). If necessary, though, I settle for good players." While it's true that many of the traits that build good players (e.g., dedication, perseverance, sacrifice, and commitment to excellence) also help to build character, I simply can't accept the notion that ability comes first. Neither can Don Shula, who equates winning and character: "You win with good people. Character is just as important as ability." Joe Gibbs of the Washington Redskins feels even more strongly about the role of character: "Look for players with character and ability. But remember, character comes first." Which way you look at the ability vs. character question depends on your priorities; if winning is everything, it follows that nothing else matters.

When he went to Clemson as head football coach, Ken Hatfield gave the players a nine-page list of acceptable and unacceptable behaviors for Tiger athletes.

When he was coaching football at Georgia Southern University, Erk Russell had two rules for his players: on the field, hit the other guys as hard as you can; off the field, *do right*. I'm partial to Erk's approach. It's easier to remember. Anyone who says he or she believes that the kids we coach don't know right from wrong is simply looking for alibis for bad behavior.[6]

In either case, though, the important point to remember is that rules should apply equally to everyone. Successful programs are not built or maintained by making exceptions to the rules.

2. FUNDAMENTAL SKILLS/ATHLETICISM

Fundamental skills can be taught; athleticism cannot. To paraphrase Bobby Knight, you can teach a kid to play football, but you

---

[6] Have you ever wondered why it's unfailingly our starters who are caught breaking team rules? Perhaps the culprit isn't Murphy (of Murphy's Law fame), but rather the fact that *starters are more likely to think they can get away with it*. Our challenge is to convince them otherwise before the temptation arises.

can't teach him to run the 40 in 4.2 seconds. In player selection, with all other factors being equal, remember the following:

(a) If forced to choose between skills and athletic ability, go with the player with athletic ability.

(b) Among players of equal skills and athletic ability, take the younger player (i.e., the one with the most remaining eligibility).

(c) If you still can't decide whom to keep, go to the next priority on your list.

3. WILLINGNESS TO WORK HARD WITHOUT QUESTION OR COMPLAINT

Vince Lombardi was right: Fatigue *does* make cowards of us all—if we let it. Erk Russell's slogan, "One more time," expressed his belief that, fatigue notwithstanding, any athlete who is properly motivated and properly trained can do anything just *one more time.* As coaches, we attempt to physically and mentally condition our players to reduce (or, preferably, to *eliminate*) the effects of fatigue on their performances. It's called "extending the comfort zone," the level at which players feel comfortable playing the game at any given point. For players who have grown accustomed to losing, *that's* where teaching players how to win begins. Simply wanting to win doesn't matter unless you're willing to put out the kind of effort that makes winning possible.

There are several ways to find out who doesn't mind working hard—the simplest and most obvious being to work them hard and find out who comes back for more. Bear Bryant said that, prior to his first season at Texas A&M, it took five buses to carry all the coaches, players, and equipment to their spring training facility, and only one bus to carry back the coaches, players, and equipment at week's end.

Along with working the players rigorously, the coach should be alert for things like grumbling, complaining, and forgetting equipment—and note which players do not work hard unless they are specifically told to. (Along these lines, many coaches do not permit players to walk anywhere during practice; some even time water breaks and punish lateness in returning to the practice area.) Conversely, noting which players practice enthusiastically, show up early—and prepared—for practice, and stay late to practice on their own if and when you let them—all of these are likely clues that such players will adopt your work ethic and stay with you during that first year.

Two other points merit attention:

(a) If you're going to drive the players physically during preseason tryouts, you should warn them beforehand to prepare themselves accordingly.

(b) Players should understand from the earliest possible moment that hard work is the minimum expected of them, and not the maximum. Among the few guarantees we're afforded in this life, two are that success will not be easily achieved, and that the players who are unwilling to give a total effort in preseason tryouts will not give a greater effort if and when they make the team.

4. PLAYERS WHO WILL MAKE YOUR JOB EASIER

Not to harp on a theme, but if *the coach* is the team initially, anything that will make his or her job easier during the difficult first-year transition period will also benefit the team he or she is coaching. If this is a selfish viewpoint, so be it, but the end result of such thinking is highly desirable: players and coaches who stand united in their desire to make the Team all that it can be. Player qualities that can make a coach's job easier include:

■ *A favorable attention span and the ability to listen and concentrate.* During your first year at a school, the changes in coaching philosophy, personality, offensive and defensive styles, and so on, are likely to be both dramatic and traumatic for the new players and veterans alike. It is important, therefore, that wasted time be kept to a minimum. In addition to getting the players in shape—which in itself is somewhat time-consuming—there are a multitude of major and minor changes to be effected, most of which require considerable concentration and thought, and must be accomplished in a very brief time span.

It never hurts to have players who pay attention to what's going on, whether by listening to the coach's instruction or by concentrating on what they're doing. Such players tend to learn quickly, and to retain what they learn. You can waste an incredible amount of time over the course of a season if you're talking to players who aren't listening to what you're saying.

■ *Players who can take criticism and acknowledge their mistakes without alibis, excuses, or blaming others.* Criticism is basically negative in the sense that it involves pointing out mistakes, faults, or shortcomings. Criticism is also necessary, since we cannot realistically expect mistakes to be corrected if they are not identified. While nobody likes having his mistakes pointed out to him, some people handle criticism better than others. Framing criticisms in positive or constructive terms can ease the tension that sometimes arises in teaching-learning situations, except with players who habitually rely on making excuses or blaming other people for their mistakes. Players should never be allowed to criticize or otherwise demean the performance of other players.

Beyond the obvious problems associated with denying responsibility for one's actions, such tactics also waste time and impede learning. A football coach was reminded of an offensive lineman he once had who refused to acknowledge his mistakes even when they were pointed out to him in game films. Said the coach, "We reran the tape of this one play *five times in slow motion,* and every time the kid insisted that he hadn't missed his block even though it was there on tape, plain as day, in living color." He shook his head at the memory. "Who'd ever have thought I'd be spending large chunks of my adult life arguing with sixteen-year-olds?"

■ *Players who enjoy competing—and winning.* Here's a thumbnail sketch of the kind of player I most like to coach: Regardless of skills level, the athlete, for whatever reason, feels basically inferior to other people. The athlete regards participating in sports as a way of proving to himself or herself that he or she is as good as everyone else. For such an athlete, losing consistently is unacceptable, because it reaffirms or magnifies that basic sense of inferiority; thus, the athlete is internally driven to compete *and win*—not as a life-or-death proposition—but simply to feel better about himself or herself. Such an athlete *can* be compulsive, obnoxious, and driven to win at all costs by any means, fair or foul; far more commonly, however, the athlete is merely *self-motivated* toward individual excellence and winning. And there is absolutely nothing wrong with *that*.

■ *Players who like—and more important, respect—their teammates and coaches.* Casey Stengel had this to say: "The secret of managing is to keep the guys who hate you away from the guys who are undecided." After your first year at a school, the way to accomplish that is to suggest to the guys who hate you that they play for someone else next year.

While I wouldn't want anyone who hates me to stay on my team any longer than it takes to say "I quit," it's not really important that the players like me. Teenagers seldom like adults, even their parents. What's important is for them to respect me, their teammates, and the team's role as a second family in their lives. It's not possible to make people like one another, but it *is* both possible and necessary to make teammates treat one another and their coaches with respect.

Respect doesn't necessarily mean being nice to one another, nor does it mean that players cannot disagree, argue, or fight among themselves occasionally. What it *does* mean is that, once the arguments and misunderstandings are over, everyone involved recognizes that we're all in this together, and we need each other if we hope to accomplish our goals. Family members argue and disagree constantly, too—especially if there are teenagers in the household—but when the battles are over they are still family, united by bonds that are stronger than the forces that might sever them.

(That so many American families are dysfunctional actually works to our advantage; after all, the players on our teams have voluntarily joined that second family. It wasn't thrust upon them biologically. I take that to mean that they also voluntarily accept the responsibilities that being a team member entails in order to reap the benefits and rewards that team membership affords them.)

My goal is to ensure that their team membership is one of the most positive, rewarding experiences in their lives. If that experience includes championships and undefeated seasons—well, that's great! But what really matters is building teams of individuals who are so committed to one another that, in Bear

Bryant's words, "They've got one heartbeat. Then, you've got a team." And the wins will take care of themselves.

- *Players who exhibit leadership qualities.* After seventeen years of coaching, I stumbled across a quick and easy way to identify leadership potential. (You probably already knew about it, but I'm a slow learner.) It consists of *giving the players the opportunity to make at least one major decision that affects the entire group.* In my case, the problem was to select a traveling outfit for the jayvee and varsity girls basketball teams. I interrupted practice the day after tryouts ended, took both teams into a classroom, tossed a stack of clothing catalogs on a table, and told them they had 30 minutes to find an outfit. They took 27 minutes to reach a decision.

What surprised me, though, was the source of the leadership: an eighth-grader, a jayvee player, who talked longer, louder, and more persuasively than any of the varsity players. As it turned out, while my varsity squad suffered from a lack of senior leadership that year, the jayvee team fairly bubbled over with it, to the extent that twice I jokingly asked the jayvee coach if he'd like to swap coaching duties with me!

3

Special Effects: Making Your Team All That It Can and Should Be

In three of my earlier books—*Coaching and Motivation*,[1] *Coaching and Winning*,[2] and *Basketball Coach's Survival Guide* (coauthored with Larry Chapman)[3]—I pursued the notion that the ideal team functions as a second family for everyone involved. While I certainly didn't invent that concept, I like to think that through my writings I've helped to popularize it, because now more than ever before, young people need family ties.

It's a law of nature that, if a void exists, something will fill it. Whether we're talking about single-parent families or families in which both parents are working full time, many young people today aren't getting what they need from their families. With too much unsupervised free time and too little guidance, many youngsters fall prey to drugs or turn to sex as a way of developing relationships. Searching for structure, security, and peer status, many of them turn to gangs.

Our task—and unquestionably one of the greatest challenges facing us today—is to build teams that meet young athletes' needs so convincingly that they won't need drugs, sex, or gang memberships to compensate for what their own families aren't giving them.

---

[1] Englewood Cliffs, NJ: Prentice Hall, 1983.

[2] Englewood Cliffs, NJ: Prentice Hall, 1988.

[3] West Nyack, NY: Parker, 1992.

How might such a team be created? That's what this chapter is all about.

Either love your players or get out of the game.

—Bobby Dodd (Georgia Tech)

THREE REASONS FOR LOVING YOUR PLAYERS

The French existentialist Albert Camus stated that the most important question in philosophy is, *Why should I not kill myself today?* Camus, a fatalist, viewed life as an ongoing process in which we find reasons for continuing to exist from one day to the next in a universe that is basically absurd and meaningless. Each of us, Camus said, must find that meaning for ourselves and reaffirm it daily.

The first time you quit, it's hard. The second time, it gets easier.
The third time, you don't even have to think about it.

—Bear Bryant (Univ. of Alabama)

In sports, Camus's question translates into *Why should I not quit the team today?* As coaches, we understand the values of sports and team membership that make dedication, sacrifice, and commitment worthwhile. We know why players shouldn't quit when the going is tough—but do *our players* know it? Most of them probably do, most of the time. If or when they don't, however, we must be prepared to remind them of how their blood, sweat, and tears shed on the team's behalf are enriching their lives and will continue to do so. Such reminders are most likely to be believed when players and coaches love each other.

Love is the strongest bond, and the greatest motivator, that exists. There are many kinds of love, starting with *self-love*, for we must love ourselves before we can love others. From self-love, I can move on and immerse myself in something more important than *me*. In that sense, then, love is the glue that binds us to something beyond ourselves. In our case, yours and mine, that something is actually two things, the sport and the players we coach.

PLAYERS WHO LOVE THE GAME

Most of us probably became coaches because we developed a genuine love for our sport as players and wanted to continue our involvement beyond our playing days. If we stay in coaching long enough, we find that many of our players feel the same way and eventually go on to become coaches themselves. At any rate, it's easy and natural to feel affection for players who love the game the way we do.

Of course, not every prospect for our teams comes to us filled with a love for the game. Genuine love for the sport usually develops slowly, as players work hard and develop skills that permit them to appreciate the game and its subtleties in ways that were largely closed to them as rank beginners.

PLAYERS WHO WORK HARD

A second basis for developing a genuine affection for the players we coach derives from our appreciation of their hard work. Good things happen to people who work hard to make good things happen; I believe that with all my heart. I also believe that, while some players are more highly skilled than others, everyone on the team who is not injured is capable of giving a total effort in every practice session and every game. Kids who prefer to decide for themselves when they will hustle and when they won't usually don't last long on my teams, because there are no free rides. Everyone has a clearly defined role, and is expected to fulfill it to the best of his or her ability. My practices are always physically demanding, and playing time in games is allotted on the basis of how hard each player works in practice. There are no exceptions. My players understand this, and they accept it because they also understand the alternatives.

My coaching is highly personal. For example, at the end of every daily practice I announce a "Player of the Day," a player who has shown the kind of hustle, determination, and spirit that I'm looking for. That player's photo goes up on the gym wall on our "Champions' Corner" bulletin board. Now, that probably doesn't seem like a big deal, but it *is*, because I always make a big deal of it. I single out players for praise when they are working especially hard, in practice or in games. Players want—and need—their coaches' approval, but I want them to know that it's conditional, and based on their work habits. I won't hesitate to get in the face of a player who is giving a half-effort and demand to know why he or she has chosen to take the day off when everyone else is working hard. It's the old "carrot-and-stick" approach—and it *works*, both ways. Like the old mule, the players will work hard, whether to earn the carrot or to avoid the stick—and the net result is the same—*players working hard.*

I love them for it—and I tell them so.

PLAYERS WHO ARE LOYAL

The third reason for loving the kids we coach is their loyalty. As Jerry Tarkanian has said, "The only *bad* kid is one who won't be loyal to his teammates and coaches." While anyone can be loyal when things are going nicely and the team is doing well, loyalty is the *only* thing that can save us when things are going poorly.

Faith is the substance of things hoped for, the evidence of things not seen.

—Hebrews 11:1

Let's face it—like it or not, we're salespeople. What we're selling is a dream or vision of what our team can become through hard work, dedication, and sacrifice. It's not always easy to sell that dream, especially when players are used to losing. "In turning a program around," UNC football coach Bill Dooley said, "the hardest thing to do is to convince players that they can win." The process starts with your dream; if your players don't accept it, they won't work hard enough to put themselves in position to win games. It becomes a vicious circle of negativity: The less inclined players are to work hard, the more likely they are to lose—and the more they lose, the less inclined they will be to work hard in the future. Like winning, losing becomes a habit.

The way out of this downward spiral is: *Build your program around the players who are loyal to you and their teammates.* Teach them to believe that hard work always breeds success. As Vince Lombardi noted, "The harder we work, the harder it is to give up."

The first thing any coaching staff must do is weed out selfishness.
No program can be successful with players who put themselves ahead of the team.

—Johnny Majors (Univ. of Pittsburgh)

The weeding-out process is, in most cases, gradual; since you don't want to run off the good kids along with the bad apples, you can't make your daily practices as grimly forbidding as the Bataan Death March. And since you don't want to be known as The Coach Who Kicks Players Off the Team When They Don't Work Hard Enough to Suit Him (or Her), you will in most cases grit your teeth and bear it until that glorious day when your problem players quit the team or graduate. (You hope it will be the former, but it will probably be the latter.)

Identify and bond with the kids who, for whatever reason, are loyal to you and your vision. Tell them at every opportunity how much their loyalty and hard work mean to you and to the team. Tell them how special they are to you—and why—and let them know that *they* are the foundation upon which the team's future rests. You can find a thousand tiny ways to show them that their loyalty and hard work are paying off, and a thousand other ways to thank them and encourage them to keep up the good work. Encourage them to talk their friends into trying out for the team next year.

To build your program from the ground up: *Start with the good kids.* If they're also good athletes—well, that's great!—but if not, if they're good kids, they'll be receptive to your teaching. You can motivate them, and in time you can teach them what they need to know to be competitive.

Over the long haul, your teams will take on your personality and you'll tend to attract youngsters into your program who accept your values and philosophy. Many of those youngsters will be good athletes—and because they already know what you stand for (and what you won't stand for) via the reputation you've built in the school and community, you won't be as likely to lose them as you were when you first set foot in the school.

BUILDING TEAM UNITY: WORKING AND PLAYING TOGETHER

Making your team special will make it easier for everyone involved to accomplish whatever goals you set for the team. First, however, we should define and delimit the term *special*—what it is, and what it isn't.

Defining your team and the players on it as special *doesn't* mean that the players deserve special treatment by their coaches, teachers, or anyone else. It doesn't mean asking teachers to change an athlete's failing grades to keep him or her eligible, or overlooking players' violations of team rules because you need them in the lineup for an important upcoming game. It doesn't mean allowing players to show up late for games or practices (or skip them altogether), to forget their uniforms or equipment, or to practice half-heartedly because they'd rather not work up a sweat today. It doesn't mean interceding on behalf of a player who breaks the law or violates school rules by fighting, cutting class, committing acts of vandalism or theft, or possessing drugs or alcohol. And being special has absolutely nothing to do with individual skills or the team's won-lost record. *Any* team can be special if the coach takes the time and effort to make it so. Under such circumstances, wins, championships, and individual honors are merely the icing on the cake that makes accomplishments even more special.

What being special *really* has to do with is attitudes—the pride that comes with belonging to a group whose members accept you as equals, without reservation, regardless of your race, religion, or social or economic background; respect your role within that select group of athletes; need you to help them accomplish team goals; and love you for yourself, warts and all, because of your commitment to them and the team.

Where else in today's world is a young person likely to find himself or herself accepted, respected, needed, and loved by so many people at one time?

In church or synagogue? Maybe—but many young people don't go to church or synagogue. In school? Most school relationships are, like on-the-job relationships, casual or shallow; deeper relationships usually develop outside the confines of classrooms, and they tend to be limited in number. Think about it: When you were in junior or senior high school, how many *real* friends (other than athletes) could you count on for support through thick and thin, good times and bad? If your answer is more than three or four at any given time, you probably were—or should have been—the class president.

At home? Perhaps if you come from a very large family. Many parents these days, however, are single parents or working parents, and are often too overworked, too overwhelmed, and too tired to spend quality time with their children.

In gangs? "Ah, there's the rub," as Shakespeare noted. Teenage gangs, once confined to the larger cities, have spread, franchise-style,[4] to smaller cities and towns across the nation. Gang membership offers security and a sense of belonging as well as acceptance, respect, and the opportunity to be needed and loved, albeit by people whose values, lifestyle, and illegal activities hardly represent mainstream America at any socioeconomic level.

Gang membership offers two things that cannot be matched or bettered by membership on our athletic teams—namely, protection from the gangs themselves and money obtained through illegal activities. Those can be—and *are*—powerful enticements for young people who see no better alternatives available.

Instead of complaining about the quality of local recreational programs and coaches, we must work with local recreation officials to find ways to expand and improve their programs, both quantitatively and qualitatively. We must encourage our local politicians to increase funding for youth recreation programs. We should, as noted in Chapter 1, explore the possibility of conducting mini coaching clinics for youth rec league coaches. We should strive mightily to improve the quality of our feeder systems.

Perhaps most important of all, we must consider the Latin phrase *in loco parentis.* Translated as "in place of the parent," it has been used in courts of law to define teachers' legal rights and responsibilities regarding the students in their classes. In building teams that young people will want to become a part of, we should bear in mind that families are civilization's basic social units.

Family structure is vital to human development. Regardless of what our other goals in coaching might be, if we cannot meet our players' needs, they will look elsewhere to have those needs met.

---

[4] From the *Griffin Daily News* (March 31, 1996), p. 1-A: "Members of the Chicago-based Gangster Disciples, the Los Angeles-based Crips and Bloods, and members of smaller independent groups are now in Griffin, according to patrolman Pat Akin, the police department's gang specialist.

"Members of the Chicago-based Vice Lords had been operating in Griffin until the police department and the Spalding County Sheriff's Department 'prosecuted them out of existence,' Akin said."

The city of Griffin has about 20,000 residents.

The day is past when we as coaches can set ourselves apart from our players, and not become involved in their lives. If we aren't prepared to assume personal—parental—roles in our players' lives, we shouldn't be surprised when their loyalties turn elsewhere and they discover that they don't really need us or our teams to find fulfillment in their lives.

YOU AND YOUR TEAM: CONTROL PRINCIPLES

1. CONTROL IS NEITHER GOOD NOR BAD. IT IS INEVITABLE.

There is nothing wrong with controlling your players, any more than it's wrong to try to control opponents. Control *is* dehumanizing in the sense that we're "using" our players to further our own ends—but they are also "using" us and the team to further their own ends. To carry the concept to extremes, we could say that we all use one another: husbands and wives, teachers and students, bosses and employees, buyers and sellers. Sometimes decisions are arrived at jointly, and sometimes not. Just because someone is in control of the decision-making process doesn't necessarily mean that someone else is being used in a harmful or negative way.

Jerry Tarkanian expressed it nicely: "I want my players to understand that I'll do everything I can to help them with their problems away from the basketball court. But they also have to understand that I need their help in solving *my* problems on the basketball court."

2. TO CONTROL OPPONENTS, YOU MUST FIRST CONTROL YOUR OWN TEAM

"Controlling your team" can mean whatever you want it to mean; generally, however, it refers to limits defined by coaches regarding what their players are and are not expected or permitted to do, whether in game situations or otherwise.

In game situations, controlling your team refers to such things as: dictating game strategies or styles of play, calling plays, making substitutions, calling timeouts, changing strategies or tactics, establishing basic expectations regarding intensity of play, monitoring players' conduct, and whatever else the coach may or may not feel compelled to control.

Some coaches prefer to make decisions themselves; others prefer to give their players broad latitudes of decision-making responsibilities (e.g., in calling plays, changing defenses, calling timeouts, signaling their desire to be taken out of the game for a breather, etc.). Either way is acceptable, provided that the head coach understands that he or she is ultimately responsible for all decisions. Allowing others to make decisions does not absolve the head coach of responsibility for those decisions. As the French philosopher Jean Paul Sartre put it, "Not to choose is also to choose."

In other situations, controlling your team means establishing performance expectations that will meet team needs and accomplish team goals. Some coaches prepare lengthy, detailed rules sheets governing player conduct on and off the court or playing field; others prefer to keep the rules to a minimum.[5] In either case, success depends on making the rules known to all of the players and enforcing them the same way for all players, regardless of their status on the team. (Equitable enforcement of team rules is often difficult for young or inexperienced coaches who do not understand the most basic aspect of control as applied to coaching: *If you don't control your players, they will control you.*

John Wooden's concept of discipline was embodied in a simple phrase: Make the rules clear and the penalties severe. This, he reasoned, makes young athletes mentally tough and willing to commit themselves to the idea of working hard, not just on the court or playing field, but in other phases of their lives as well. It all starts with the rules: We should not expect the athletes we coach to control themselves unless we clearly define the rules we expect them to live by.

3. WE'RE SMARTER THAN OUR PLAYERS ARE

This is a statement of fact, not a throwaway line intended to make us feel good about ourselves. If you stay in coaching for a decade or more, you're likely to find many of your ex-players becoming doctors, lawyers, engineers, scientists, and the like. Some of the youngsters we coach have absolutely brilliant minds, but I have yet to meet

---

[5] "Keep rules to a minimum and enforce the ones you have." —Vince Dooley (University of Georgia)

a teenager who can realistically assess her or his athletic potential as well as the coach can do it. That's our job—and *we're better at it than the kids we coach*! That's why I tell every player I coach never to listen to or believe *anybody's* assessment but mine regarding their ability or potential, including that of their friends, their parents, the media, and especially themselves. If they believe those assessments, they'll grossly over- or underrate themselves, depending on how much self-confidence they have. Either way, outside assessments tend to limit the distance a given player is willing to go toward reaching his or her potential.

In most cases, our players are equally unable to assess the team's potential properly; they usually fail to comprehend the strengths of the team in all its complexities, except as they relate to it individually. They may accept our philosophy or coaching style at any stage of their development, but they usually understand it only after a lengthy and prolonged exposure to it. They are, in the vast majority of cases, too close to the trees to see the forest.

That's why I believe so strongly in developing a personal coaching philosophy; without it, we're no smarter than our players who accept our offenses and defenses unquestioningly. If we know where we're going—and if we have a plan for getting there—we're light years ahead of all those who don't understand where they're going or how they intend to get there. Without adequate preparation and attention to detail, coaching is a hit-or-miss proposition, and few of us can afford to coach like that.

4. WE CAN'T CONTROL HOW OUR PLAYERS THINK, BUT WE CAN CONTROL HOW THEY ACT

We can't control whether they get base hits in key situations, but we *can* make them treat each other with respect. We can't make them like each other, but we can make them act as if they do.

He chasteneth whom he loveth.

—Proverbs 13: 24

WE'RE ALL IN THIS TOGETHER

HARD WORK AS A UNIFYING FORCE

Our players may not like it if we work them extremely hard in daily practice; however, hard work can (and will) serve as a bond that helps to mold individuals into a team.

Vince Lombardi's coaching style consisted of driving his players relentlessly while constantly explaining to them why he was doing it. His players regarded him—initially, at least—as a brutal, uncaring taskmaster in the Green Bay Packers' daily practices. But their mutual misery tied them together emotionally in ways that the greatest motivational speeches ever devised could not have done. Coach Lombardi's players developed tremendous pride in themselves for having survived his demanding practice sessions—and their initial dislike of the coach gave them a common target for their complaints among themselves. Later, when they saw their hard work paying off in wins that previous Packer teams would have let slip away, they no longer regarded Lombardi as an ogre. His players may not always have liked the man, but they respected him immensely, and they were fiercely loyal to him and to their teammates.

Lombardi's style isn't appealing to every coach, of course. Few of us like the idea of our players' hating us. But if your players, like Lombardi's, are used to (a) giving a halfhearted effort and (b) losing, the only way out of the downward spiral is to teach the players to work harder than they're used to working. Working players hard either drives them off—in which case you didn't really need them anyway (although common sense might dictate otherwise)—or else it unites them in the sense that "we're all in this together." Your own hard work and preparation should serve as a model for what you expect from your players.

A mile of extra effort. In my basketball coaching, I've always had my players run a mile before practice. I run it with them. Running that mile is primarily a symbolic act; beyond its minimal condition-ing value, it permits me to say to the players, "Do you really think (our next opponent) is running a mile before practice today to get ready for us? If I thought so, we'd be running *two* miles. They may be more experienced or highly skilled than we are; if so, we can't help that. But we *can* work harder than they are working. Nobody can stop us from doing that but ourselves."

My running with the players shows them that we're all in it together. This doesn't extend to the drills we do, of course, since those drills are intended to get *them* ready for the next game, where-as *my* game preparations are of a far different—and primarily men-tal—nature. It's still hard work, however, and I make sure to remind them of it occasionally. I've done some of the conditioning drills with the players from time to time (e.g., step-slides and running stairs and doing wind sprints); and while I wouldn't advise every coach to do likewise, I'll say this: "No matter how poorly you per-form, the players can't seriously complain that you're overworking them if you're out there huffing and puffing along with them."

PLAYERS KEEPING IN TOUCH

I have, in previous books, described a "touch system" wherein team-mates are required to touch hands with each other whenever they meet anywhere in the school except the gym. (Nowadays, the touch probably should be upgraded to high- or low-fives.) The penalty for failure to do so is running an extra mile after practice for each infraction. I've used this system with great success over the years as an overt symbolic gesture of acceptance between teammates. It tells, not just the players involved but anyone who sees it as well, that *we are teammates; we are special to one another.* Any player of mine who is unwilling to show such symbolic acceptance of his or her teammates can waive the requirement by running five extra miles a day instead of one. So far, I've had no takers.

The touch rule applies to coaches as well as players, of course.

HANDLING RACISM

It's desirable, but hardly feasible, to expect all of our players to like one another. It *is* possible, however, to expect them to get along with their teammates. Beyond the fact that racism can tear a team apart like a concealed explosive device, racism is inexcusable and should be dealt with swiftly and harshly.

In my remarks to the team immediately after completing the player selection phase of preseason practice, I tell the assembled squad and assistant coach(es) that if any of them harbors racist thoughts, they'd better keep them strictly to themselves. The penalty for being overheard uttering a racist remark is 50 miles of running—and an apology sincerely delivered to the offended person as well—before the guilty party will be permitted to rejoin the team in daily practice or suit up with the team in games.

THE EXCEPTION TO THE RULE

Racism is vile because it is rooted in the belief that one person or group of people is inherently superior to another person or group. Such beliefs are always negative and counterproductive—with one important exception: *the special nature of the team.* Players should regard their team membership as something that sets them apart from everyone else. We—players and coaches alike—are investing considerable time and energy in a joint enterprise that will give everyone involved a great sense of accomplishment, whether because we win a lot of games, because we have developed very special relationships among team members, or, preferably, both. That feeling of being part of something special is the payback players receive for their dedication, commitment, and sacrifice on the team's behalf. Nothing should be allowed to interfere with the process whereby that sense of being special is achieved, because *anything* is possible when you believe in miracles.

If the team is to be special to your players, it will be because of what you have gotten them to *give* of themselves, not because of what they expect to *receive*. It takes a lot of giving to make a team truly special, as opposed to being just a collection of individuals. A collection of students is a class, but there's nothing special about that.

HANDLING PLAYER DISPUTES AND OTHER PROBLEMS

Family members don't always get along—but they are always family, before disputes arise and after they are settled. Handling player disputes involves identifying problems promptly and taking the long view that the team is more important than the dispute. Players must be encouraged to bring their problems to you—or, in the event that they fail to do so, other players must be willing to alert you to problems involving their teammates. Since tattling goes against the grain of most teenagers' code of conduct, the only way to achieve such a state of concern for the team is to create and maintain an atmosphere of openness in which players are not afraid to risk their teammates' disapproval for the sake of the team. It's another of the million-and-one reasons for emphasizing *The Team Above All* in everything you do.

In my experience, the vast majority of disputes among teammates have resulted from problems with the opposite sex—two girls after the same boy, or vice versa. I've often envied coaches who coach in all-girls or all-boys schools, and thereby avoid the friction of "girl problems" or "boy problems." While every such case is unique—and agonizingly serious, as well—to the participants, there's a sameness to them that is frankly boring. My approach to such problems, which probably leaves much to be desired, lies in pointing out that, while I don't care who they date or think they're in love with, I care very much about anything that threatens the team's well-being. I'll do whatever it takes to protect the team; that means that the disputing players must find a way to solve their problem *right now*, while we're together discussing it, and in a way that is mutually satisfying to them, or else I'll do it for them in a way that they might not like. Putting it that way gets my point across without having to say exactly what I might do.

That sets the tone for the discussion. To ensure that a positive mood prevails throughout, I'll begin by asking each of them if he or she likes the other. Of course they answer "yes," since for either of them to say "no" would immediately set that person at a two-to-one disadvantage. They know that I could never support them if they openly admit to disliking a teammate.

Before turning the discussion over to them, I'll also point out that, while player relationships such as ours usually extend to life-long friendships, boy-girl relationships among teenagers are as changeable as the weather and last about as long as a hiccup. And because the object of their attention is not a part of the team, he or she cannot, should not, and *will not* replace the team among the players' natural priorities (i.e., God, family, team).

It's all part of what might be called "ultimate decisions" that young athletes have to make. They include such things as: doing drugs or living a straight life; dropping out of school or continuing to graduation; working hard and accepting responsibility, or hardly working and looking for someone to blame for their failures; and pursuing team goals or paying lip service to the team while following individual agendas. Such decisions are "ultimate" because, when wrong choices are made, they are unmade only with great difficulty, if at all.

All of us make decisions every day—but every now and then we face major decisions that will change our lives for better or for worse. No one can make those decisions for us; we have to live with them, regardless of how they turn out.

As coaches, we counsel our players regarding responsible decision making—but we should also challenge them every day to reaffirm their commitment to the team and the sport. The major decision they face in this regard involves thinking, "I'm going to dedicate this portion of my life to basketball or football (or whatever sport)." The minor decision is harder because it is both ongoing and specific: "I'm going to do it *today*." Saying it—and meaning it—every day isn't easy; the pursuit of excellence is a full-time job and there are no days off where dedication and commitment are concerned. Teaching your players to live that way is the greatest favor you can ever do for them.

To handle player disputes or other player problems, you want them to feel comfortable in coming to you with their personal problems, and to know that you're interested in their lives—but they must also understand that the team comes first. Don't give anyone special consideration where violations of team rules, school rules, or the law are concerned. Beyond that, do everything in your power to help them through the rigorous ordeal of growing up and becoming responsible adults.

TEAM CONTROL PRIORITIES

1. CONTROL YOURSELF

There are different levels of interpretation regarding this statement. First, like it or not, as the team's nominal head, you are a model for your players' behavior. If you encourage cheating (e.g., by sending the wrong player to the free-throw line when a poor shooter is fouled), lying (e.g., by suggesting that a player fake an injury to give the team an extra timeout), or dirty play (e.g., by suggesting that a pitcher hit an opposing batter or hinting that it would be nice if the opposing quarterback were to be hurt on the next play)—your players will have little respect for rules, fair play, or honesty.

If you expect your players to work hard, model your expected work ethic in your preparations for daily practices and games. If you want your players' respect, you must show respect for them—not necessarily by being nice to them all the time, but at least by allowing them to retain a measure of basic dignity—first, as team members, and second as humans.

A second level of self-control concerns avoiding the temptation to speak or act impulsively. All of the apologies in the world, no matter how sincerely delivered, are unlikely to undo the damage done by a single racial epithet or slur of any kind. One Georgia high school football coach was suspended from his duties for the rest of the 1995 season when, on the sideline in an early season game, he grabbed the quarterback's face mask—*and the player involved was his son!*

Admittedly, it's easier to talk about thinking before you speak or act than it is to *do* it; but, like paying taxes, it must be done. The best way to do it is to adopt a mind-set that always considers the *team's* needs before your own. Don't succumb to that impulse to give someone a well-deserved, expletive-undeleted tongue lashing! (As serious drinkers will tell you, the pleasure they get from an evening with Jack Daniels or Jim Beam is more than compensated for by the misery of the following morning's hangover.) What is more important to you—controlling your impulses, or paying the price for losing control?

2. CONTROL YOUR SENIORS

"To be good," University of Pittsburgh football coach Johnny Majors said, "a team must have good seniors." Having been with your program longer than the other players, your seniors should be thoroughly familiar with you and the intricacies of your system or style of play. It follows, then, that they should be capable of providing leadership, helping their younger or more inexperienced teammates, and setting a positive example in terms of attitude and behavior.

Of course, the situation is radically different in your first year at a school. In such cases, the players' loyalties may be to the former coach; if so, you may face the resentment of upperclassmen who blame you for the previous coach's departure. Unless it is handled properly, such resentment will undermine everything you try to do, the team will be racked with dissension, and players will form cliques according to players who like you and others who don't.

A cozy chat with your seniors. Coaches often complain about how hard it is to come up with new motivational talks that the players haven't heard before. Whether in a new or established coaching situation, however, there's one speech that my players never hear but once, since they are seniors only once. It's what I call my "cozy fireside chat,"[6] although there's no fireplace in the coach's office.

My "chat" with the current year's seniors takes place almost immediately after final squad selections are announced. I begin by telling them how much I (or the team and the school, if it's my first year) appreciate their hard work over the past few years. I express my belief that we're going to have a great year, working and playing together with the seniors leading the way. We can't have the kind of year that all of us want the team to have unless they—the seniors— show the younger players how *real* athletes go about improving themselves and the team. I know they can do it, I tell them, because I know they want this year and this team to be special. It is, after all, their last time around, so all of us have to work extra hard to make it a year that they will look back on fondly and with pride for years to come.

That's pretty standard stuff, right? But then comes the kicker— the fine print between the lines:

> You're a great bunch of kids, and the team and the school owe you a lot, I wish we could have you here on this team for four more years, but we can't. So you need to understand one thing: My job is to do what's best for the team. Team needs are always more important than the needs of any individual or group of players. This means two things for you.

---

[6] After Franklin D. Roosevelt's "fireside chats" to the nation's radio audience during the 1930s–1940s.

First, the team needs your leadership in terms of spirit, dedication, and hustle. Whether you're in the game or on the sidelines, the younger players will be watching you to see how you behave. Because you're seniors and you've been through it before, I expect more from you than I expect from them in terms of spirit, enthusiasm, and a positive attitude.

Second, I won't start you or give you playing time just because I like you, or because you're a senior. If you were a starter at the end of last season, the job is still yours, but you have to prove that you're better than the younger players or I'll have to give them the starting job and playing time. It's nothing personal, but I have to think of the team. A sophomore with three years to play will gain more from the playing time than you will with one year left to play. So you're gonna have to outplay (him or her) or I'll have no choice but to go with the younger player.

The seniors don't always like what I've told them, but they can't argue with the logic involved. I've used this approach with four high school teams that were new to me and others that I had coached before, and it has always worked for me. I've also used it in coaching at the junior high level—addressing my remarks to the players who will be moving up to high school the following year.

Regarding the statement, "It's nothing personal. . .": I believe strongly in giving players all the personal attention, encouragement, and individual coaching I can find time for; when it comes to making decisions on the team's behalf, though, no coach can afford to let personal feelings interfere with team needs. As a friend says he reminds his players from time to time, "I'd bench my *mother* if she wasn't getting the job done!"

Earl (Campbell) may not be in a class by himself, but whatever class he's in,
it doesn't take long to call the roll.

—Bum Phillips
(Houston Oilers)

3. CONTROL YOUR SUPERSTARS

I've coached three bona fide superstar athletes in my nineteen years of coaching: one in track, one in basketball/track, and one in basketball. In addition to making me look like a much better coach than I am or ever could be, these superlative athletes have shared one common trait beyond their uncommon skills: All of them ranked among the most coachable athletes I've ever been around. I'm not saying that I never had problems with them; every athlete I've ever coached has presented problems of one kind or another. To paraphrase Notre Dame football coach Lou Holtz, coaching is a matter of solving problems (he used the phrase *correcting mistakes*) before you get fired.

The two biggest problems with superstar athletes. First, there is what football coach Mike Koehler refers to as the "Tyranny of Talent." He explained,

> Like Mozart and all other artistic geniuses, uniquely gifted athletes are controlled by their genius. It assumes an identity of its own and places unusual demands on them. As Mozart heard symphonies in his head and simply wrote them down, Michael Jordan and other athletic geniuses, even young ones, are controlled by the demands of their talent. They *must* compete and occasionally find themselves in "zones" that even they don't understand.

> So superstars may be easy to coach, but they (may also) experience great difficulty fighting the demands of their talent, often to the point of failing in school or of de-emphasizing other aspects of their personality development. . . . Such athletes require a different kind of control that enables them to fight the imposition of their own bodies.

Second, there is the familiar "Big ME, little you" syndrome; it results from a young athlete's constantly being told by friends, fans, the media, etc., that he or she is God's gift to that particular sport. Seeing superstar professional athletes pampered, idolized, paid untold millions of dollars, and generally treated as if the world revolves around them, envious young athletes sometimes develop the attitude that *this team needs me more than I need the team.* From there, it's only a short step to thinking, if I can't get a million dollars, *I at least deserve a different set of rules from everyone else.* That is why some coaches prefer not to have superstars on their teams. I'll take all the superstar athletes I can get, however, and be grateful for the opportunity to coach them. I happen to believe that, at the high school level, at least, superstar athletes are the easiest of all athletes to coach, and I'm going to tell you why.

The good news about superstars. First, of course, they possess the skills that can make anything you do look like brilliant coaching. Beyond that, they also tend to have a well-developed work ethic and they understand the concept of making sacrifices. Isiah Thomas once said that the fans in the stands who marveled at his ballhandling and passing skills had no idea of the thousands of hours that it took for him to develop those skills to the point where he made them look easy. Superstar athletes generally have tremendous drive to excel and improve, and they usually love playing the game. Baseball great Ted Williams used to stay at the ballpark after practice, taking extra batting practice for as long as he could find people to pitch and shag balls for him.

Not every gifted athlete is so dedicated. Some players may think, for example, that quickness and vertical jumping ability are all that they need to become NBA superstars. Bad attitudes and lazy or indifferent work habits are *learned* traits, however, and you can ensure that your superstars learn the positive attitudes toward self-improvement and hard work.

The key, if there is one, to working with highly gifted athletes lies in recognizing and coming to terms with their talent. Don't pretend that the superstar is like everyone else—"just another one of the guys"—or try to fit the superstar into a team-oriented system that doesn't use his or her skills to full advantage (e.g., using an Emmitt Smith in a triple-option attack).

By definition, superstar-caliber athletes are capable of doing things that the rest of us can only dream about. They may be homey and down-to-earth, and they may be highly team-oriented as well—let's hope so, anyway—but if you've ever coached a superstar you're acutely aware of how different they are. Injuries are always regrettable, but regardless of how much you care about your players, a third-stringer's sprained ankle doesn't raise your blood pressure to the critical level that the same injury to your superstar performer will do.

What you do with your franchise player depends on two factors—coaching preferences (or philosophy) and the number of talented athletes you have in addition to the superstar. I've known football coaches to limit a star running back to 8–10 carries a game because they—the coaches—don't want any of their players to compile the sort of stats that might overshadow the team's accomplishments. That's one coaching preference, but I'll take a Bo Jackson and I'll give him the ball every play if that's what it takes to beat you. It's easier to control a superior player's ego than it is to control opponents without taking full advantage of the superior player's skills.

Handling superstar athletes. The huge salaries doled out to professional athletes have made it difficult to sell them on the idea of working hard; after all, if you're guaranteed $5 million a year in salaries alone for the next decade, regardless of your production, what incentive is there to improve? The attitude of many pros—"I'm a superstar, so I don't have to do what you (the coach) say; and I'll work when I feel like it, and at whatever pace I choose"—sometimes filters down through the college ranks to the high school level and below. It is most likely to take hold in situations in which the coach fears losing the superstar if he or she isn't treated with kid gloves. Such fears lose sight of what being a superstar *really* means.

> *For of those to whom much is given, much is required.*
> —John F. Kennedy, speech (1961),
> paraphrasing Luke 12:48

As St. Luke's (and later, President Kennedy's) words suggest, instead of expecting less from our superstar athletes for fear of offending them, we should be demanding *more* from them than from other players, by virtue of the fact that they have more to give. They should be made to see that their talent is both a gift and a responsibility.

My approach to dealing with superstars is simple and basic. It involves an easily understood message, stated as often and in as many ways as necessary for it to sink in:

> You have a rare and wonderful talent. I want to develop that talent in such a way that you—and more important, the team—get maximum benefit from it. As long as you're willing to work hard and follow the rules, I won't hold you back. If you'll work with me, I'll give you every chance to use that talent as much as possible and we'll have every college coach in the world beating down the doors to get you. But you have to work with me, not against me. You have more to give, so you'll be expected to give more. The team needs 100 percent of you in practice and in games, not 50 percent or even 80 percent. I can't bend the

rules for you, and I wouldn't do it even if you were twice as good as you are now. I hope you won't expect me to, because I want you to be the player that people around here brag about for the next fifty years. You can be, too, if you let yourself—and if you'll let me help you.

Expect from the superstar athlete the same two things that you expect from everyone else on the team: hard work and loyalty to the team. As long as you get those things, the wins will take care of themselves. Don't expect the superstar to win games—or even to take a leadership role on the team—unless that player wants to. It is the voice of the coach—your voice—that he or she must respond to, not some inner voice—and not the voices of parents, fans, the media, or anyone else.

Coaching superstar athletes is tremendously challenging, and highly rewarding as well. The challenge lies in steering them along the straight and narrow path that leads to developing their full potential; like teaching a gifted class, it takes constant hard work to stay ahead of the gifted player. The reward lies in the thousand and one ways that such athletes can surprise you just when you think you've seen everything they have to offer.

They also serve who only stand and wait.

—John Milton, *On His Blindness* (1652)

4. CONTROL YOUR BENCHWARMERS

Not everyone is, or can be, a superstar, a member of the starting line-up, or even a second-string player. It would be nice if it were otherwise; it would also be nice if every player were highly skilled and capable of helping the team achieve maximum performances every game.

There are two aspects of controlling your benchwarmers: controlling them during games, and controlling their attitudes toward the team, playing time, and their roles.

Game behavior. I've never bought into the idea that bench-clearing brawls can be excused or justified as "players going to the aid of their teammates." That's a cop-out, purely and simply; in reality, such brawls are nothing more than mass loss of control by players whose involvement in the game should stop at the sidelines or baselines.

During his glory years at UCLA, John Wooden's players were routinely manhandled and mauled by opponents who tried to substitute brute strength and unsportsmanlike tactics for whatever athletic skills they lacked, yet you never saw the Bruin players or subs duking it out with opponents in bloody brawls. It doesn't take a rocket scientist to figure out why Wooden's players never displayed a tag-team wrestling mentality on the sidelines, or who was responsible for their self-control.

Football and hockey are violent, collision-oriented sports, but remember: *Players will do what the coach lets them do (or, in some cases, encourages them to do).* Fights erupt from time to time; there's no way of predicting their occurrence—but there *is* a way to forestall them by warning players of the severity of the penalties involved. And there *is* a way to reduce the chances of their recurring by rigidly enforcing rules against fighting.

Self-control is the essence of team play. If, for example, a certain play is called and one player doesn't like the call, he still must carry out his responsibilities for *that* play, and not the play that he wanted to be called. As coaches, we try to extend that concept to every other phase of our players' performances, yet I've known football coaches to goad their players into fighting in practice. At least one basketball coach had a policy that no daily practice was over until someone drew blood; it was supposed to make his players "game tough."

You want your bench players to be supportive on the sidelines. One of the many ideas I've borrowed from coach Larry Chapman (AUM) is having the players on the bench stand up, applaud, and touch hands with every teammate who comes out of the game. It signifies that *whether your performance was great, mediocre, or downright awful, we're still behind you all the way.*

Fostering positive attitudes among benchwarmers. If you want your benchwarmers to support their teammates, take pains to make them feel that they are important to the team. Look for opportunities to cite them as examples of how you want your players to perform. Unused to being singled out for praise, a seldom-used benchwarmer will be embarrassed by the attention initially—but the pride that the player takes away from that brief moment in your spotlight will cement his or her loyalty to you and the team forever.

At the University of Alabama, the most prestigious award presented by Bear Bryant at the football team's annual banquet was named for an obscure fifth-string running back whom Bear chose to immortalize for his "100 percent hustle" attitude at daily practice throughout four years. The player's name escapes me, but you can bet that Bear's subtle message didn't escape his players: *It doesn't matter how good you are; it's what you do with what you've got.* As Bear liked to say, "I can reach a kid who doesn't have any ability as long as he doesn't know it."

Another way of making your subs feel important is to allow them to develop an identity apart from the rest of the team. For example, one football coach let his third-string defense call itself "The Battering Rams." (The school's nickname was the "Rams.") The players on that unit selected their own captains who, along with other team leaders, led the team in pregame warmup exercises and occasionally represented the team at midfield for the pregame coin toss. The unit had its own designated warmup area in practice, and the captains were permitted to schedule a few minutes of extra practice on days when they felt that their unit hadn't functioned up to their expectations. The coach assured the captains that, as long as their group worked hard and enthusiastically in practice, he would give them two full opponents' possessions of playing time per game. The players on that unit understood that the team couldn't afford to give up two touchdowns per game via the third-stringers, so their game preparations were almost always far more intense and demanding than the other players'.

Admittedly, such a strategy was somewhat risky on the coach's part, but his team was deep and powerful and he could afford it. In addition, it broadened his team's depth by giving the third-stringers much more game experience—and more responsibility within that context—than might have been possible otherwise. The players on the "Battering Rams" defensive unit developed a fierce loyalty to one another that strengthened their ties to the team and rendered them extremely competitive in games.

"On one occasion," the coach said, "it was a fairly important game for us, and the second unit wasn't getting the job done. The other team was driving steadily down the field on us. Instead of putting the first team back in, I called for the Battering Rams. Darned if they didn't go out and stop the other guys dead in their tracks. Those kids were sky high; when they came off the field, you'd have thought we had just won the state championship.

"They didn't always play that well, of course," he went on. "But what they accomplished as a unit was pretty incredible. Once, when I elevated one of their captains to second string, the boy came to me after practice and asked if he could keep working with the Battering Rams because they needed him to help them get ready for the next game. In all my years of coaching, I've never heard anything like that before or since."

> *It's amazing how quickly a message can travel from the right buttock to the lower base of the brain.*[7]
>
> —Kevin O'Neill, Tennessee basketball coach, on using pine time (i.e., bench duty) as a teaching tool

Playing time. Like Coach O'Neill and many other coaches, I use the threat of increased bench time to motivate my starters and the promise of increased playing time to motivate everyone else. Because I keep my promises, the players have relatively few grounds for complaining about their playing time. If everyone hustles every day, everyone plays in the next game. Some will play more than others, of course, because some players are better than others and we are, after all, trying to win the game. If every player knows that he or she will get to play, however briefly, all that remains is to remind them that (a) they must be ready when their turn comes, and (b) how long they play depends on how well they produce.

There aren't enough minutes in the game to give everyone the playing time he or she needs—but in most cases there *are* enough minutes to give them the playing time they deserve.

If everyone is playing hard and playing well, I'll shuffle players in and out of the game so fast that it'll look like a rapid transit station at rush hour, but that is not everyone's way. Adolph Rupp coached basketball at the University of Kentucky for thirty-eight years, and he seldom went deeper into his bench than the first six or seven players until mop-up time when the outcome was no longer in doubt.

---

[7] *Sports Illustrated*, Vol. 83, No. 23 (November 27, 1995), p. 28.

One of the advantages of substituting freely *when you can do it safely* is that no one but the starters can seriously complain about their lack of playing time. In all my years of coaching, no player has ever come to me complaining that he or she should be in the starting lineup or getting more playing time. I'm very confrontational and I tell my players, "If you think you can do better than the player who is currently ahead of you, start proving it *right now.* I've been wrong before, and maybe you've got skills I haven't seen. But if you can't back up your words with deeds, I'd better not hear any complaints from you about increasing your playing time or not starting."

Being confrontational has the advantage that problems are not allowed to linger like unwanted houseguests; it's your job to decide who starts and who plays at any given time. Take that job seriously; unless a player has accumulated impressive statistics, you should be able to make convincing arguments favoring the status quo. Start— or play—anyone who can get the job done; let the players who can't (or won't) carry their load look for a splinter-free section of the bench.

Defining roles. Not every player can do everything equally well. Defining roles consists of telling players exactly what is (and is not) expected of them. Those expectations should be realistic, specific, and limited to what each player is capable of accomplishing.

For example, if a basketball player is a poor ballhandler or shooter it's important to let the player know that she or he will not be expected to excel at those skills, or to perform them more often than occasionally. (You will, of course, work with the player to improve those skills in daily practice, because an opposing coach will attempt to steer the ball into that player's hands as often as possible when your team has the ball. For games, structure your offense in such a manner that your best ballhandlers handle the ball most of the time, your best shooters take most of the shots, and everyone else fills complementary roles such as setting picks and rebounding.)

You may or may not want to tell certain players not to shoot or dribble except in emergencies, but you should understand that there is nothing wrong with doing so. You're not belittling the player or showing a lack of confidence in her by limiting her shooting or ballhandling opportunities; in fact, you're doing precisely the opposite by protecting your player from situations that might further weaken her confidence in those areas. If a player is a weak ball-handler or poor shooter, she knows it—and in most cases she isn't any more enthusiastic than you are about the possibility of exercising her limited skills in those areas.

Your subs should understand what they will be held accountable for in games, and they should be given ample opportunities to practice those skills daily. For example, if you expect your running backs to function effectively as blockers as well as runners, they need to practice blocking regularly. Players don't have to be proficient in all phases of the game to develop pride in performance; they need to focus on the goals you set for them in those areas where they are most likely to succeed.

Finally: Many coaches send in the scrubs for mop-up duty in the latter stages of blowouts and act as if what the subs are doing doesn't matter because the team has an insurmountable lead. The message they are giving their players is this: "I've already done all the coaching and teaching I'm going to do tonight. The quality of your play isn't important to me because your teammates have played well enough to win the game for us." That attitude is condescending and demeaning to the players involved.

It is, of course, unrealistic, unwise, and self-defeating to expect the same level of skills execution from first-stringers and third-stringers, but it is by no means unrealistic to expect or demand the same level of intensity and concentration from *all* players in *all* situations.

The players will regard their own contributions to the team's success as important if the coach regards them as important. Don't sit around joking with the players on the sideline and generally ignoring the action on the court or playing field just because the outcome of the game is no longer in doubt. Pay attention to your players; encourage them to hustle and to pay attention to what they're doing. Regardless of the game situation, the score, or the players involved, the team *and every player on it* deserves the coach's best efforts.

Coach with intensity, and teach your athletes to play with intensity at all times. Treat every player's game and practice performance as if each of them is important to the achievement of team goals. Let every player know that, when her time comes, she must be ready to give a total effort for as long as is necessary.[8] It is the players' willingness to give their all on the team's behalf, and without question or regard for their own physical comfort, that makes them special to you and to their teammates. That's as true for the last player on the team as it is for the starters.

---

[8] You don't have to try to extend a 60-point lead to 90 points or more. You're not interested in humiliating your opponents. Your goal should be, rather, to improve every player's game performances in specific directions, regardless of the situation. One way to do this without further running up scores is to have the various substitution units practice phases of your offense that aren't necessary now but may come in handy in other situations (e.g., late-game or last-second ball protection or come-from-behind strategies, or new plays or patterns that you've been practicing but haven't used in games).

4

EFFECTIVE TEACHING AND PRACTICING

No coach ever won a game by what he knows; it's what his players have learned.
—Amos Alonzo Stagg

There was no coaching this year. (It was) All teaching.
—Nolan Richardson (Univ. of Arkansas)
on starting four freshmen in 1996

I had no trouble communicating. The players just didn't like what I had to say.
—Frank Robinson (Baltimore Orioles)

What makes a good coach?

According to some parents, a good coach is one who understands that winning or losing is secondary in importance to giving their son or daughter adequate playing time. For some fans, a good coach is one whose teams not only win all of their games, but do so in a manner that is exciting and crowd pleasing. A basketball coach complained, "I asked the father of one of my ex-players why he (the father) had stopped coming to our home games. He said, 'It's boring. I like close games, and you're winning every game by thirty points.' That's when I realized that I would never be able to satisfy anyone but myself in my coaching."

Some good coaches are close to their players; others are aloof. Some of the good ones are mild-mannered like Lenny Wilkens, others are volatile and explosive. Some are conservative in their approaches to offense and defense, others are relentlessly aggressive. Some coaches are more organized than others, or know more about their sport, or are better recruiters or game coaches. But *all* good coaches share two characteristics—their teams play hard and unselfishly, and they are good teachers.

Stripped to its barest essentials, coaching consists of bringing athletes into our program and teaching them what they need to know in order to prepare them for competition. Some coaches are better at teaching fundamental skills, and some are better at teaching team patterns. The best coaches are equally knowledgeable and adept in both areas. In any case, if this were the textbook for Coaching Philosophy 101 we might begin with the following syllogism: *Coaching is teaching. Teaching is communicating. Therefore, coaching is communicating.*

TEACHING: CONCEPTS AND PRINCIPLES

As coaches, we believe that competition is a positive force for making people stronger, more confident, and self-reliant. We believe that mastering fundamental skills is a prerequisite to learning advanced skills and techniques. We require our players to memorize plays, patterns, formations, and other essential knowledge. And because we believe that the more you do something, the better you get at it, we rely on repetition and drills as mainstays in the teaching-learning process. Most of us believe that this approach works as well in the classroom as it does on the court or playing field. The following concepts and principles relate to coaching, teaching, and communication:

1. THERE IS NO ONE RIGHT WAY TO TEACH

Successful teaching is largely a matter of trial and error. While coaching experience brings confidence in certain approaches to teaching skills, the individual nature of each of our players indicates that what works with one player isn't always equally effective for others. We tell; we demonstrate; we distribute playbooks, game plans, and scouting reports; we study game films; we use drills, slogans, competitive activities, chalkboard explanations and discussions, and whatever else we can think of—and all for the purpose of teaching players what we want them to do or to know. When those methods fail, we try them again or look for new or better ways to get our points across. As baseball's Paul Richards (Baltimore Orioles) said, "Tell a ballplayer something a thousand times, then tell him again, because that might be the time he'll understand something." Or it may be the time that he's listening.

2. LEARNING IS A MATTER OF DOING SOMETHING UNTIL IT BECOMES A HABIT

We'll begin with what might be called "The 10,000 Times Principle": If you want to become expert at something or master a given skill, do it 10,000 times.

After my sophomore year in high school, I had a summer job as an instructor at the Savannah (GA) YMCA. Every morning, I arrived early enough to practice shooting free throws by myself in the gym before classes began. I shot 25 at a time and recorded the scores in a notebook, repeating the process until I'd shot at least 250. Writing down the scores forced me to concentrate on each shot. If there was still time remaining, I shot more free throws or worked on other phases of my game.

Whether I was a slow learner or my high school coach wasn't very good at teaching offensive fundamentals is unimportant; all that matters is that I wasn't what you'd call a good free-throw shooter when the summer began. Around the time I reached 3,500 free throws, though, something incredible began to happen; I noticed that, whenever I did certain things (i.e., held the ball in the same place every time; spread my shooting fingers; cocked my wrist; supported the ball on my hand pads—the callused area—and fingertips rather than my palm; kept my eyes on the target and didn't watch the ball in flight; extended my arms as fully as possible before releasing the ball; and uncocked my wrist in following through—called "making a swan")—whenever I did all those things, I made most of my free throws.[1] Of course, you already understand all that if you're a basketball coach, but for me, as a high school junior, it was an act of discovery on a par with the invention of the wheel.

---

[1] It sounds complicated, but it's not. Of the seven checkpoints cited, only the last three involve movement. The others should be done prior to starting the shot.

I made 643 of my first 1,000 free throws in early June. I improved rapidly after that, though. By September, having fulfilled my goal of shooting 10,000 free throws, I was disappointed whenever I didn't make at least 45 out of every 50 shots. But what really mattered was that, in shooting so many free throws in a relatively brief time span, I became so attuned to my shooting form that I learned to recognize what felt wrong about a missed shot. That's the sort of thing that can happen when you practice a skill 10,000 times! Of course, you have to concentrate on what you're doing, and concentrating is difficult if you're not used to it. Still, concentrating while performing a skill that many times offers the added bonus of extending your ability to concentrate in other areas, thus doubling the activity's effectiveness.

Habits. There are good habits and bad habits. Invariably, bad habits involve laziness, whether in the form of the athlete's looking for a less physically demanding way to perform a skill (e.g., hand-checking in basketball) or the athlete's failure to concentrate on the skill he or she is performing.

In teaching individual skills, your goal is to find a way to help your players form mental images of themselves performing certain movement sequences correctly. The thinking process involved in learning to shoot a jump shot in basketball is the same as that in learning to perform a complex movement in diving or gymnastics. Your role in this process is to identify the elements in the skill that are associated with timing, accuracy, and efficiency of movement, and to correct errors as they arise. The outcome of such instruction, rigorously applied on a regular basis, is players who can perform a skill the same way every time—the ultimate *good* habit!

Such outcomes are rather easily achieved in gross motor movements such as jumping or running, and less easily mastered in skills involving hand-eye coordination such as hitting a baseball. In the latter case, having a "feel" for the skill involves both mental imagery and a kinesthetic sense of what the muscles are doing—and when—in order to execute the movement successfully. Athletes who develop such acute neuromuscular sense may actually learn to monitor their own performances without the coach's help.

Many coaches, unwilling to face the daily resistance that accompanies trying to teach skills to players who don't want to learn them, opt for the easy way out and accept raw athleticism as a substitute for improving fundamental skills. Such an approach will work as long as you have more and better athletes than your opponents; it *won't* work when it's the other guys or gals who are bigger, stronger, and faster. In the absence of superior athletes, having players who are sound fundamentally is the only thing that can save you. That's why Chapter 2 stressed the importance of finding players who believe in you and love to play the game; they are the ones you can motivate to do things like practicing on their own.

Ignorance. If you don't understand the fundamentals yourself, you won't recognize errors or know why they are occurring, and you won't know how to correct them.

Ignorance can be an acceptable excuse initially, but continued ignorance is a sin of omission; every sport has fundamentals textbooks and videotapes by experts who know what the sport is all about. Anyone who has been in coaching for two years or more and still doesn't know how the basic skills of his or her sport are properly executed hasn't bothered to find out. If you know any such coaches, get their teams on your schedule as soon as possible. You may not defeat them every time, depending on their players' athleticism, but you can rest assured that you won't be outcoached!

3. THE ONLY WAY TO IMPROVE FUNDAMENTAL SKILLS IS THROUGH REPETITION AND DRILL

There aren't enough hours in the day for all the coaching that needs to be done—but learning takes time and proceeds at its own pace. You can't speed up the learning process by teaching faster.

Every coach's worst enemy is wasted time; the good news here is that attention to fundamentals is never wasted. The offenses and defenses we use are nothing more than the coordinated, synchronized movements of players executing various basic skills simultaneously. The need for fundamental soundness is shown in the frequency with which plays break down when one or more players fail to execute the responsibilities of their positions.

Drills and scrimmaging. There are two basic approaches to practice organization: drills and scrimmaging. Whereas scrimmages generally simulate game conditions, drills create specific, repeatable situations that focus on selected fundamental skills or aspects of team play. Both drills and scrimmaging have their rightful place in daily practice; both possess advantages and disadvantages that can aid or hinder a team's progress, depending on the players' skills or the team's needs:

■ Because scrimmaging basically amounts to playing an actual game (or a portion thereof), it is challenging and exciting to players in ways that drills cannot be.

■ While scrimmaging provides a suitable format for familiarizing players with the broad range of situations they will encounter in actual games, its effective use depends on (a) whether you've installed your offense and defense, and (b) whether your players are fundamentally sound. Because of the fluid nature of game situations, scrimmaging does not allow the coach or players to concentrate on specific situations, nor does it lend itself well to correcting mistakes.

■ Drills may or may not duplicate actual game conditions—although many of the best drills do—but they permit the coach to focus on specific situations in ways that scrimmaging cannot match. Drills can be repeated as often as necessary for players to learn to execute skills or movement sequences without thinking about what they're doing. Because most drills are of relatively short duration, they allow coaches and players to correct individual mistakes without interrupting the flow of the activity.

■ Most important, drills offer the only effective format for teaching individual skills. UCLA's John Wooden contended that every coach's goals should be the same, namely, getting the best players you can find and using the best drills you can find to teach them how to play the game the way you want it played.

Regarding the use of drills to teach skills, Larry Chapman (Auburn University at Montgomery) contends that a five-step process is involved:

1. Specify (what is to be learned)
2. Simplify
3. Repeat

4. Repeat

5. Repeat[2]

Specify. Say exactly what you mean to say in a way that can be understood. In giving instructions, I've sometimes felt as though I were speaking in one language and my players were listening in another. Invariably, the fault has been mine—in failing to specify exactly what I meant, what I wanted to be done, or how it was to be done. In many cases, I haven't searched diligently enough for the simplest way to explain, describe, or analyze a given skill or movement.

Veteran high school football coach Mike Koehler *(Football Coach's Survival Guide)* concurs: "Any time something goes wrong on the team, the first thing I do is grab a mirror to take a good, hard look at myself, to determine, first of all, what I might be doing to cause it."

Simplify. What do you do when an offensive play or pattern starts misfiring like a $250 used car? In the old days, coaches went "back to the basics" to practice the fundamental skills upon which plays and patterns are based. While that's never a bad strategy, it has been supplanted in recent years by the notion of using *breakdown drills* to give a sputtering offense a kick start.

The concept underlying breakdown drills is that it's easier to teach and to learn an offense in parts than it is to teach and learn the whole thing at once. This concept is strengthened by the fact that, when an offense misfires, it's usually only one or two aspects of the total play or pattern that need treatment, not the entire package. If you break down the offense—or even a single play within an offensive system—into bite-sized, easily digestible segments, the players gain a thorough understanding of each part that will make learning the entire offense much easier. And later, when problems arise, you simply identify the aspect(s) of the offense that need fine-tuning and go back to the breakdown drills that cover the area needing work. Unless you're using an offense that you created, there probably are books available in your sport that break down

---

[2] Chapman, Larry F., and Warren, William E. *Basketball Coach's Survival Guide.* West Nyack, NY (Parker Publishing Company, 1994), p. 130.

your offense into instructional blocks. Still, if you understand your offensive system as well as you should, you probably can do as good a job as anyone else in devising your own breakdown drills.[3]

Regarding points 3–5 and the teaching of drills, there are two aspects of those *repeats*: repeating your instructions as often (or in as many different ways) as necessary to be absorbed, and repeating the drill until errors are identified and corrected and the players' actions or reactions are both habitual and correct. Coach Chapman believes that, regarding the latter point, it is better to follow your scheduled time allotment for a given drill when it's not working than to extend the drill for a few minutes longer.

"We think that, if a practice schedule is important enough to prepare, it's important enough to follow," Larry says. "We've found that, if we start cheating on the time allotments we've set for our drills, we wind up running out of practice time before we've covered everything we meant to do. We think it's better to leave it, go on to the next activity, and come back to it tomorrow when the players and coaches have a fresh outlook." The only exception he makes is occasionally "borrowing" an extra minute or two from a later activity to make a coaching point, or to allow the players one or two more tries at executing the skill or movement after such instruction has taken place. But he *won't* extend the drill ten to fifteen minutes longer than planned. If it's working, the players don't need that extra time; if not, the players and coaches tend to become increasingly frustrated, and their frustration and negativity are likely to carry over into the rest of practice. And when (or if) the players finally perform the skill as desired, the atmosphere is likely to be a feeling of relief rather than a sense of accomplishment.

How much is too much? As for the ratio between drills and scrimmaging in daily practice—well, it depends on what you're comfortable with. Some coaches scrimmage during part of every

---

[3] A nine-step method of installing an offense via breakdown drills: 1. Teach your players the basic pattern or movement sequences by walking them through it until everyone is familiar with it. 2. Drill the players in isolated segments of the basic pattern. 3. Add defense to the drill sequences, but don't let the defenders overplay the pattern. 4. Introduce options to the pattern one at a time in walk-through fashion. 5. Break down the options into drill segments. 6. Add passive defense to the options drill segments. 7. Practice the basic pattern, options and automatics, first in breakdown drills and then in team form. 8. Add full-scale defense to the breakdown drills and team run-throughs. 9. Whenever you encounter problems, go back to the breakdown drills in practice. (Source: Chapman and Warren, *Basketball Coach's Survival Guide*, pp. 139–146.)

daily practice, starting on Day One and continuing throughout the season. A veteran basketball coach explained, "It's never too early to give your kids a feel for the game and actual playing conditions." But his program was established, his players experienced and fundamentally sound in most areas, and they were already familiar with his offense and defense. It's unlikely that he would have felt that way with an inexperienced squad, or with players who were learning a new offense or defense.

That coach's approach is far superior to that of other basketball coaches, who do nothing but scrimmage throughout every daily practice. That's like allowing your five-year-old son or daughter to skip grades K–2 and start school in the third grade. A coach is hired to teach and train young athletes, not to referee—or worse, *play*—in daily full-length scrimmages). The only advantages to the full-time scrimmage approach are that (a) the players are usually in great shape physically, and (b) they aren't in any danger of being overcoached.

Drills are for players who need them. Scrimmaging is for players who don't need the sort of repetitive practice that drills provide. If your players are fundamentally sound and understand your offense, defense, and the strategies associated with them, there is no reason why you can't or shouldn't devote at least part of your daily practices to scrimmaging. After all, when the skills, patterns, or strategies break down you can always go back to the drills.

4. Concentration Is a Habit, Not a Talent

Unlike, say, slam dunking or driving a golf ball 350 yards off the tee, the ability to concentrate is a skill that every athlete can master through practice. Although concentration is a mental process, it does not require a high IQ or intellectual giftedness. It requires merely that players focus their attention on the task at hand. Still, there are several aspects of teaching players to concentrate that we as coaches must understand.

Because concentration is a learned skill, it must be taught. Teaching players to concentrate is not so much instructing them as it is creating situations that require them to concentrate. And it's not a matter of saying "Here's how you concentrate," but rather "Here's what I want you to think about." Players can be taught to concentrate even when they know almost nothing about the skill they're performing.[4]

The problem here is that many of today's young athletes don't really want to think about what they're doing; they'd rather Just Do It, as the Nike ads suggest, and rely on their athleticism to get them by. Thinking and paying attention can be difficult, especially when the action is intense and the game is on the line—but they are also necessary. Assuming that athletes will stay focused and concentrate without being taught to (and required to) is somewhat akin to expecting children to say "please" and "thank you" without being taught or required to.

Concentration of any sort increases players' ability to concentrate in other areas. If, through practice, a player can learn to concentrate intently while executing a given skill or movement a number of times in drills, it follows that the player should, within limits, be able to concentrate intently for the same amount of time in other phases of the game. In football, blocking isn't the same as tackling; pitching is totally unlike hitting in baseball; yet the level of focus necessary for successful skills execution is identical for all of them.

The term concentration *can refer to either short- or long-term concentration.* While our goal is to extend our players' ability to concentrate in both ways, short-term concentration comes first. For example, since most football plays last no more than six to eight seconds, players must be able to concentrate at least that long in order to ensure carrying out their responsibilities in a given play. On a long-term basis, they must also be able to maintain that same level of focus throughout every play during the entire game.

Team sports are not static; they are based on creating or reacting to situations involving movement. Those movements are generally fluid, with one set of movements preceding another, and those movements in turn leading to others—the "flow" of the game in progress. Short-term concentration involves analyzing the situation

---

[4] A familiar example: The coach gathers her basketball players around the free-throw lane at the end of practice and says, "There's no time remaining in the game, the score is tied, and you're at the line to shoot one-if-one. If you make your first shot, we win the game and you can go home. If you miss it, the game goes into overtime and you stay after practice to shoot 25 more free throws." The coach has surely taught her players the elements of proper form, but even if she hasn't done so she can rest assured that the players will be concentrating on *something* when their turn comes at the line.

in regard to one's responsibilities within it, and changing one's assessment and subsequent actions or reactions as the present becomes the past and new situations arise.

There's more to it than that, though: Depending on their fundamental soundness, players may or may not have to divide their attention between the skill involved and the situation in which the skill is being executed. For example, in dribbling to keep the ball away from a defender a basketball player must divide her attention between the ball, the defender on the ball, other defenders, her teammates, her court position, and possibly the game clock as well. While a skilled dribbler can protect the ball quite easily in most situations by focusing on the situation rather than the ball, the opposite is true of an unskilled dribbler who has to watch the ball in order to control her dribble. Dribbling drills can be used to teach players to master protective dribbling techniques; situational drills familiarize players with the various situations they will encounter in games; and constant repetition causes the players' actions and reactions to become habitual.

Drills are superior to scrimmaging for improving short-term concentration; scrimmaging is superior to drills for improving long-term concentration. In this area, the art of coaching is knowing which your team needs the most at any given time.

To improve short-term concentration, use incentive drills that reward or punish players for correct or incorrect execution of a skill. A high school football coach and I have an ongoing debate as to whether coaches motivate. His position is that coaches cannot motivate their players because all motivation is self-motivation. No matter what we say or do, he contends, the players will decide for themselves when they will hustle, and how hard they will work, and for how long.

Searching for ways to motivate kids to do things they don't want to do can be difficult, time-consuming, and frustrating—especially if you confine your motivation to pregame and halftime speeches—but there are other motivators: In games, the fans and the scoreboard motivate; in daily practice, drills and scrimmages can motivate players to concentrate and perform at higher levels. By using competitive drills, rewards, and punishments, you can make your players want to concentrate, work hard, and avoid making mistakes; all you need is a competitive drill that offers rewards and penalties *for both of the competitors every time the drill is performed.* The rewards don't have to be great or the punishments severe in order to ensure the drill's effectiveness; they need merely be important enough to make your players want to succeed.

In football, as Stan Scarborough[5] has noted, one of the many problems coaches face is that—over the long haul of a season—so much repetitive drill goes on that it's virtually impossible to get players to give a total effort every time. In the line, for example, offensive and defensive players may attempt to go through the motions of executing their assignments in practice by leaning against each other halfheartedly, a technique Coach Scarborough referred to as "brother-in-lawing."

To combat brother-in-lawing, you can add a bit of competitive spice to the drill. The offensive line coach might tell his players, "We're going to practice protecting the passer, who will be using a (3-, 5-, or 7-step) drop. Your job is to keep the other guys away from the quarterback for *X* seconds on each snap. We'll go for twenty-five snaps. You're starting out with *no wind sprints at the end of today's practice.* For every time a defensive lineman touches the tackling dummy at the quarterback's drop site within *X* seconds, all of you will do one wind sprint with the rest of the team. If the other guys go 0-for-25, you can pack it in and hit the showers while they're doing twenty-five 40s."

At the same time, the defensive line coach is telling *his* players the same thing, with modifications: "You're starting out with twenty-five wind sprints at the end of today's practice. Every time any of you gets to the quarterback within *X* seconds, we'll subtract one wind sprint. If you go 25-for-25, you won't have to do any 40s at all." All of the players involved must use legal techniques. Failure to do so would result in one wind sprint for that team for that trial.

In basketball, when practice is going poorly because no one wants to hustle or concentrate, I'll occasionally scrap my practice schedule altogether and go to our half-court three-on-three drill. Here's how it works:

Line up all of the players in three rows at half-court. The first player in each line is a defender. The three defenders can press at

[5] Scarborough, Stan, and Warren, William E. *Option Football: Concepts and Techniques for Winning.* Boston: Allyn & Bacon, 1983.

half-court or set up closer to the basket, whichever they prefer. The second players in each line are the offensive team. Their goal is to score, or at least to take a shot that hits the rim before the defenders get the ball via a steal, turnover, or rebound. The rest of the players await their turns, moving toward the front of the lines as the teams change. Rotation is from the waiting lines to offense to defense to the back of the waiting lines, and so on.

When play begins, the offensive team has twenty seconds to shoot and either score or hit the rim. If they fail to do so within the allotted time—or if they lose possession prematurely via a steal or turnover—play stops, all three offensive players leave the court to perform whatever penalty is set (e.g., running laps or sprints along the sidelines, doing hops over benches or other obstacles, jumping rope, running up and down bleachers) and then go to the back of the lines. Meanwhile, three more offensive players take their place and a new twenty-second sequence begins.

If three consecutive offensive teams fail to score or maintain ball possession, the defenders' reward is to move to the back of the waiting line without penalty. The next six players in line take over the defense and offense, respectively.

If a player commits a foul, whether offensive or defensive, that player is replaced by the next player in line and a fresh twenty seconds begins. The player who committed the foul performs the penalty and goes to the back of one of the lines.

When the offensive team scores, the defenders leave the court to perform their penalty, the offensive players move to defense, and the next three players in line go to offense. If the offensive team rebounds a missed shot, a fresh twenty-second possession begins. If the defense rebounds a missed shot that hits the rim, play stops, neither team is penalized, and both teams rotate as usual.

If the ball goes out of bounds and the offensive team retains possession, the twenty-second count stops momentarily until they inbound the ball from the sideline or baseline and try to score within whatever time remains in that twenty-second possession.

In simple terms, then, play begins with a twenty-second time limit and continues until (a) time expires, (b) the offensive team scores, (c) the offensive team commits a turnover or loses the ball without having shot and hit the rim, (d) someone commits a foul, or (e) the defensive team rebounds a missed shot off the rim. In all cases except (e), someone is penalized.

Time is kept by a manager, using a stopwatch if the game clock cannot be reset immediately. (Another manager should monitor the penalty phase to ensure that every player completes the penalty.) Using a stopwatch means that the players won't always know how much time is remaining in a given twenty-second possession, but that will hasten the players' efforts to set up a good shot quickly, and thus reduce the waiting time in line by the extra players.

These drills are examples of what I call *self-motivating drills*. Their principal value lies in the fact that you don't have to constantly urge your players to hustle, or to think about what they're doing, in order to ensure a total effort on their part. Motivation and concentration are inherent in the drill itself. Even if you never say a word except in terms of refereeing the action, teammates will motivate one another to hustle and to concentrate.

There are several points to consider regarding the use of self-motivating drills:

a. Not every drill can or should be self-motivational, especially in the sense of the football drill and its penalties. After all, you don't want players doing 250 wind sprints after practice as the result of failures in ten drills. Most drills are teaching drills, whether in terms of teaching individual fundamentals or aspects of team offense or defense, and players should never be penalized for not learning as quickly as you want them to.

b. Players must possess the skills necessary to carry out their individual responsibilities. Where team concepts are involved, players must understand the offense or defense thoroughly enough to be held accountable for its eventual success or failure. Without these prerequisites, players will fail most of the time, regardless of how motivated they are or how hard they try to concentrate.

c. Two such drills were described; virtually *any* competitive drill in any sport can be used as a self-motivational drill, but it's wise not to overdo it. Self-motivational drills are not a substitute for teaching or coaching; their effective use is limited to motivating players to work hard and concentrate in competitive situations.

Mistakes lose games. Everyone knows that. Still, there's a big difference between hustling mistakes and lazy mistakes. Nobody likes mistakes, but even the most driven of coaches I've known can at least accept, if not entirely overlook, their players' hustling mistakes.[6] Erk Russell's "One More Time" slogan suggests that neither mental fatigue nor pressure is an acceptable excuse for failing to concentrate on a short-term basis.

To improve long-term concentration, use scrimmaging or controlled scrimmaging. Just as we use drills to practice skills that will make our players more effective in a variety of game situations, we also attempt to extend their ability to focus more intensely and for longer periods of time in order to put those skills to best use at any given moment. We approach the *depth* of concentration through drills, but to extend its *length* we need action sequences that are longer than most drills. *Scrimmaging* refers to any extended team activity that simulates actual game conditions.

Scrimmaging allows players to see how the individual and situational drills they do relate to game situations. It permits players to use a broad array of offensive and defensive skills in an equally broad array of game situations. That same breadth of skills and game situations, however, tends to limit the effective use of scrimmaging to teams and players who can deal with the unpredictability that is inherent in game situations. Players who must consciously think about the skills, techniques, plays, or patterns they are executing are unlikely to be able to concentrate on anything else simultaneously.[7]

A vast gulf lies between the ability to concentrate on the execution of a single skill or movement in a particular situation and extending that concentration to include all of the situations that make up a game or any of its subdivisions (e.g., a half, quarter, or inning). The difference between what drills and scrimmages are intended to accomplish is equally broad: repetitions of specific skills or situations versus the random unpredictability of game situations. If those two choices were all there were, coaches in continuous action sports such as basketball, hockey, and soccer would be hard pressed

---

[6] A hustling mistake is an error that occurs when a player is earnestly trying to make something good happen. Lazy mistakes arise when players aren't paying attention to what they're doing, or to what is going on around them.

---

[7] This does not contradict my earlier contention that concentration of any sort improves players' ability to concentrate in other areas. A player may be able to walk, and to chew gum, but that doesn't mean she can do both at the same time.

to bridge those gaps. Fortunately, there's an intermediate step between drills and scrimmaging. It's called *controlled scrimmaging*.

In controlled scrimmaging, teams practice two sequential phases of their overall game under scrimmage conditions, stopping to reset the offense and defense when the second phase is completed. For example, a basketball coach might want to practice half-court defense and fast breaking after scores or transitions, or getting back on defense quickly after scores or transitions. In either case, the sequences would begin the same way every time, with the same teams on offense and defense—and they would end the same way (i.e., with the shot at the end of the break in the former case, and the team stopping the opponents' fast break and settling into its half-court defense in the latter instance).

Any two sequential phases of a sport can be used for controlled scrimmaging.

Limiting the scrimmaging to two specific situations offers the sort of immediate, continuous repetition that makes drills effective; performing under simulated game conditions adds a sense of reality—and thus urgency—that may be missing from drills that are less specifically game-oriented. Controlled scrimmaging requires players to extend their concentration beyond that which is necessary in most drills, yet it falls short of requiring them to concentrate on every phase of the game for long stretches at a time. The repetitions and breaks in the action to reset the offense and defense allow ample time and opportunity for instruction; the action itself, albeit isolated and controlled, provides excellent preparation for actual game experiences.

Incidentally, the sequences can be made more competitive by keeping score. Controlled scrimmaging can be made self-motivational by, say, offering an extra water break to members of the winning team.

> *I don't know why anyone would be surprised that I was a first-round (NBA) draft pick. After all, I played every day for four years against the best center in the world.*
>
> —Swen Nater
> (backup center at UCLA behind Bill Walton)

5. TO INCREASE PERFORMANCE, INCREASE THE RESISTANCE

This adaptation of the *overload principle* suggests that, in drills and scrimmages, the weaker opponent should be given all the advantages. One of the problems associated with coaching superior athletes is providing competitive challenges for them in daily practice, especially when one athlete is far superior to his or her teammates. Without sufficient challenges, such athletes may develop a half-hearted work ethic that inhibits their progress. The solution to this problem lies in creating competitive situations in which the athlete's skills are taxed beyond what he or she might normally expect. If your superstar isn't sufficiently challenged in your drills and scrimmages, perhaps a permanent double-team can increase the resistance enough to provide a suitable challenge.

With one outstanding player, you can have him or her play one-on-two in your competitive drills. With two superior players at the same position, you can pit them one-on-one against each other or have them go two-on-three against their teammates. In track, give your slower distance runners time or distance advantages; in the sprints, stagger the starting blocks as much as necessary to make races competitive.

If there is a noticeable drop-off in quality beyond your first string, add one or more extra players to the other team in scrimmages. The more pronounced the disparity, the more advantages you may need to equalize the teams. In baseball, you might give the weaker team an extra fielder, start their innings with a baserunner on first, and give them four outs. Conversely, you could limit the stronger team to only two outs per inning and start their players' at-bats with a 1-2 count.

In practicing half-court defense in basketball—zone *or* man-to-man—try stationing a sixth offensive player in the middle of the lane (and ignore the three-second rule, of course). In full-court pressing defensive drills, I almost always put at least six players on offense, including a snowbird under the offensive basket. More commonly, we've gone 5-on-7 or 5-on-8 because I've seldom had the luxury of coaching ten quality players at a time. I tell my starters, "That's the price you have to pay for being a starter. *If you're a starter, you work harder.*"

In every case, your ultimate goal is to make your drills and scrimmages more demanding than your games will be. Admittedly, this isn't always possible, but it *is* always desirable.

6. Organized Practices Facilitate Teaching and Learning

Know what you want to accomplish; set daily goals and devise an organized plan for accomplishing those goals. Sometimes those plans fail, as with drills that just don't work the way we intended them to. Sometimes it's our fault or our players', and sometimes it's just the wrong drill. Again, teaching is largely a matter of trial and error; that's why it's important to sit down with your assistant coaches for a few minutes after every practice to evaluate the results while the practice is fresh in your mind.

Most successful coaches organize their daily practices into time blocks. How rigorously you structure and adhere to your time allotments is your concern, but players should never be permitted to waste time with horseplay at the expense of learning. Activities should be structured in such a manner that no one has time to stand around loafing, chatting, or daydreaming. (My apparent exception to this rule, the 3-on-3 basketball drill I use occasionally, reminds even the most casual observers in the waiting line of how intense their effort and concentration must be when their turn comes if they are to avoid the penalties involved. Their waiting time between turns seldom exceeds ninety seconds, and we wouldn't be doing the drill in the first place if their collective effort and concentration had been better!)

Beyond organizing daily practices into time blocks, there is also the notion of *organizing your teaching for maximum effectiveness*. For example, preparing copies of your daily practice schedules for your managers as well as your assistant coaches will reduce the transition time between drills; you will have the necessary personnel and equipment in place when and where they are needed. Whether you're using special equipment for station drills or a portable chalkboard to diagram plays, it should be available and ready for use at the desired location and designated time.

Team managers. Whether your team is of state championship caliber or destined to absorb more losses than a failed savings & loan institution, *you deserve good managers*. Conscientious, hardworking managers[8] can make your job easier in a thousand ways.

The best time and place to look for managers is in your preseason tryouts; they're the ones who give the proverbial 110 percent throughout every second of practice, but lack the basic athleticism needed for development into effective players. Rather than cut such players, if there's a managerial opening available, talk with them

---

[8] And student trainers too, for that matter.

about joining the team in that capacity—with the understanding, of course, that their new role, while demanding, will be unlike that of the players.

Good managers are very important. To underscore their importance, I give my managers a whistle just like mine and tell my players that the managers' duties always come first. Whether they're running the clock in scrimmages, keeping stats in games, or otherwise attending to their regular duties and responsibilities, no one is allowed to interfere with, inhibit, or question their authority. I consider my managers an extension of *me*, and as long as they take their responsibilities seriously I'll back them the same way I back my assistant coaches. Such an approach tends to build strong loyalty and encourages the managers to use initiative in developing their team roles to the fullest extent possible. Everything they do that helps me helps the team and vice versa; emphasizing the importance of their contributions (which might otherwise be overlooked and thus minimized) is one more avenue for building the sort of pride in performance that I want every member of the team to have.

A second aspect of organizing your teaching for maximum effectiveness is *teaching new skills or concepts early in your daily practices, while the players are fresh both mentally and physically*. Fatigue, whether physical or mental, saps concentration and inhibits retention; that's why it's better to work with players on an individual basis either before practice or during its early stages than to work with them after a lengthy scrimmage or the conclusion of conditioning drills. Besides, early work permits the player(s) to practice those skills in situations arising later in the practice.

Finally: A basic tenet of coaching suggests that you teach players skills they can use, and patterns—or a style of play—that incorporate those skills. But since you cannot teach everything at once, what you teach should be arranged sequentially in terms of priorities. This in turn suggests that *long-range planning should precede short-range planning*.

To cite an obvious example: In many cases preseason practice is too brief to install every phase of your offenses and defenses to the extent that you'd like in order to be ready for the first game of the season. (That's why most coaches prefer to start the season with one or more nonregion or nonconference games.) The problem isn't insurmountable, especially if you have experienced, talented players returning from last year and you anticipate no major changes in your offense and defense. Even then, however, your approach should be the same, namely, covering the bases as thoroughly as possible in the allotted time. Setting priorities facilitates the process.

In basketball, for instance, there are nine general areas to consider: conditioning; fundamentals; individual offense and defense; team defense; team offense; beating the presses; fast breaking; delay tactics; out-of-bounds plays; and special situations such as last-shot scoring plays. Prioritizing those areas doesn't necessarily mean deciding which ones you'll cover in preseason practice and which will have to be postponed until after the first game; if possible, you'll cover all of them in preseason. Prioritizing them means *deciding which ones are most important and thus deserve the most practice time.*

Because every team is different, priorities may change considerably from one season to the next. Still, conditioning is always a high priority, and with an inexperienced team, beating the presses usually ranks second on the list, followed by fundamentals drills, individual offense and defense, team defense, and team offense. The more highly skilled and experienced a team is, the more preseason practice time can be allotted to the other areas.

New priorities. One of the main reasons for resisting the temptation to discard an offense or defense that isn't working and start over from scratch after the season has begun is that, once league or conference play begins in earnest, a new priority arises: *preparing the team for each upcoming opponent in succession.* Such preparations may or may not be extensive, depending on how you feel about scouting or adapting your offense or defense to counter opponents' offenses and defenses. Whatever practice time is spent in this regard, however, is time that would otherwise be spent attending to other facets of your game preparations. If you decide to, say, install a new offense after your third game of the season, you should expect it to consume from one-third to one-half of your practice time for at least a month. That's a heavy price to pay for doing what should have been done during the off-season.

To compound the problem, many coaches recognize a need for reducing the length (but not the intensity) of their daily practices as the season progresses. Preseason and early regular season practices tend to be longer because there's a lot for the players to learn while they're getting in shape. Because long seasons tend to wear players down both physically and emotionally, many coaches cut back the length of their practices by as much as one-fourth by midseason, and even more in late season as tournament time approaches. Such compression requires that all of the prioritized areas be in place by then in order for the new priorities—working on options and variations within your offense and defense, and preparing for upcoming opponents—to receive adequate attention.

Weekly practice schedules. If you start with the premise that there are nine areas of team preparation to be taken into account, one way to cover them in an organized manner is to highlight a different area each week. Continue to work, of course, with the various areas in daily practices, but giving more time, attention, and in-depth treatment to one area per week offers flexibility that might not be possible in other forms of practice planning. All it takes is willingness to sit down and list all of the drills and teaching activities you'll use, and deciding how much time to allot to them in your daily practices.

A high school basketball coach listened as I explained the planning process. His response: "That sure seems like a lot of work to me. I just don't have time for all that planning." He had time to play golf or tennis every weekend, and every afternoon after basketball practice, however.

I've known a lot of coaches like that over the years; you probably have too. We should be grateful to them for making the rest of us look better by comparison. It's a matter of priorities.

HINTS FOR EFFECTIVE TEACHING

1. BE PATIENT

Perhaps this rather obvious bit of advice should have a qualifying addition: Be patient *with players who want to learn, and are willing to work hard to do so.*

Once, I got so fed up with my junior high basketball players complaining "I can't do that" whenever I introduced a new skill that I assessed a penalty of an extra mile of running after practice for anyone who said it. What "I can't do that" *really* means is, "I don't want to try to do it your way; I'd rather do it *my* way, even if it's wrong." My coaching time—and yours—is far too valuable to waste it arguing with fourteen-year-olds (or anyone else, for that matter) about what they need to know in order to become more effective players.

Having said that, however, I hasten to add that, along with a knowledge of your sport and its fundamentals, patience, a positive attitude, and a sense of humor are indispensable virtues in teaching situations.

Much as we would like to speed up the learning process, it can't be done.[9] All we can do is create conditions favorable for learning, motivate our players to want to learn, and show and tell them how to do the things we want them to learn, as often and in as many ways as necessary for learning to take place.

Learning is unpredictable. Some players learn faster than others—but even so, learning does not occur with prescribed regularity. In many cases it occurs spontaneously, like seeing the cleverly hidden figure of a rabbit or a fox in a woodland drawing. Patience is vital to the teaching-learning process because you never know when the learner is going to make the necessary connection. Great teachers always believe that *this* will be the time when learning occurs—and if not this time, then next time.

Patience is necessary because players who want to learn tend to become quickly discouraged when confronted with repeated failures. A coach's patience tells a player, "I believe in you. Don't give up on yourself, because I'm not going to give up on you. We'll keep trying until you get it right."

It's not always easy being patient or finding new ways to teach something when the first 999 ways don't work, but the alternatives—losing our tempers and bawling out players for not learning as quickly as we'd like, or giving up and abandoning the skill, or the player, as unteachable—are unlikely to improve our team.

And therein lies the key to patience, a positive attitude, and everything else: *The Team Above All.* If you keep that phrase in mind in everything you do, you'll find a way to smile through gritted teeth when your players find creative new ways to botch up your carefully planned instructional segments. If the skill is important (and obvi-

---

[9] Not by us, that is. Players can speed up their development by listening and trying to absorb information during practice, and by practicing on their own time to master the skills we teach them.

ously it is or else you wouldn't be devoting practice time to it)—and if your players are honestly and earnestly doing their best to do what you say—then there is no reason to give up on the skill or lose faith in your players' ability to master it sooner or later. As one coach put it, "There are no defeats, only temporary setbacks. That's why God created tomorrows."

2. DON'T ASSUME THAT PLAYERS UNDERSTAND SOMETHING JUST BECAUSE THEY DON'T ASK QUESTIONS

Many young people regard asking questions as a sign of ignorance. Others fear having unwanted attention focused on them. Encourage your players to question whatever they don't understand; they are most likely to do so when the team atmosphere is one of openness and mutual respect among the players, and when you have carefully explained to them that there is no such thing as a dumb or unimportant question.[10]

In the absence of questions from the players, the best way to initiate two-way verbal communication is to question the players about why certain skills or movements are executed in a particular manner. The first time I tried it, I was shocked to find how much of what I thought my players understood was actually their unquestioning compliance with what I wanted them to do (e.g., running a pattern the way I told them to).

The difference between the two may seem insignificant, but the players' lack of understanding of what the pattern was designed to do limited their ability to take full advantage of freelance opportunities created by the pattern. (The solution, of course, is to break down the pattern into segments and option situations for drill and practice. Unfortunately for me, this occurred back in the 1960s when continuity patterns were all the rage in basketball, and breakdown drills were yet to be popularized.)

3. KEEP IT SIMPLE

In one sense, this advice refers to breaking down complex patterns, movements, concepts, etc., into smaller, more easily understood

---

[10] I tell my players, "The only question I never want to hear is, *How much longer do we have to practice?* If you ask that one, the answer will be *Forever.*"

segments; in another sense, it refers to avoiding complexity altogether except when your players are experienced and talented
enough to handle it without adverse effects. Finally, it can refer to
using slogans or easily remembered words or phrases to remind
players of what they should be doing. (The latter can be particularly useful in live-action game situations and timeouts when crowd
noise or time limitations render lengthy explanations ineffective.)

In all three cases, simplicity increases the chances of your
players' doing the right thing at the right time, especially in pressure situations when mistakes limit a team's chances of winning
games.

Regarding complex offenses and defenses: They are intended
to confuse your opponents, not your own players. If you intend to
use a complex system, you need players who are smart enough to
master its complexities and still play aggressively without losing
their competitive edge.

Not every player possesses the necessary blend of physical skills
and mental acuity to make adopting a complex offensive or defensive system worthwhile. You may have devised the cleverest offense
since Hannibal's Carthaginian army crossed the Alps with elephants
to surprise the Roman legions in 218 B.C., but it won't work without
players who can make it work.[11]

If you have the horses—or, in this case, *elephants*—you can do
whatever you like and it will probably work, but you don't *have* to
use a complicated system. Vince Lombardi's Packers teams used a
relatively unsophisticated offensive system built around his famous
Green Bay sweep; Tom Landry's offensive playbook with the
Cowboys resembled the Greater Dallas-Ft. Worth telephone book.
Both coaches were highly successful, although their approaches to
team offense were radically different.

Complex systems are, by definition, harder to teach and harder to learn, and they take longer to install. The best offensive or
defensive system is the one, whether simple or complex, that fits
your players like a glove. If you're not sure which way is best, make
it easy on yourself and your team and *keep it simple.*

---

[11] It didn't work for Hannibal, either: most of the elephants died while crossing the Alps;
the rest, frightened in battle by the shouting and blaring of Roman trumpets, turned and
fled, trampling Carthaginian soldiers in their paths.

Be pragmatic. If a drill works, use it; if not, either refine it or discard it. Study the available drills books in your sport; if you still can't find what you need, invent it yourself. That is, in fact, how the drills in the drills books and coaching magazines came into existence, through the efforts of coaches who were—and *are*—dissatisfied with the drills they're using.

Bobby Bowden or John Thompson may use a certain drill but that doesn't mean you need it, or that it will work for you the way it works for them; if that were the case, every college basketball coach would use John Wooden's UCLA drills and win NCAA titles every year. His drills *may* work for you—or they may not.

Conversely, Tom Osborne or Rick Pitino may not use a particular drill, but that doesn't mean you shouldn't be using it, either. The best drills are those that teach *your* players what they need to know to play the game *your* way. If you're satisfied with your present drills, *great!* If you're not, keep looking around—or devise drills of your own. Encourage your assistant coaches to do likewise. Even if you don't consider yourself a creative individual, *you* know your team and its needs better than anyone on the face of the earth (except for a few parents and disgruntled fans, of course).

Players occasionally must be reminded that *they can do more than they think they can;* sometimes it doesn't hurt to remind ourselves that we can, too. If you keep your daily practice schedules—and if you take time to sit down with your assistant coach(es) for five to ten minutes after every practice to evaluate what transpired—you'll have detailed information regarding all your drills and activities, and their relative effectiveness. You can also build files of drills you've used (or considered using), for handy reference at a later date.

No matter how long you've coached, it's amazing what you'll forget if you don't write it down and save it. That's one of the many lessons I learned in coaching the hard way—by failing to write things down.

4. Don't Let Daily Practices Become a Drudgery

Back in the bygone days when athletes scheduled p. e. for the last period of the day and practice started before school was out, I once had three players show up late for practice because they had been watching a movie in their fifth period class that carried over into sixth period. I had no problem with that until I discovered that they had asked to stay and watch the same movie over rather than come to the gym to get ready for practice. I felt that they had betrayed me and their teammates.

Later, when I was able to consider the problem objectively, I realized that I was to blame as well as the players. *Yes,* those particular players had developed a case of "senioritis"; but I had to admit, too, that as the pressures mounted in a long, stress-filled season, I had unconsciously but systematically stripped my daily practices of everything that the players might conceivably find enjoyable. In my zeal to Get the Team Ready For the Playoffs, I was conducting practices in which the players were essentially beating up on each other for one and a half to two hours a day.

As noted earlier, coaches look for the best drills we can find. When we find them, it's only natural that we should want to stay with them because they *are* the best drills. When you use those same drills regularly, however, they tend to become boring to the players; combined with other, equally effective (but equally repetitious) drills, they can turn what might otherwise be productive daily practices into stale routines that are as exciting as study halls or as eagerly awaited as trips to the dentist's office.

Variety is the spice of life, or so they say. There are a number of ways to inject a measure of variety or vitality into daily practices, among them:

- Give the starters a day off. In addition to appealing to your starters, this will give you more time to work with the other players on an individual basis.

- Emphasize different areas of the game every week.

- Shorten practice time as the season progresses. From a maximum of 120–150 minutes of daily practice in preseason and early season, AUM basketball coach Larry Chapman progressively cuts back on his practice time until, by the end of the regular season, his Senators are practicing between 45 and 75 minutes daily. Admittedly, this conflicts with the notion that *there's so much that we have to do to get ready for the playoffs,* and it *does* require a great deal of organization in order to ensure that all the necessary preparations are seen to. But Coach Chapman believes that cutting back practice time keeps his players fresh mentally and saves their legs as the playoffs loom closer. He believes, too, that it's not the length of the practice that counts, but what you accomplish in the time you spend practicing. If, as should be the case by the end of the season, you can accomplish everything you need to in 45 minutes or an hour, there's no need to extend practice for another 60–75 minutes just for the sake of practicing.

■ Scrimmage more frequently. Players always like scrimmaging. To be productive, however, the scrimmaging should be directed toward specific goals involving specific time allotments. For example, a thirty-minute football scrimmage might be devoted to defensing next week's opponent as follows: five minutes of special team strategies, ten minutes of defense outside the 20, ten minutes of red zone defense, and five minutes of goal-line defense. Conversely, it might be devoted to implementing the offensive game plan in a similar manner. At any rate, the time allotments help to ensure that whatever needs to be covered, *is* covered.

■ Give your players a break they'll remember. Water breaks are nice—and necessary, too—but once or twice a season I like to interrupt practice unexpectedly for an ice cream or popcorn and soft drinks break. Yes, it wastes time that could be spent practicing free throws, pickoff moves, or working on receivers' timing in pass routes—but such unusual breaks are always greeted with enthusiasm and delight by the players. It's a nice way of saying "thanks" to them for the long hours of hard work they've put in.

Occasionally, after a particularly satisfying win, we'll drag out the popcorn machine and let the players eat popcorn while we're watching the game tape. Left unspoken is the inference that we might do it again if we win our next game. (We won't do it, but it doesn't matter since we never promised anyone anything.)

■ Stage a brief "fun" competition such as a Home Run Derby in baseball or softball; an NBA-type three-point shooting or fancy layup competition in basketball; or a touch football game with linemen and backs swapping roles, or a punt, pass, and kick competition in football. Such activities need not consume an entire practice, nor should they be held regularly; they merely provide a brief but interesting diversion when players are under a lot of pressure or practice sessions seem to be getting in a rut.

- Give the team a day off from practice late in the season. Some coaches might object that the players already have weekends off (except for Saturday games, of course), and they don't need another day to help them get out of shape. I'll concede their point, as long as it's based on *what the players need*, but most 9-to-5 workers get weekends off, too, and they seem to benefit from an occasional holiday from work.

If the players seem listless or uninspired, maybe it's just the effects of a long, hard season taking its toll. And maybe, instead of racking your brain for yet another motivational approach to reignite their competitive fires, all you need to do is give them a day off and start afresh the following day.

PART TWO

THE NATURE
of
CONTROL

5

COMPETITIVENESS AND CONTROL

COMPETITION

There is a sizable number of people out there who deeply resent everything you stand for as a coach. I'm not talking about referees, disgruntled ex-players who quit your teams (or were thrown off), parents who judge your coaching ability by their child's playing time, or angry fans who blame you for every loss that your teams suffer. Those are the obvious crosses you bear for having decided that it might be fun to spend a large portion of your professional life wearing shorts, coaching shoes, and a whistle around your neck.

No, the people I'm referring to have a more basic objection to your coaching than simply questioning your professional competence. These individuals would prefer to do away with your job altogether, on the grounds that competitive sports create stress, subject young people to unnecessary pressure to succeed, unfairly label children as *winners* or *losers* and consign those in the latter category to unproductive, unhappy lives.

They're wrong, of course. If you've never been involved in sports beyond the activities in your high school physical education classes, it's easy to overlook the values of competitive sports and leap to the broad generalization that for every winner there must be a loser. That might be true *if* sport seasons consisted of only one game, or *if* final scores were the only yardstick by which the quality of one's athletic performance were measured—but neither of those *if*'s is even remotely accurate. The true winners in sports are the coaches and athletes who have dedicated themselves to the pursuit of personal excellence and team goals—not just for themselves but for the betterment of everyone concerned. That includes the overwhelming majority of participants, past and present, who have played and coached competitive sports. Many of them might not be able to express in precise terms what their athletic participation has meant to them, but it's a safe bet that they wouldn't regard themselves as losers because they didn't win every game they played. If that were so, competitive sports would have vanished from the scene long ago.

Sports has always had its detractors, and always will have them. Perhaps our best response to criticism of any sort is to show, through the depth of our commitment to the young people we coach, that we are earnestly striving to make a difference in their lives. Our players are our most important critics; if we have taught them properly, they understand that winning and losing involve far more than points on a scoreboard, and that competitiveness is a virtue, not an evil. The competitive spirit is the vehicle by which we reach from where we are toward where we want to be. In the words of Vince Lombardi,

> Not everyone can be a winner all the time but everyone can make that effort, that commitment to excellence. And if we fall a little short of our goals, at least we have the satisfaction of knowing we tried. . . .
>
> The spirit, the will to win and the will to excel—these are the things that endure and these are the qualities that are so much more important than any of the events that occasion them.[1]

CONTROL

In a coaching context, *control* refers to either of two very different things, i.e., coaches' attempts to control the variables relating to their teams, or a team's status relative to controlling opponents or being controlled by them. While both areas will be addressed at length in later chapters, our present concern involves three preliminary points.

---

[1] Lombardi, Vince. *Vince Lombardi on Football, Vol I.* New York (Graphic Society Ltd., 1973), p. 16.

1. There is nothing wrong *per se* with exercising control over the athletes you coach, as long as it is done for professional rather than personal reasons and directed toward the accomplishment of team goals. In fact, you are doing your players a grave disservice if you do *not* attempt to influence their behavior, shape their values and attitudes, and control their athletic performances. Such control is no more dehumanizing than a teacher's attempts to control student behavior in the classroom.

   Now, more than ever before, with single-parent families becoming the rule rather than the exception, young people need control, guidance, discipline, direction, stability, and order in their lives. Few people in our society have a better opportunity to make a real and lasting difference in the lives of young people than coaches who genuinely care about their athletes.

2. There are varying levels of controlling opponents, with the upper range consisting of domination. For discussion purposes, we'll define *dominance* as "a team's ability to overpower an opponent in a game, or a series of opponents over the course of a season, whether by exploiting its own strengths or attacking opponents' weaknesses."

   At the upper end of the dominance scale, *total dominance* is achieved when the superior team's offensive and defensive effort is so overwhelmingly successful that the opponents lose their will to compete. For example, sometimes in blowouts, the trailing team's coach will take out his or her starters before the other team does likewise, thus signifying the team's unconditional surrender. This symbolic gesture, made to spare one's team or starters further humiliation, is traditionally (but not necessarily) followed by wholesale substitutions by the other team. Failure to do so in a reasonable amount of time is considered unsportsmanlike behavior.

   Many coaches feel that perhaps the truest indicator of a "great" team is the ability to dominate most of its opponents and at least control the rest of them in *all* phases of the game. But it is also possible for a team to dominate opponents either offensively or defensively, but not in both phases of the game.

Dominance tends to lose a certain amount of its potency when it is confined to offense or defense, since opponents may win games (or at least keep them uncomfortably close) by exploiting the other, weaker phase. A team may have the greatest offense since Attila the Hun decided to extend his real estate holdings to include downtown Rome, but it won't matter much if the team can't get its hands[2] on the ball more often than occasionally.

3. Another aspect of controlling opponents relates to the word *control* itself. Controlling opponents doesn't mean making them do whatever we want them to do, nor does it mean stopping them from doing whatever they want to do; both of those situations involve *domination*, not control. Controlling opponents simply means finding ways to minimize the effects of their strengths.

An excellent example of basic control-oriented strategy can be seen in football's "bend-but-don't-break" defensive strategy. As applied to opponents whose offensive firepower is equal or superior to your team's defensive ability to contain it, this strategy is based on playing the percentages. Those percentages indicate that, the more plays from scrimmage it takes opponents to drive upfield and score, the greater the chances become that they will make a costly mistake along the way and turn the ball over, or otherwise stall the drive somewhere short of paydirt.

"Bend-but-don't-break" means that you'll concede them 3–4 yards per rushing play or 5–7 yards per pass completion if necessary to string out the drive until either they make a mistake or you are forced into goal-line defense, but you *won't* give up the long bomb or the big play that gets them downfield in a hurry. They may still defeat you, of course, and they may compile some impressive yardage numbers in the process of marching up and down the field. Offensive statistics don't win ball games, however; *points* do. Unless their performance is relatively error free, the opponents might find it difficult to translate those statistics into points on the scoreboard.

---

[2] Or feet, in soccer.

LEVELS OF TEAM QUALITY AND CONTROL

This chapter is largely definitional, and the following section offers five levels of quality—"Great," "Very Good," "Good," "Fair," and "Weak"—to describe teams' relative ability to compete, to control opponents, and to win games. These terms will serve as broad and easily recognizable indicators of team quality. They should be regarded not as changeless or beyond question like the Ten Commandments, the Bill of Rights, or referees' calls, but rather as flexible guidelines toward understanding what teams might be capable of accomplishing at any given stage of their development.

GREAT TEAMS

Badness you can get easily, in quantity: the road is smooth, and it lives close by.
But in front of excellence the immortal gods have put sweat, and long and steep
is the way to it, and rough at first. But when you come to the top,
then it is easy, even though it is hard.

—Hesiod (a Greek poet), c. 700 B.C.

Greatness is both relative and subjective. While such lofty accolades usually are conferred upon teams after they have achieved great successes, it is the *potential* for great achievement that we're investigating here. A team's potential may be estimated by considering the various elements that combine to render it beatable or unbeatable at any given point. In that sense, a Great team is one that has no weaknesses, or else its strengths are so overwhelming that opponents cannot ignore, avoid, or play around them.

Greatness starts with the players, of course: players whose superior skills permit them to dominate the majority of their opponents and force opposing teams to adopt strategies that they wouldn't consider using otherwise. A *Sports Illustrated* cover photo from the early 1970s showed UCLA center Bill Walton at low post without the basketball, surrounded by four Oregon defenders; it remains my all-time favorite image of desperation coaching tactics, especially considering that the Bruins' lineup also contained future NBA all-star Jamaal Wilkes.

The "no weaknesses" angle also implies other things about Great teams. For example, while it does not require that every player be a superstar, it means that all of them are skilled enough in their main or complementary roles that they cannot be singled out for special treatment by the opposition without substantially weakening their—the opponents'—offensive or defensive strategy elsewhere. It means that the team is using a style of play that the players are comfortable with and that allows the team to control if not dominate every opponent. It also means that the players are versatile enough to adapt their basic playing style to opponents' strategies or tactics and still control the flow of the game, individual matchups, and other factors upon which winning is based.

Great teams possess other qualities that tend to render them virtually unbeatable: effective leadership, a strongly developed sense of team purpose combined with a high degree of self-motivation among the players, depth, experience, adaptability, confidence, consistency, conditioning, and the ability to concentrate for long periods of time. Great teams simply have too many weapons to lose more often than rarely. Under normal circumstances, the only team that is capable of defeating a Great team is a Very Good team that is playing to its maximum potential—and even then the Great team will win most of the time.[3]

It's nice to consider incredible success stories such as Hawaii's tiny Chaminade College (enrollment: 800 students) upsetting no.-one-ranked Virginia and Ralph Sampson in basketball, 77–72, in December, 1982; still, that that game is remembered after more than a decade shows how rarely such upsets occur.

> *The price of greatness is responsibility.*
>
> —Winston Churchill

Great teams thrive on competition. They tend to play their best games against their toughest opponents because they are motivated by challenges and they enjoy rising to the occasion. Great teams play as if they are obsessed with winning, but that's not generally the case; in reality, the players simply expect to win every game they play, and the caliber of their play almost always fulfills their expec-

---

[3] Except perhaps in sports such as college baseball, in which the length of the season, playing single games or doubleheaders several times a week, travel, fatigue, and other factors tend to drain players physically and emotionally.

tations. They find ways to win the close games, whether by elevating their performance physically at crunch time or by maintaining a high level of concentration in pressure situations. They don't think about losing; as a result, their minds are free to concentrate on doing whatever it takes to win.

Can a team be considered "great" if it loses or ties a game? If undefeated, does a team have to win every game convincingly to achieve greatness? Such questions, answerable only in the context of opinion, are part of the mystique of sports. As Mark Twain noted, without differences of opinion there would be no need for such things as horse races—or for *any* competitive sport, we might add.

> *All excellent things are as difficult as they are rare.*
>
> —Benedict Spinoza
> *Ethics* (1677), pt. V,
> proposition 42: note

On the basis of skills alone there are fewer Great (or potentially Great) teams than teams in any other category. Not every Very Good team that aspires to greatness achieves such lofty goals—not by a long shot. Being part of a Great team is an unforgettable experience; every coach should have that experience at least once in his or her career.

VERY GOOD TEAMS

> *If you see a tennis player who looks as if he is working very hard, then that means he isn't very good.*
>
> —Helen Wills Moody
> seven-time Wimbledon champion

For our purposes, a Very Good team may be defined as "a team whose weaknesses can be successfully attacked or exploited only by Great teams or other Very Good teams." Most championship teams are, by definition, either Great or at least Very Good; however, many nonchampionship teams are also Very Good teams. (In many leagues, you have to be either very good or very lucky—or both— even to make it to the playoffs.) Let's consider the specifics that render a team potentially Very Good:

▪ The team has mastered a recognizable, identifiable style of play, and is capable of successfully imposing that style of play on most opponents.

▪ Enough of the players are highly skilled or fundamentally sound to afford the team the luxury of attacking or controlling opponents in a variety of ways (and of dictating or controlling game tempo and taking advantage of individual matchups or opponents' weaknesses as well). While the Very Good team prefers to play to its strengths, it is equally capable of winning games by exploiting opponents' weaknesses.

▪ The team possesses no glaring weaknesses beyond those that a better team might be able to exploit. Whatever individual weaknesses exist are generally compensated for by the team's style of play and the superior skills of other players on the team.

▪ Teams in the Very Good category seldom beat themselves. They play with confidence and high expectations for winning, and they handle pressure situations well. They are usually easy to motivate, and they seldom lapse into the sort of lackluster or dismal performances that even Good teams experience occasionally. Like Great teams, Very Good teams can win games either by virtue of their individual and team skills or by the intensity of their play. They may not always play up to their potential, but they are always capable of finding ways to win. Whether aggressive or conservative in their approach to offense and defense, they are fundamentally sound, and opponents normally find it difficult to upset their rhythm or take them out of their game plan.

Very Good teams need top-notch competition, both to prepare them for the challenges of post-season play and to keep them mentally and physically sharp along the way. At least 15 percent of their schedule should consist of tough road games.

In concrete terms, a Very Good team should be capable of winning at least 70 percent of its games. Admittedly, such a figure might be misleading; for instance, a Good team might win three-fourths of its games by scheduling a number of weak nonconference teams to pad its record—a common practice in NCAA Division I basketball—or by playing in a relatively weak conference. But since, as will be seen in the next section, the upper limit of teams in the Good category is 67 percent wins, the three percentage points separating the two categories provides a measure of leeway regarding borderline teams in either category that play up to (or below) their potential.

Those percentages, and others that appear in these analyses of team quality, are not infallible, nor are they meant to be absolute measures of team potential or success. They are offered merely as aids to understanding differences in team quality and performance. If the win-loss percentages are not appropriate to your own concept of what a Good or Very Good team is, ignore them.

GOOD TEAMS

The word good *has many meanings. For example, if a man were to shoot his grandmother at a range of 500 yards, I should call him a good shot, but not necessarily a good man.*

—G. K. Chesterton

A result-merchant might arbitrarily define a Good team as one that is capable of winning from one-half to two-thirds of its games. While the validity of either or both of those figures is debatable, they will suffice in depicting the Good team as one whose strengths are at least as great as its weaknesses. A Good team might also be thought of as a Very Good team with one or more key elements missing.

What might those elements be? It depends on the team; there are a number of ways that a team might be capable of winning half to two-thirds of its games. For example:

- It might feature one or two outstanding players and a supporting cast of mediocre players.

- It might depend heavily on young, talented players who are inexperienced at that level of play.

- It might be a squad of experienced, fundamentally sound players, none of whom possesses outstanding skills to consistently dominate opponents.

■ It might be a potentially Very Good team that, for any of a variety of reasons (e.g., team disharmony, "problem" players, lack of motivation, injuries to key players, etc.) fails to play up to its potential more often than occasionally.

Several salient points regarding Good teams should be noted:

■ Whatever their makeup, Good teams require careful coaching. All teams, even the very greatest of them, profit from superior coaching; however, Good teams simply cannot do the sorts of things that Very Good or Great teams can do—at least, not consistently—because their inherent weaknesses limit their ability to dominate or control opponents. Failure by the coach to recognize that limited ability can cause a Good team to lose games that it should have won, by failing to hide or compensate for its weaknesses adequately.

■ Because most teams fall within the Fair to Very Good range of the win-loss continuum, Good teams tend to play a lot of close games. To win their share—or more—of those games, they must find either ways to win or ways to avoid losing—or both.

> *Before you can win a game, you have to not lose it.*
>
> —Chuck Noll (Pittsburgh Steelers)

Many—and possibly most—coaches tend to believe that more games are lost through mistakes than are won through spectacular plays in pressure situations. It isn't always true, of course, but it's true often enough to sway many coaches toward adopting a conservative coaching style. Such coaches tend to prefer basic styles of play that emphasize error-free performance, rather than high-risk approaches to offense and defense that can get them blown out of games. "Playing within yourself" is the antithesis of the dreaded "playing out of control." It doesn't mean that the Good team won't abandon its basically conservative approach in the waning moments of games when winning is on the line, nor does it mean that the team won't play aggressively at any given point in the game. What it *does* mean is that the coach will most likely choose *very carefully* when to attack and when to defend (e.g., when to blitz a linebacker and when to keep him back in pass coverage) in order to avoid making the kinds of mistakes that lose games prematurely. It's what might be called the "fourth quarter" approach to coaching and winning: If you can keep the game close until the fourth quarter, you can find a way to win.[4] Such a philosophy is perfectly suited to Good teams since, as we noted, they play a lot of close games.

▪ While Good teams occasionally have outstanding games, they are equally capable of playing far below their potential. Unlike Great or even Very Good teams, they cannot count on winning games on talent alone when they are unmotivated or their concentration is poor.

FAIR TEAMS

A Fair team is one whose weaknesses generally outweigh its strengths. This creates obvious coaching problems in terms of finding ways to win games, since before you can win by playing to your strengths, you must find ways to keep opponents from beating you by taking advantage of your weaknesses. This in turn tends to limit the coach's ability to change tactics or provide a diverse attack that keeps opponents off balance.

The further a team strays from what it does best, the less likely it is to succeed in preventing opponents from doing what *they* do best. The ability to counteract opponents' strengths and strategies is a basic defining characteristic of team quality. Fair teams are limited in the extent to which they can make meaningful changes without further weakening their control—whether offensively, defensively, or in both phases of the game.

> *A thing moderately good is not as good as it ought to be.*
>
> —Thomas Paine
> *Rights of Man* (1791), pt. II, ch. 5

Having arbitrarily defined a Good team as one that is capable of winning at least half of its games, we might define a Fair team as one that can reasonably be expected to lose more games than it

---

[4] "Winning isn't imperative, but getting tough in the fourth quarter is." —Bear Bryant

wins. If we assume that a Fair team plays two-thirds of its games against opponents who are at best marginally superior—a not unreasonable assumption, since it is unlikely that more than one-third of the teams in a given league are Very Good or Great—it becomes obvious that Fair teams tend to lose more close games than they win. The major culprit here is usually a lack of skilled players, especially at key positions. The problem sometimes goes deeper than that, however, encompassing such factors as: lack of motivation, concentration, or effective team leadership; inexperience; lack of depth; absence of a take-charge player who is willing to step up his or her performance at crunch time; or players who don't perform well under pressure.

Whatever the case, Fair teams are usually missing one or more of the elements necessary to control opponents consistently. Fair teams are more likely to find themselves being controlled by opponents, rather than being in control and dictating how and where confrontations arise and how they will be resolved.

> *You cannot run away from a weakness, you must sometimes fight it out or perish; and if that be so, why not now, and where you stand?*
>
> —Robert Louis Stevenson

To rise above Fair status, a team must win all (or most) of the games it is supposed to win and at least half of the close games. Such a goal may or may not be realistic—and it certainly isn't easy; if it were, there would be no teams in the Fair category.

WEAK TEAMS

> *We definitely will improve this year. Last year we lost ten (football) games; this year we scheduled only nine games.*
>
> —Ray Jenkins (Montana State)

Two good ol' boys were sitting in the shade at the base of a tall oak tree. Every now and then one of them would cry out in pain and swat at one of the insects that were bothering them.

"What's these insects that keeps bitin' me?," Billy Bob asked. His friend replied that they wuz hossflies.

Billy Bob yelped, swatted again, and rubbed his arm. "Hossflies? What's that?"

"Oh, they's insects that lights on hosses an' jackasses an' stuff like that," his friend drawled.

Billy Bob eyed the man suspiciously. "Are you callin' me a jackass?"

"I ain't callin' you nothin'," his friend responded, "but you cain't fool them hossflies!"

In like manner, you're not likely to fool a really weak team about its chances of winning games; at least, you won't fool it for long. Such teams understand losing in ways that don't normally occur to other teams.

> *Bad teams are creative. They can always find a new way to lose.*
>
> —Archie Manning (New Orleans Saints)

A Weak team might reasonably be defined as one that has few if any strengths with which to control opponents. To the extent that it must adjust its basic style of play in order to control opponents, the Weak team tends to become mistake-prone and to give up a succession of easy scores that further reduce its chances of winning or remaining competitive. Lacking the kind of skills that afford players self-confidence, Weak teams do not handle pressure well, and thus are unlikely to find ways to defeat teams that are more than marginally superior to them. Weak teams function best when using a basic, no-frills playing style against other Weak teams that are incapable of taking full advantage of their shortcomings.

Basically, there are two kinds of Weak teams: those whose players are inexperienced and have not yet developed the skills necessary to render the team competitive in a broad range of game situations, and those whose players—whether inexperienced or not—are used to losing and have adopted a losing attitude. Of the two, teams in the latter category are infinitely more difficult to coach.

> *This is the only way a team improves—by working on their mistakes, correcting their weaknesses.*
>
> —Red Auerbach (Boston Celtics)

Coaching is teaching. Team quality aside, players on all levels must be taught how to execute the fundamental skills associated with their sport and their position. They must also be motivated to adopt and maintain a work ethic that will permit them to execute those skills successfully in a variety of game situations. Players who adopt a losing attitude tend to resist efforts to extend their mental or physical comfort zones. Losing begets losing; when a team is mired in an extended losing streak, its players may unconsciously prefer being blown out of games to losing close decisions. That way, they can avoid the pressure situations and frustrations resulting from losing games that they might have won.

The same negative attitude tends to prevail regarding their work ethic. After all, why should the players work hard, whether in practice or in games, when they're going to lose anyway? For a new coach entering a situation where players expect to lose games, *this* is precisely where coaching starts: teaching basic skills and changing attitudes about playing to win.

6

INDIVIDUAL MODES
OF CONTROL

In this chapter, we'll investigate the factors that affect individuals' and teams' ability to control their opponents: speed and quickness; size (height/weight); athleticism and fundamental soundness; and other factors (experienced/veteran players, depth).

SPEED, QUICKNESS, AND AGILITY

Speed refers to the ability to get from Point A to Point B in a hurry. In track and field, the title "World's Fastest Human" is given to the person who wins the Olympic 100-meter finals. In football, coaches use 40-yard sprint times as a standard gauge of foot speed because that distance is considered the maximum a player will have to run on most plays from scrimmage. In baseball, it's how fast a player can cover the 90 feet from home plate to first base. Mickey Mantle did it from his left-handed batting stance in 3.1 seconds.

Quickness is speed concentrated in a confined area.[1] *Agility* refers to the ability to use quickness effectively, whether moving forward, backward, or laterally. A running back or receiver cutting to daylight; a baserunner stealing second; a ballhandler driving past a defender: All of these skills ultimately rely on speed to get them where they're going, but it's anticipation and quickness in the first

---

[1] As a friend, Fred Rossi, put it, "Speed is what gets you to the outhouse door; that's where quickness takes over."

few steps that make the rest possible. Without explosive quickness to create and exploit an advantage, the opportunity is likely to be lost.

Many coaches consider quickness the single most important attribute an athlete can possess. When combined with height, weight, or strength, quickness opens doors of opportunity that do not exist for slower athletes. All other things being equal, the good quick player will beat the good slow player most of the time. This holds true whether we're talking about quick hands, quick feet, or both.

A good example of the effects of speed and quickness can be seen in two recent Atlanta Braves baseball teams. In 1993, possessing an outstanding pitching rotation and excellent team speed, the Braves dominated the National League regular season with 106 wins. A year later, with their starting rotation intact but their three fastest players—Deion Sanders, Otis Nixon, and Ron Gant—lost to free agency or trades, the Braves ended the strike-shortened 1994 season $6 - 1/2$ games behind the Montreal Expos in the NL East. No longer able to mount the sort of big-inning rallies that speed and quickness on the basepaths afford, Atlanta had to rely instead on the long ball and a largely one-dimensional approach to team offense. Add to that the team's bullpen woes and lack of an effective closer, and the result was a lot of low-scoring games that put added pressure on the starting pitchers to pitch longer than usual and produce error-free performances.

All of the Braves' problems in 1994 stemmed from their dramatic—and sudden—reduction in team speed. With three highly effective speed merchants in 1993, they were able to apply early-inning pressure consistently to opposing teams offensively; with virtually no speedy players in the lineup in 1994, it was the Braves who felt the pressure to outscore their opponents or play catch-up ball.

Unfortunately, speed and quickness aren't the sort of qualities that lend themselves to dramatic improvement through coaching. In gross terms, at least, speed is hereditary. It has to do with fast-twitch muscle fibers; either you're born with them or you spend most of your running time trying to catch up. Any athlete's foot speed or hand quickness can be improved to a certain extent through practice and coaching in efficient movement techniques; however, no amount of practice or coaching is going to increase a pitcher's fastball from 75 mph to 95 mph, or improve a 100-meter time from 11.7 to 9.5. If that were so, someone considerably wiser than you or me would already have copyrighted the technique and earned millions of dollars from it!

IMPROVING SPEED, QUICKNESS AND AGILITY

Having noted what cannot be done to improve speed, quickness, and agility (i.e., turn a tortoise into a hare), let us consider what *can* be done.

Regarding quick hands: *Any exercise or skill that improves hand-eye coordination also improves effective hand speed.* Juggling comes to mind readily in this regard, as does handball. In World War II, Japanese pilots practiced catching houseflies with their bare hands to improve their hand quickness and manual dexterity. Although none of those activities is directly related to team sports, all of them improve hand-eye coordination.

Every sport has its own quickness drills, available in coaching books. Baseball's "pepper" drill is basically a quick-hands drill; football has its tip drills and basketball its bad pass drills.

Regarding quick feet, there's the obvious: *Feet move fastest when the athlete moves on the balls of her or his feet, with the heels contacting the ground lightly if at all.* To speed up a slow runner, first check to see whether she's running on her heels. Heel-to-toe weight transference is fine for race walkers—and it's less tiring for runners, too—but it is also considerably slower than running on the balls of the feet. Time spent transferring the weight from the heels to the balls of the feet is largely wasted, since the force that propels the athlete forward or laterally is generated from the balls of the feet.

A second checkpoint in evaluating the running efficiency of the slow runner is to stand in front of him and watch him run toward you. His toes should point straight ahead, or even slightly inward in pigeon-toed fashion, when his feet contact the ground. Power generated in the stride is dissipated somewhat when the runner's feet are splayed outward like a duck's.

This problem is rather easy to identify and resolve. In extreme cases of splay-footedness, the athlete's head will sway or bob from side to side with every walking or running step. To correct the problem (which actually is a minor form of birth defect resulting from faulty alignment of the femur in the hip socket), the athlete must concentrate on rotating his feet inward in mid-stride. Of course, he should begin by practicing the rotation movement at a slow trot or walking pace before trying it at a faster pace.

Assuming that the previous points have been attended to, the next step—and the hardest one—is *lengthening the athlete's running stride.* When you tell her that you want her to take longer steps on the balls of her feet, she'll probably adopt a bouncing lope that looks as if she's practicing triple-jumping. That's not what you're after. Instead, tell her to lift her heels higher than normal and reach out 3–8 inches farther with her toes than she's used to doing. You're not trying to make a sprinter out of her; that would be self-defeating because she's *not* a sprinter and never will be. Sprinters generally feature a knee lift–toe reach running stride that emphasizes their big, fast-twitch quadriceps muscles. All you're trying to do is teach her to use her slow-twitch quads in a comfortable, longer stride *in the same amount of time per step as she was running previously.* In doing so, she will travel farther in the same amount of time and steps—or else she will travel the same distance in fewer steps at the same rate of speed per step, which amounts to the same thing. Either way, the longer stride has forced her to move faster than before.

Of course, it's not *quite* as easy as all that. The athlete is also expending more energy than she did earlier, and her pulse and respiratory rates are increased as well. The first time she tries to run, say, a series of 40s with a longer stride, she'll find out what track athletes mean by the phrase "hitting the wall." It isn't fatal, but it isn't exactly enjoyable, either. Continued practice and conditioning will soon acclimatize the athlete's body to the increased demands she's making on it, and she'll be faster than before—not quicker, but faster. On the best day of her life she won't be a threat to FloJo in the 40 or the 400, but she'll outrun her former self by a few yards or tenths of a second. In terms of what that can add to her performances, it's certainly worth the effort.

Regarding agility, changing directions rapidly requires shifting one's balance without overbalancing; in many cases, it also involves quick starts and stops. Because balance is involved, the keys to success in changing directions quickly are to lower the center of gravity and widen the base of support.

Consider, for example, the basic defensive stance in basketball (or that of a linebacker in football): *feet spread, knees bent, tail down, back straight, head and shoulders up.* From this balanced stance, the defender can move quickly in any direction without losing his balance *as long as he maintains his low, wide stance.*

Changing directions while running also involves lowering the center of gravity and widening the base. In running, however, the change-of-direction step itself serves to broaden the player's base. Bending the knee of the planted leg lowers the center of gravity and redirects the force in the desired direction.

Whether the player is running or sliding defensively, agility can be improved through rigorous drilling and practice. Every sport has its drills involving start-stop movements and change-of-direction sequences. John Wooden described the art of coaching as getting the best players you can find, finding the best drills to teach them how to do what they need to learn, and drilling them in those movements until they do them automatically—without thinking about what they're doing.

ANTICIPATION

The previous paragraphs refer not to making slow athletes fast—but to making them faster than they were. While many drills exist in the various team sports to improve quickness, the best approach of all is to improve the athlete's *anticipation.* Such a goal is not accomplished overnight, but results from the process whereby players are taught to recognize familiar situations and respond to them automatically.

For example, consider rebounding a missed perimeter shot in basketball. Of the ten potential rebounders on the court, only one—the shooter—has immediate visual and tactile input regarding whether the shot might be long, short, or off-line. The other nine players can guess or play the percentages in going to the boards, positioning themselves and blocking out when the shot is missed, but the initial edge belongs to the shooter. When he (or she) fails to anticipate a missed shot and decides to "fall back, baby!" as ex-Knick Dick Barnett put it, rather than following the shot to the boards, the advantage, however slight it may have been, is lost.

Anticipation plays an important role in rebounding for the other nine players, too. Rebounding technique generally involves either (a) positioning oneself immediately to claim the rebound or block an opposing player away from the boards, or (b) moving to where you think the ball will rebound before blocking out. In the latter case, the majority of missed perimeter shots rebound to the weak side; players who are aware of that can "steal" a lot of cheap rebounds (and easy baskets via offensive follow-shots) by positioning themselves accordingly. Anticipating a weak-side rebound generally gives a player a step or two advantage over players who merely react to the bounce of the ball off the rim or backboard.

The more thoroughly players understand their roles and responsibilities within a given offense or defense, the more likely they will be to act (and react) decisively and accurately. Your task is to teach players, not merely how to react, but how to initiate action on their own, based on anticipation of what they expect to happen.

In full-court zone pressing in basketball, the trapping defenders must be taught where and how to set up their traps—but their teammates must also be taught to play the passing lanes and anticipate the ballhandler's response to the trapping movement. Hesitation or indecision on the part of any of the defenders most likely will result in failure to contain the ball, much less steal it.

Remember, though, that reaction comes first. Teaching players to react quickly and decisively should precede allowing them to act on their own, or else they won't know how to handle situations that are new or unfamiliar to them. Anticipation is an advanced mental skill; it arises out of familiarity and recognition, not unfamiliarity and confusion.

> *Luck follows speed.*
>
> —Frank Broyles (Univ. of Arkansas)

SPEED AS A CONTROLLING AGENT

Speed is a *tool*, and not a goal, for the team player. Speed is helpful only to the extent that it can be controlled. Playing under control at a slower speed is preferable to playing out of control at full speed.

In football, when speedy members of the punting team race downfield to cover the punt and, without breaking stride or breaking down into a defensive posture, allow the return man to sprint past them untouched—*that* is playing out of control.

In basketball, where teams often employ a deliberate, ball-control style of play, the players must be able to operate at their own effective top speed, if for no other reason than to deal with quicker opponents who are capable of forcing them to adopt an up-tempo pace. Fast teams and players can always slow down their pace without losing control; slower teams and players cannot speed up and maintain control.

All teams and players, even the very slowest of them, should be trained to function effectively in situations involving high-speed decision making. This doesn't necessarily mean abandoning a control-oriented game plan; but if your slow basketball team is playing an opponent who uses speed and tempo to control opponents, your game preparations had better include information regarding how and where their defensive pressure will be applied, how to handle the traps and full-court pressure, organizing your defense quickly when transitions occur, and avoiding the temptation to run-and-gun with a run-and-gun team.

The first prerequisite of control as applied to team sports is to keep opponents from playing the game at their tempo rather than yours. This isn't normally a problem when both teams prefer the same tempo; when one team is appreciably faster than the other, however, the slower team is the one at risk.

SIZE (HEIGHT/WEIGHT)

It's not the size of the dog in the fight; it's the size of the teeth in your leg.

—William Warren

Size is what you make of it, and what you make of it depends on the sport involved and how much size you have to work with. Short basketball teams and lightweight football teams normally attempt to compensate for their lack of size by emphasizing quickness or whatever other advantages they can muster. (The operant word here is *compensate*, because the need for size is more basic to basketball, volleyball, and football than to other sports where it may or may not be advantageous (e.g., baseball, hockey, golf, or tennis), or to sports such as soccer in which it is seldom a factor at all.)

In football and basketball, size has always been important. Prior to the 1960s, it was possible to win championships largely on the basis of size alone, because there just weren't many effective "big" players in those sports. Between 1948 and 1954, the Minneapolis Lakers won five NBA championships in six seasons, due largely to the talents of basketball's first dominating center, 6'10" George Mikan. Forty-one years later, in 1995, the Chicago Bulls' starting guards in the NBA playoffs were 6'6" Michael Jordan and 6'11" Toni Kukoc.

In 1960, a college or professional line that averaged 240 pounds per man was considered large, or at least a healthy *average*; today, high school offensive lines routinely equal or surpass that figure by as much as 20–45 pounds per player.

Today's players are not only taller and heavier; they are also faster and stronger. Whereas 250-pound linemen once were slow afoot, many of today's 285+ pounders are fully capable of chasing down a speedy little running back and rearranging his anatomy. In every sport, you're far more likely to find kids who possess the total package—size, speed, and strength—than you were, say, fifteen to twenty years ago.

HEIGHT

> *The sort of girl I like to see*
> *Smiles down from her great height at me.*
>
> —John Betjeman
> *The Olympic Girl* (1954)

While having tall players is not an absolute essential in any sport, it can be a valuable or helpful commodity in most sports. Its importance varies directly with the necessity of reaching upward with the hands (e.g., basketball, volleyball) or achieving height with the feet (e.g., hurdling, high jumping).

In basketball and volleyball, height alone doesn't do the work; it just makes the job easier. If your standing reach is 8'2" and mine is 7'6", the first eight inches of my vertical jump will be devoted to equalling your standing reach.

Other factors besides vertical jumping ability come into play in using one's height effectively. Players cannot be taught to be tall, but they can be taught the fundamentals of efficient movement (balance, stance, footwork). They can be drilled in activities to improve their coordination, reaction, and timing. They can be taught how to execute the skills of their position. Their strength can be improved in the weight room, their stamina and endurance on the court, track, or practice field.

Incidentally, in basketball, body width can sometimes be an acceptable substitute for height. Watching 6′7″, 240-lb. Wes Unseld, basketball's original hefty widebody, average 18–22 rebounds per game throughout his NBA career in the 1970s suggested to this observer that a wide, bulky frame can be the equivalent of three or more additional inches in height—at least when it is combined with muscular strength and an aggressive attitude toward rebounding. Trying to rebound against Unseld's broad-based and determined inside positioning must have been somewhat akin to jumping flat-footed over a parked car—possible for some people, but not likely for most.

WEIGHT

Not to bore you with what you already know from high school physics, but here's the formula for generating force:

Force = mass × acceleration

In the equation, "mass" refers to a *muscle's* mass; however, it can also refer to the athlete's *total body weight*—a far different proposition.

In the same way that basketball coaches tend to prefer tall players, football coaches seldom object to the presence of hefty widebodies in their offensive or defensive lines. Especially desirable are those earthmovers whose body weight is complemented by sufficient muscular power or quickness to dominate or control opponents. The development of earthmovers results, of course, from the hefty widebodies' exposure to a rigorous weight-training, nutritional, and conditioning program over a period of time sufficient to create a favorable ratio of muscle to body fat. Body weight does not in itself confer muscular strength, or else every 280-pound lineman would be an All-State candidate. A 6′7″ basketball player can lack the leg strength and timing to dunk a basketball, and a 230-pound football player's bench press prior to initiating weight training may be 75 pounds.

Without muscular strength sufficient to render it effective, increased body weight can be a hindrance to athletic performance, sapping muscles of their speed of movement and endurance. Still, among athletes of equal quickness, force is determined by mass; a quick, big athlete in a contact sport will beat an equally quick, smaller athlete most of the time. Exceptions arise when the smaller athlete has, through rigorous strength training, increased his or her ability to sustain that speed of movement throughout extended contact situations.

Where mass is equal, however, speed is likely to be the determining factor. Many of major league baseball's finest home run hitters have been big men, but the greatest of them all, Henry Aaron (755 homers) was only 5'11", 185 pounds in his prime. Ted Williams (521 homers) was nicknamed the "Splendid Splinter" for his youthful spindly frame, and Cincinnati's Ron Gant, a fine present-day power hitter, tilts the scales at about 200 pounds. All of those men generated prodigious bat speed that more than offset their relative lack of weight. Aaron's strength lay in his powerful forearms and wrists; Williams' secret was a fluid, seemingly effortless swing—that, and 20/10 vision that must have made the ball look like a pumpkin floating toward the plate. Gant is simply an incredibly muscular young man whose swing generates tremendous force. If he were the size of, say, the White Sox' Frank Thomas, Gant probably could hit a baseball 700 feet.

SIZE AS A CONTROLLING FACTOR

Another in my seemingly endless attempts to describe the coaching task, this time in the form of a parody of the scouting oath as drawn from the misspent days of my childhood:

> *On my honor I will do my best*
> *To take what they give me and steal the rest.*

"To take what they give me . . ." In one sense this refers to opponents' throwing away games through costly mistakes at inopportune moments (as if there could be an opportune time for making costly mistakes). In another sense—and the way we're using the phrase here—it refers to the old gamblers' adage that you play the hand you're dealt, not the one you wish you'd been dealt. Size is a bonus for you when you have it and can use it effectively. When you don't have it, it's an obstacle to be overcome.

No matter what sport you're coaching, or where, or at what level, if you stay in the profession long enough to be blamed for your players' athletic shortcomings you're going to have some big teams and some small ones. You'll find, if you don't know it already, that *every* team presents problems. While size presents different problems—depending on whether you have it or not—those problems are solved by taking what you're given and playing the hand you've been dealt. There is no single road to success in coaching, but there are many ways to accomplish the same goals. It all depends on your team: what it needs to succeed, and how willing you and your players are to work to fill those needs.

Size is most effective in controlling opponents when it is combined with mobility (read: quickness and agility). If size were the sole criterion for athletic success, 7'8" Manute Bol would be the greatest basketball player in the world; at 450 lbs. and a height of 7 feet, the late professional wrestler Andre the Giant would have had a stellar career in the NFL *or* the NBA.

Admittedly, such exaggerated examples don't mean much when your tiny defensive line is facing two-thirds of a ton of interior offensive linemen on the other side of the ball. Still, the principle remains true: *If everyone concerned has done everything possible to minimize the effects of whatever size disparity exists, no one has anything to apologize for when things don't go as we'd like.*

Size helps, but if forced to choose between height, weight, and quickness—with all other things being equal—I'll take the quickness every time. To paraphrase the old Typing I drill, *The quick brown fox jumps over, runs past, or otherwise outmaneuvers the lazy or largely immobile dog.*

ATHLETICISM/FUNDAMENTAL SOUNDNESS

You may be able to get by in the short run on your raw talent or ability;
but in the long run, you have to improve your weaknesses if you expect to win.

—Howard E. Ferguson[2]

ATHLETICISM

To my mind, at least, talent and potential are not synonymous. They should not be used interchangeably because potential precedes tal-

---

[2] *The Edge* (Cleveland, Ohio: Getting the Edge Company, 1991), pp. 3–21.

ent. Talent is what you have when you possess the skills necessary for success in a given sport or activity; potential is merely an estimate of how good you might be if you develop those skills.

Athleticism refers to the raw tools and general sports ability that an athlete brings to the court or playing field. Some of those tools, such as height and body type, offer natural advantages for players in certain sports; others involving skills and ability are developed, improved, or refined through training or practice.

Two basic aspects of athleticism are: gross muscular strength in its various forms (e.g., running, jumping, lifting, pushing, throwing) and such finely tuned neuromuscular movements as balalnce, timing, and hand-eye coordination.

Generally speaking, gross athletic skills are largely one- or two-dimensional. That's all right within limits, too, because not every player needs to be a complete athlete. Stripped to its barest essentials, football consists of blocking and tackling; if your team does a better job of it than mine does, you'll beat us most of the time. In basketball, a player's defensive or rebounding skills can at least partially compensate for whatever offensive skills he or she lacks. A coaching colleague once told me, "Give me a kid who can clean the boards like Windex, and I don't care if he's so clumsy he can't tie his shoes. If he can give us double-digits on the boards, he can play in loafers."

Gross muscular strength alone will not help an athlete to make a free throw or field a ground ball. In some cases, strength may even be a drawback, as in the case of two of basketball's greatest big men, Wilt Chamberlain and Shaquille O'Neal. Both men are 7-footers and tip the scales at 300 pounds, and both have been spectacularly inept free-throw shooters. I've always believed that their difficulties at the line stemmed, not from a lack of practice or desire to improve, but from their prodigious strength and the size of their hands. (Chamberlain's spread fingers spanned an incredible $13 \text{-} \frac{1}{2}''$— equivalent roughly to halfway around an NBA basketball.) In the hands of a Shaq or a Wilt the Stilt, the ball must feel like a miniature beachball—thus their relative inability to consistently apply "touch" to their free throws.

At the highest levels of athleticism, at least, it doesn't take long to recognize that you're in the presence of greatness. In 1962, Russian high jumper Valeri Brumel, the world record holder, walked onto the basketball court in UCLA's Pauley Pavilion and, after a short approach run, jumped up and touched the rim—*with his foot!*

At all levels, athletic talent can be assessed through objective tests, measurements, and statistics. How such assessments are translated into meaningful estimates of performance depends, however, on the coach's subjective evaluation. No one has ever devised an objective scale for defining the absolute limits of talent or potential.

Athleticism is a valuable asset for any athlete. It can be refined through conditioning, practice, and attention to proper form and technique in skills execution, but it cannot be taught. It's either there, or it isn't.

In the Middle Ages, alchemists tried unsuccessfully to convert ordinary metals into gold. Today, while coaching can make a noticeable difference in a player's skills, it cannot convert ordinary athletes into Michael Jordans, Jerry Rices, or Tony Gwynns, any more than the brand of athletic shoe they wear could do the trick.

As a senior at N. C. State University in 1974, All-American basketball player and future NBA all-star David Thompson visited track practice one spring day. After being shown how to triple-jump, Thompson set an unofficial school record in his first and only attempt. *That's* athleticism in its purest form.

Athletic ability provides a wonderful foundation for the development of specific sport skills. As has been noted repeatedly, every athlete can benefit from effective coaching; still, young people who are naturally gifted athletically have a huge initial advantage over others who must constantly compensate for whatever they lack in speed, quickness, strength, jumping ability, hand-eye coordination, or other basic components of athleticism.

That is one of the reasons why most coaches agree that you can't treat every player alike. Sometimes an extra measure of patience is necessary in dealing with naturally gifted athletes who either have not yet mastered the skills associated with their playing position or have not yet developed a deep and abiding commitment to that sport. In squad selection, choosing between the inexperienced natural athlete and the one who wants desperately to succeed but is limited in talent or potential is always a tough call, since you don't want to lose either of them. With all other things being equal, though, most coaches tend to go with the naturally gifted athlete who possesses skills or attributes that can be refined but not taught.

FUNDAMENTAL SOUNDNESS

While *athleticism* refers to raw physical ability or general sports skills, *fundamental soundness* is the ability to execute specific basic skills in a given sport in a manner that approximates proper form and technique.

Many sports skills are properly executed in a manner that is unnatural and awkward for the beginner. Examples abound: the jump shot (and imparting backspin to shots) in basketball; the catcher's behind-the-ear throwing motion in baseball; the passing motion in football; swinging a baseball bat without having the elbows locked in place at the sides; kicking a soccer ball with the instep rather than the toes. All of these and many other basic sport skills are *learned* skills, acquired through patient coaching and diligent practice. Because many youngsters start out in sports at a very early age under the tutelage of recreation league coaches who may know little or nothing about fundamental skills or how to teach them, our job is made more difficult at higher levels of play by players' having to unlearn improperly executed skills before we can teach them correct form.

Poor teaching and misunderstanding the fundamentals aren't confined to rec league coaching, however. One junior high coach was known to tell players to shoot free throws from their shoulders; presumably, the coach felt that the girls did not possess the necessary arm strength to shoot free throws properly. Somewhere along the line, another coach at a higher level will have to "unteach" improper form and substitute proper form, at the expense of teaching-learning time that could have been put to better use if it had been done right the first time. If you work closely with the coaches in your feeder system to see that kids coming up through the program are learning the fundamentals correctly, your teaching-learning time will be more productive when they get to your level.

My mother was a deeply religious person; her favorite saying was, "Be sure, your sins will find you out." If we substitute the word *shortcomings* for *sins,* her statement applies as well to athletics as to the moral principles she believed in. Sooner or later, your shortcomings will catch up with you.

A player may possess a wealth of athletic potential or ability, but athleticism alone can take a player only so far. Without a firm grasp of the basics, the player eventually reaches the point where recurring mistakes render further improvement impossible. Building a career on athletic ability alone, without attention to form and execution, is as impractical and fruitless as building a house without a solid foundation.

Fundamental soundness can permit players of limited athletic ability to compete on an equal footing with opponents who are athletically superior to them but inferior in terms of technique. If you are building a successful program from the ground up, take heart; teaching the fundamentals provides a short cut to success in the early stages of program development. You may not yet have succeeded in attracting the most gifted athletes in your school into your program; if that's the case, make the best of your current situation by sticking to the basics, adopting a conservative approach to offense and defense, and emphasizing individual improvement and achievable team goals, rather than focusing on winning as the chief criterion by which your team's success is judged.

The same holds true even after your program is established. You don't need superstar athletes to build or maintain a strong program; all you need is good athletes who are firmly grounded in the basics, and who thoroughly understand your system and style of play. In Bobby Knight's twenty-three years at Indiana, only eight of his players have gone on to play as many as five seasons in the NBA, and of those, only one, Isiah Thomas, has been a bona fide NBA superstar. That hasn't stopped Knight from developing one of the most highly successful men's basketball programs in NCAA history, however.

ATHLETICISM/FUNDAMENTAL SOUNDNESS AS CONTROLLING FACTORS

Ideally, every team should be composed of players who are strong, quick, naturally gifted athletically, and fundamentally sound, but that's not how it is for most coaches most of the time. Our players and teams possess those qualities in varying degrees, and in that sense coaching is like putting a jigsaw puzzle together. We try to find the proper fit for the individual pieces of the puzzle, hoping that, when we're finished, all of the edges will blend into a satisfying pattern. When it doesn't work out, we compensate for the missing pieces by adopting styles of play that permit our players to do whatever they do best, or by devising game plans that are meant to minimize opponents' attempts to exploit our shortcomings.

Athletic ability and fundamental soundness are vital components of team and individual play, and neither one by itself will take a team to the pinnacle of success in team sports. Athletic ability may permit a player to recover quickly from mistakes, but fundamental soundness reduces the chances of mistakes being made in the first place. Whereas athletic ability allows players to take chances that less gifted athletes cannot risk, fundamental soundness offers possibilities for controlling opponents without taking undue risks.

Athleticism is an important factor in the player selection phase of preseason tryouts, especially in considering players who may or may not have a firm grasp of the fundamentals. Coaches are always on the lookout for players with athletic potential.

Later, the need for proper skills execution increases in importance as you seek to extend your players' effective use of whatever athletic ability they possess. This need extends throughout the athletes' playing careers; if you forget that and overlook the basics, you are shortchanging yourself—and the team as well.

While you can't do a great deal to improve a player's basic athletic ability beyond fine-tuning its individual components, you can improve basic skills. Effective teaching of fundamental skills can make *any* player effective within the limits of his or her athletic potential. It is there, in the realm of *teaching basic skills*, that the very best coaches excel. They teach the basics, and relate them to whatever the team is doing offensively and defensively. Whenever things go wrong, they go back to the basics.

The problem with that type of coaching—and the reason why many coaches (especially in basketball) prefer scrimmaging to teaching fundamentals—is that, with exceptions, many of today's players don't want to learn the fundamentals or practice them. They prefer to do it their way, using their God-given abilities in whatever way is natural for them. Hank Aaron still believes that he would have been a better hitter if his coaches had let him bat cross-handed throughout his professional career. He made the change, though, because he wanted to play pro ball.

Basketball coaches don't have it that easy. Even at the pro level, you're lucky to find a team with three players who can successfully execute a jump stop. The stride stop's the thing because it's easier and more natural (never mind that it's slower). Vertical jumping ability can make up the difference. Like many of basketball's basic skills, the jump stop is becoming a lost art—*lost*, because it's easier to ignore it than to teach it to kids who don't want to learn it.[3] Nevertheless, the best coaches are those who teach the game—including its fundamentals.

To control opponents, athleticism and fundamental soundness make a powerful combination. All Great teams and players excel in both categories. In terms of team quality, as defined in Chapter 2, the best that teams or players who are deficient in athleticism or fundamental soundness can hope for is Very Good status if their deficiencies are minor—less if they are major.

OTHER FACTORS

1. EXPERIENCED/VETERAN PLAYERS

While filling out a personal information questionnaire, an NFL training camp attendee wrote in the space marked Educational Background: *Hard Knocks U.* If experience is such a good teacher, why do so many people have to repeat the course so many times?

Simply being in a program for four years does not make an athlete an experienced player. Experience comes through quality playing time amassed over a period of time sufficient for players to learn to function comfortably and effectively in a broad array of game situations.

Ideally, experienced players are fundamentally sound and understand how their individual skills relate to team strategy, patterns, and style of play. This isn't always the case, however; some players never master the fundamentals, and sweeping changes in a team's customary playing style can be confusing to veteran players and novices alike.

Although basic skills don't change, regardless of who is coaching the team, the way those skills are applied can be radically different from one playing style to another, or from one coach to the next. The worst-case scenario arises when a team has four different head coaches in four years, each of whom has a different philoso-

---

[3] Other basketball skills on the Endangered Species List: bounce passes; using fakes to pass the ball beyond a defender; catching the ball with both hands at the end of one's dribble prior to passing or shooting a layup; hook shots; underhand layups; and dribbling without turning the hand sideways or under the ball to catch it between dribbles.

phy of how the game should be played. In such cases, players are unlikely to develop the kind of confidence that comes from playing in a program that offers consistency in coaching expectations.

The same holds true to a lesser extent when a coach decides to change styles of play. The coach's basic philosophy and expectations may remain constant, but every style of play has its own rhythm and timing. Some offensive and defensive styles are aggressive (action-oriented), while others are conservative (reaction-oriented). Major changes of this sort require time for players to learn their new roles, since neither action nor reaction is likely to be effective when players have to think about what they're supposed to do at any given point. Such changes are usually made during the off-season, and then only *very* carefully. Major midseason changes in a team's style of play are a sure sign of coaching desperation.

Experience and personality form the basis for most effective team leadership. New or inexperienced players often follow the example of the team's veteran players regarding conduct, attitude, and general approach to playing the game. It is important, therefore, that veteran players and the head coach agree on team goals and how they are to be accomplished. A coach who cannot control the team's veteran players will be unlikely to handle anyone else effectively, either.

Many of the factors that go into making a team successful have little to do with scoring points or making game-winning plays, but are found instead in the ways in which players relate to one another and their coaches, and the pursuit of team goals. Having spent more time associated with your program than the younger players or transfer students, your veterans are ideally suited to assuming leadership roles. Such leadership can be demonstrated actively by virtue of dynamic, forceful personalities, or passively through the example of their work ethic, positive attitude, and commitment to the team and the program.

2. DEPTH

Back in the 1960s, the tiny farming community of Brooklet, Georgia (population: 185, give or take a stray dog or tomcat), produced two of the finest Class B teams in Georgia high school football history. Over a two-year period, Coach Fred Shavers and his Southeast Bulloch Yellow Jackets lost only one game, won a state title, were runners-up the other year, and steam-rollered their opponents by nearly 50 points per game in the process—and accomplished all that with only *thirteen* players on the team! Those two SEB teams of Shavers' routinely scored 60–80 points despite the coach's efforts to hold down the scores against clearly outclassed opponents.

Unable to substitute freely, all Shavers could do was make token substitutions and move players around in the lineup. But since all thirteen players were highly skilled, gifted athletes, it didn't matter much where they played. It was not at all uncommon in those very uncommon seasons for an SEB center playing quarterback to throw a touchdown pass to a guard playing wide receiver, or for a defensive tackle playing safety to return an interception for a touchdown.

Punting on first down didn't necessarily solve the problem, either, since the Yellow Jackets' aggressive, swarming defense was even better than their offense. During that two-year span, Southeast Bulloch averaged nearly two touchdowns per game in turnover returns alone.

Shavers' only real concern was that injuries might require him to forfeit games, since he needed eleven players to fill a starting lineup. As a hedge against problems of that sort, he usually brought along extra uniforms for his team managers.

Amazingly, only one injury severe enough to keep a player out of a game occurred during SEB's incredible run: The quarterback was hurt in the championship game that the team lost.

From the opposite end of the spectrum of depth-related problems: At the height of his dominance of NCAA men's basketball at UCLA between 1964 and 1975,[4] John Wooden's chief source of discomfort was having too many talented players. While Coach Wooden probably didn't spend too many sleepless nights wrestling with the problem of satisfying his players' desire for increased playing time, it *is* a problem, or at least it can be.

One way of handling an overabundance of talented athletes is to use a platoon system, substituting entire units at a time. Another is to count minutes played and follow a prearranged schedule in allotting playing time, a system used by a number of NBA coaches.

---

[4] Which produced ten championships in twelve seasons, including seven in a row between 1967 and 1973.

A third method—and one that I've employed over the years with all of my better teams—is to use the (promise/threat) of (additional/reduced) playing time as a motivational tool to ensure maximum effort from all players in anticipated blowouts. When it works, you merely keep a steady stream of substitutes going into the game, whether individually or in groups, until the victory is assured by whatever margin you feel comfortable with. Then you let the scrubs take over entirely, as a reward for their hard work in practice.

In professional baseball, managers often platoon at specific positions on an individual basis. Usually, such platooning is done late in the game for defensive purposes, or else to combat left- or right-handed pitching.

At any rate, depth—or, more accurately, the lack of it—is a legitimate concern for every coach sooner or later. The most common way of dealing with the problem is to use players in a variety of ways, even to the extent of switching them from one position to another when necessary to fill the gaps created by injuries or lack of talent. Moving players around is seldom an exciting prospect for the athletes involved, since they are assuming new roles that present new and unfamiliar challenges to them; still, as the coach, you are ultimately answerable to the team for your decisions, not to any given player. Individual concerns are important only after team needs have been addressed and satisfied.

In Part Three, "Controlling Opponents," we'll investigate ways that individual skills and the coach's philosophy relate to the process of selecting and implementing effective offensive and defensive playing styles. Some of the material in these chapters may seem mundane if you're a veteran coach with fifteen to twenty years of experience under your belt, but you'll also find certain theories regarding playing styles and their traditional use being challenged along the way. Consider them with an open mind. No one has all the answers regarding coaching or anything else, but as we'll see in Chapter 7, it helps to know what questions to ask.

PART THREE

CONTROLLING OPPONENTS

7

BLENDING PHILOSOPHY AND STYLE

While working on my doctorate at the University of Georgia in 1970, I was asked what my dissertation was about. The questioner was Earl Fales, head of UGa's physical education service program. I explained to Earl that my research involved applying existential philosophy to physical education.

"Gee, that's wonderful, Warren," Earl's voice was dripping with sarcasm. "Just what the world needs—another philosopher." From a coaching standpoint, at least, he was right both ways, sarcastically *and* seriously.

Coaches don't have time for the word games and semantic arguments that philosophers enjoy. We don't need to consider how many angels can dance on the head of a pin, or whether reality exists apart from the observer, in order to get ready for tomorrow's game or next week's opponent. We need to know what is important in coaching and playing the sports we're associated with.

Simply stated, philosophy consists of what we believe, and why we believe it. Philosophy serves as our guide to decision making and action, because what we do is determined by what we believe.

That's what this chapter is all about: relating styles of play to the way we believe our sport should be coached and played. Doing so should help to ensure consistency between what we believe in and what we're actually *doing*. We'll also be laying the groundwork for selecting a playing style that accommodates our beliefs and the skills, talents, abilities, and limitations of our players as well.

A QUIZ TO DETERMINE YOUR COACHING PHILOSOPHY

No matter what sport(s) you coach or how long you've been in coaching, you have a coaching philosophy. You probably haven't given it much thought, and you may not even know it's there, but it is.

The eight-item questionnaire that follows is an expanded (and greatly improved) version of a similar quiz I constructed for an earlier book.[1] Reading and checking off your responses will take no more than five minutes of your time. When you're finished, you should know more about yourself as a coach than you did before; you'll also know what's important regarding the sport(s) you coach, and why it's important to you as well.

Before we start, let's go over the ground rules:

First, please remember that this exercise is for you as a *coach*, not as a player or a fan.

Second, there are no incorrect responses, only choices between contrasting points of view, with which you are free to agree or disagree. All you need to do is place a check mark in the space provided for the choice you agree with. If you agree with both statements, select the one that you identify with most strongly.

Third, unless otherwise noted, all statements refer to Good (read: average) teams with average players. Your basic coaching philosophy probably won't change much whether you're coaching a Great team or one that is so Weak that you choose your starters by searching for vital signs of life—but *the way you apply your philosophy will vary considerably with the quality of your team.*

THE NO-JIVIN', HIGH FIVIN', ALL-PURPOSE TEAM SPORTS COACHING PHILOSOPHY TEST

A   B

_____ _____   1. Assuming that your team will win anyway, which would you consider a greater accomplishment:

(a) holding a Great team to a very low score, or (b) outscoring it by a wide margin?

---

[1] Warren, William E., and Chapman, Larry F. *Basketball Coach's Survival Guide* (West Nyack, N.Y.: Parker Publishing Co., 1992).

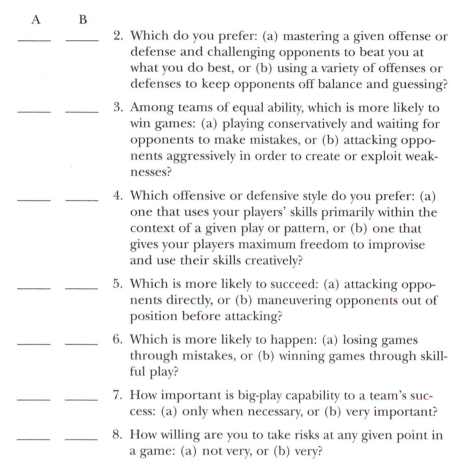

A   B

_____ _____   2. Which do you prefer: (a) mastering a given offense or defense and challenging opponents to beat you at what you do best, or (b) using a variety of offenses or defenses to keep opponents off balance and guessing?

_____ _____   3. Among teams of equal ability, which is more likely to win games: (a) playing conservatively and waiting for opponents to make mistakes, or (b) attacking opponents aggressively in order to create or exploit weaknesses?

_____ _____   4. Which offensive or defensive style do you prefer: (a) one that uses your players' skills primarily within the context of a given play or pattern, or (b) one that gives your players maximum freedom to improvise and use their skills creatively?

_____ _____   5. Which is more likely to succeed: (a) attacking opponents directly, or (b) maneuvering opponents out of position before attacking?

_____ _____   6. Which is more likely to happen: (a) losing games through mistakes, or (b) winning games through skillful play?

_____ _____   7. How important is big-play capability to a team's success: (a) only when necessary, or (b) very important?

_____ _____   8. How willing are you to take risks at any given point in a game: (a) not very, or (b) very?

Scoring: Give yourself one point for each A response and two points for each B response you checked.

IF YOUR SCORE WAS 8–10 POINTS

Your approach to coaching is no-nonsense and practical. Because you already have a pretty good idea of what works and what doesn't, you don't waste a lot of time experimenting with every new offensive or defensive fad that comes along. Your game plans generally don't change much from one game to the next—or your style of play from one season to the next, for that matter. You like to keep things simple and basic, and to force opponents to beat you at what you do best. You believe that defense wins games, and your teams are always solid defensively.

Offensively, you believe that mistakes lose games; thus, you take chances only when the odds are clearly in your favor to do so, or when no safer alternative exists. You'd rather do a few things, and do them correctly, than try a lot of different things and worry about executing them properly. You and your players believe strongly in your style of play and take considerable pride in the workmanlike quality of the team's performances. Whether winning or losing, your teams always look well coached.

In daily practice, you probably spend more time teaching and drilling than scrimmaging; as a result, your teams are always fundamentally sound and hard to beat. Controlling the variables that affect your team's performance is very important to you. You're a very good communicator, motivator, and disciplinarian, and your athletes understand your system so thoroughly that they probably could recite it in their sleep.

You're not really comfortable coaching superstar athletes who require special treatment, especially those whose work ethic or devotion to the team is questionable. You work hard and your players play hard, and you have little patience with players who don't fit into that scheme. You are regarded by your peers as a coach who always gets the most out of players of average ability, and as a coach who can turn a losing program into a winning program in a hurry.

IF YOUR SCORE WAS 11–13 POINTS

You're a pragmatist who uses whatever works. You have a broad understanding of your sport, its rules, and styles of play. You don't mind experimenting with new approaches; in games you like to add a new wrinkle or two offensively and change defensive looks frequently to keep opponents off balance.

You're a very good game coach who relishes the challenge of matching wits with other coaches. You always have a gimmick or a trick play or two up your sleeve, and your willingness to use them at the most unlikely of times makes you unpredictable to other coaches. You're at your best when coaching superior athletes who are smart as well as physically talented, and when you have team leaders whom you've trained to think the way you do in game situations. You like the idea of having a quarterback who is capable of checking off plays at the line of scrimmage in football, or a point guard who functions as a "coach on the floor" in basketball. With such athletes, your approach to styles of play tends to be adaptable and selective, your game plans complex, and your playbook lengthy and detailed.

In daily practice, having experienced, fundamentally sound players permits you to devote more time to team patterns and concepts than you might otherwise enjoy. Even with lesser-skilled players, though, you take pains to ensure that they understand not just the techniques involved but the *whys* underlying their use.

With inexperienced or unskilled athletes, you most likely would revert to a conservative offensive and defensive style with as few frills as possible (e.g., a simple passing game offense and low-risk zone defense in basketball), and extend or broaden it as your players grow in skills, confidence, and understanding. Your ultimate goal is the same for *all* players, namely, developing physical *and* mental skills that will render them effective in a wide range of game situations and strategies.

You relate well and easily to your players, and you're adept at handling superior athletes and superstars. You don't mind adapting your playing style and patterns to take full advantage of their unique skills; to the extent that your sport allows, you encourage your players to freelance and use their creativity. You're flexible enough in your thinking to put the team's best interests ahead of any preconceived notions you might have as to how the game should be played. You tend to think of your sport as a players' game, and of yourself as a players' coach.

IF YOUR SCORE WAS 14–16 POINTS

You're a gambler who is willing to take chances because you believe that great achievements require great risks. You enjoy coaching high-scoring teams, and you believe in taking your teams to the limit of what they're capable of doing. With highly skilled athletes, you tend to favor high-speed or high-risk offenses and pressure defenses that attack opponents aggressively in an attempt to take the ball away from them. You encourage your players to take chances, and you don't mind their mistakes as long as they are "hustling" mistakes, whether physical or mental. You're more interested in dominating or controlling opponents than in imposing the kind of offensive or defensive controls on your team that might hold your players back. You respect the role that defense plays in winning games, but not necessarily in the traditional sense. For you, defense also serves as an integral part of your offense, a way of getting the ball back in a hurry so your offense can take over. It's nice to hold opponents' scores down, of course, but you also recognize that the team who scores the most points wins the game. Your teams are always superbly well conditioned physically, and they are usually excellent in transition phases of the game. Your athletes tend to handle pressure situations better than most.

Although somewhat complex, your game plans don't often change much from one game to the next. Your teams may or may not look well coached, depending on your style of play, but that doesn't matter much to you. When your players play with intensity, it is extremely difficult for opponents to force you out of your basic game plan—much less defeat you. You don't call as many timeouts as most of your coaching peers.

You probably are a better practice coach than game coach; that is, you win mainly by virtue of your extensive game preparations and teaching skills in daily practice rather than the changes you make in games in response to opponents' strategies and tactics. Your style of play is popular with your players; as a result, you have little difficulty in motivating your players to work hard in practice or in games. Your daily practices are extremely rigorous, and your players pride themselves on their physical and mental toughness. They probably consider games easier than your daily practices.

ANALYZING THE QUESTIONS

1. ASSUMING THAT YOUR TEAM WILL WIN ANYWAY, WHICH WOULD YOU CONSIDER A GREATER ACCOMPLISHMENT, (A) HOLDING A GREAT TEAM TO A VERY LOW SCORE, OR (B) OUTSCORING IT BY A WIDE MARGIN?

This question identifies your position relative to whether defense or offense wins games.

To control a Great team defensively, you need to keep the ball away from it for long stretches at a time (e.g., by grinding out long, time-consuming drives in football, or by emphasizing careful ballhandling and shot selection in basketball) and play excellent defense the rest of the time.[2]

There's nothing wrong with being offensive-minded, of course, as long as you're willing to risk swapping scores with opponents or losing possession of the ball whenever your scoring drives or attempts to score fail. But Great teams don't get that way without a potent offense; the more often (or sooner) they get the ball back the more likely (and faster) they will be to solve whatever problems your defense presents for them.

The strongest argument against using aggressive offensive tactics against a team that is clearly superior to yours offensively is that, if you give them enough opportunities to beat you, they'll probably find a way to do it.

2. WHICH DO YOU PREFER, (A) MASTERING A GIVEN OFFENSE OR DEFENSE AND CHALLENGING OPPONENTS TO BEAT YOU AT WHAT YOU DO BEST, OR (B) USING A VARIETY OF OFFENSES OR DEFENSES TO KEEP OPPONENTS OFF BALANCE AND GUESSING?

Either approach will work with highly skilled, experienced players, but (b) will work only with players who possess a broad understanding of the game and its nuances. During his years as head basketball coach at the University of Maryland, Lefty Driesell often alluded jokingly to Dean Smith's "47 ways of playing man-to-man defense" at UNC; it's a safe bet that Coach Smith wouldn't use such technically refined tactics with a junior high basketball team. You shouldn't either.

---

[2] Until recently when the U.S. national soccer team began to emerge as a force to be reckoned with in international competition, our strategy against major opponents basically consisted of holding the ball and playing keep-away from powerful teams such as Brazil, Italy, and West Germany. (I say this, not to be demeaning, but to point out that, when you're in danger of being overpowered by a Great opponent, you can't do the same things you'd try against a weaker opponent.)

Now that soccer is no longer a four-letter word in the United States, we're producing more and more world-caliber players every year, and we no longer have to resort to ultra-conservative tactics such as attempting only two shots on goal in an entire match.

3. AMONG TEAMS OF EQUAL ABILITY, WHICH IS MORE LIKELY TO WIN GAMES, (A) PLAYING CONSERVATIVELY AND WAITING FOR OPPONENTS TO MAKE MISTAKES, OR (B) ATTACKING OPPONENTS AGGRESSIVELY IN ORDER TO CREATE OR EXPLOIT WEAKNESSES?

This question relates to a problem that will be addressed later in this chapter, namely, "Which should take precedence in selecting a style of play, the coach's knowledge of the game or the players' skills and athleticism?" At this point, all that is necessary to know is that the first step in the process of selecting a style of play is to identify your own beliefs and preferences. Those beliefs may change considerably over the years through experience, but unless you're comfortable with what you're doing you're unlikely to inspire any great confidence in your players that what you're doing is right for them.

4. WHICH OFFENSIVE OR DEFENSIVE STYLE DO YOU PREFER, (A) ONE THAT USES YOUR PLAYERS' SKILLS PRIMARILY WITHIN THE CONTEXT OF A GIVEN PLAY OR PATTERN, OR (B) ONE THAT GIVES YOUR PLAYERS MAXIMUM FREEDOM TO IMPROVISE AND USE THEIR SKILLS CREATIVELY?

This question might have been stated, "Which is more important, the *play* or the *player*?" It refers to the amount of control you prefer to exercise in game situations; while all players are expected or required to improvise as necessary in carrying out their individual responsibilities in any given action sequence, you may or may not want them to improvise *except as the need arises.*

If you chose response (b), you're a "players' coach" who doesn't object to players' freelancing, or operating more or less spontaneously in a system such as basketball's passing game offense; if you chose (a), you tend to trust your own judgment over that of your players.

5. WHICH IS MORE LIKELY TO SUCCEED, (A) ATTACKING OPPONENTS DIRECTLY, OR (B) MANEUVERING OPPONENTS OUT OF POSITION BEFORE ATTACKING?

Your response identifies you as being either (a) basically power-oriented, or (b) basically finesse-oriented. You probably use both approaches—most coaches do, at least occasionally—but here's the *real* question: Which style do you use to control opponents, or to set up the other as an alternative to your basic approach?

6. WHICH IS MORE LIKELY TO HAPPEN, (A) LOSING GAMES THROUGH MISTAKES, OR (B) WINNING GAMES THROUGH SKILLFUL PLAY?

Besides determining whether you're basically a pessimist or an optimist, this question also reveals your conservative or aggressive nature. If, along with most coaches, you believe that games are more often lost through mistakes, you probably don't need to adopt a high-risk, aggressive style of play unless you're absolutely certain that the majority of those mistakes will be made by the opponents. When aggressive styles go sour, they are somewhat akin to digging your own grave.

7. HOW IMPORTANT IS BIG-PLAY CAPABILITY TO A TEAM'S SUCCESS, (A) ONLY WHEN NECESSARY, OR (B) VERY IMPORTANT?

We're back to the conservative/aggressive question with this one, with a touch of power/finesse thrown in for good measure. Both answers are correct, of course, depending on the score and the time remaining, but (b) asks if big-play potential is important in situations other than those in which the game or ball possession is on the line. Aggressive tactics (and sometimes those associated with finesse as well, such as passing attacks in football) are designed to offer ongoing big-play potential that conservative or power strategies emphasizing ball control and patience cannot match. (This is not to suggest that the latter cannot incorporate big-play alternatives, of course; rather, I'm saying that, for example, Jimmy Johnson would be a fool to have Dan Marino passing only on third-and-long situations. The big-play, quick-strike potential would still be there in a run-oriented offense, but not to the extent that it currently exists with defensive backs knowing that Marino is likely to pass short *or* long on every play.[3])

---

[3] Incidentally, this explains why Don Shula had trouble incorporating a viable running attack into Miami's offense: Pass blocking and run blocking require different temperaments (i.e., a protective mentality in pass blocking and a hostile, don't-get-in-my-way attitude toward run blocking) that are rarely found in one player. Coach Shula necessarily recruited pass blockers to protect Marino from mayhem and murder while he's standing in the pocket choosing between his thirty-five or so receivers in their pass routes.

8. HOW WILLING ARE YOU TO TAKE RISKS AT ANY GIVEN POINT IN A GAME, (A) NOT VERY, OR (B) VERY?

This question restates the previous one in different form. Either taking *or* avoiding risks is acceptable, as long as you understand that you can't have it both ways at the same time. "As the farmer said, 'I'm not greedy, all I want is the land next to mine.'"[4]

WHICH SHOULD TAKE PRECEDENCE—THE COACH'S KNOWLEDGE OR THE PLAYERS' SKILLS?

There are basically two ways to approach the task of installing a style of play: fitting the players into a given playing style, or selecting a style that fits (or can be adapted to) the players' skills. Whichever approach they use, most coaches have rather strong feelings that their way is best.

ADAPTING PLAYERS TO A STYLE OF PLAY

The first reason a coach might prefer to fit his or her players into a style of play rather than the reverse is limited knowledge of the game.

When I started out in coaching at the junior high level in 1964, the sum of what I knew about basketball plus what I *thought* I knew about it was greater than the combined knowledge of everyone else who had ever coached the game. It didn't take long for me to discover the truth, though; I wound up teaching my kids a simple style of play because it was the only one I understood well enough to teach them. Eventually, I learned enough to branch out and try other things, but until I reached that point, I was severely limited in what I was capable of teaching effectively.

The second reason a coach might want to adapt players' skills to fit a given playing style is that he or she believes very strongly that that style of play is the best way to play the game. Adolph Rupp, John Wooden, and Bobby Knight (who between them won seventeen men's basketball championships at Kentucky, UCLA, and Indiana, respectively) absolutely refused to play zone defense with

---

[4] Peter, Dr. Laurence J. *Peter's Quotations: Ideas for Our Time* (New York: Bantam Books, 1979).

their teams because they felt that man-to-man defense was superior.[5] That's not to suggest that zones are necessarily inferior to man-to-man, of course, or that every basketball coach who aspires to win championships should emulate Rupp, Wooden, and Knight and use man-to-man. Many coaches and teams have had outstanding success with zone defenses over the years. But if you believe that man-to-man *or* zone is *the* way to go, you won't be comfortable using the other style and the results will show in the way your team plays it.

A third reason for adapting players to a style or system is *consistency* and *continuity*. Retaining the same basic style from one year to the next simplifies your teaching and permits your players to gain a greater understanding of what they're doing than when they are constantly having to adjust to new and unfamiliar situations.

On the college level, having your program identified with a given playing style can be an effective recruiting aid, or it can be a hindrance. High school prospects who are familiar with your program may like their chances for showcasing their skills, or they may fear that their potential will be wasted in your particular offensive or defensive style.

Because recruiting normally is rather limited at the high school level and below, those coaches are far more likely to have to make major adjustments in their style of play in any given year than their college counterparts. A winning program or a popular playing style (e.g., fast breaking in basketball) may attract potentially gifted athletes into your program. But no matter how strongly you believe in a given playing style, you still need players who are capable of making it work.

Early in his basketball coaching career, Jerry Tarkanian was ultraconservative offensively. Later, when he became nationally known for his freewheeling, high-scoring offenses at UNLV during the 1980s and early 1990s, he acknowledged the positive effects of his change in philosophy on his ability to recruit top high school prospects such as Stacey Augmon, Greg Anthony, Rod Foster, and Ed O'Bannon.

---

[5] Wooden used a full-court zone pressing defense with devastating effectiveness, however, and in his latter years at UK, Rupp adopted a "stratified, modified, parabolic man-to-man half-court defense"—in short, a zone defense, although he refused to call it that. Knight once toyed with the notion of using matchup zone defense at IU, but quickly abandoned the idea. It was obvious—to me, anyway—that an aggressive coach like Knight wouldn't be comfortable with such a passive defensive style as a matchup zone. If forced to use a zone defense, Knight probably would have found help-and-recover zone defense more to his liking.

"I hope I never have to go back to the old way of playing," Tark said, referring to his offensively conservative coaching roots. It's important to note, however, that he didn't discount the possibility of having to do so in the future (which, as I write this in November, 1995, is a distinct likelihood in Tarkanian's new job as head men's basketball coach at Fresno State. I'll be *very* surprised if Tark doesn't use a methodical, power game offense and 1-2-2 help-and-recover half-court zone defense until he establishes his program at Fresno State.)

To recap: Start with what you know, and master a given style of play that your athletes are capable of learning. Regardless of how committed you are to your beliefs, however, your professional growth requires that you extend your understanding to include other ways of playing the game—whether because you may need to go in other directions someday or simply because you need to understand what your opponents are doing. It's hardly an overstatement to suggest that, if you stay in the coaching business long enough, eventually the kind of talent you're now winning with will run short and you'll have to find new ways to win or remain competitive with different kinds of talent than you're used to coaching.

ADAPTING PLAYING STYLES TO PLAYERS' SKILLS

No two teams are exactly alike. Graduation, players' failure to meet eligibility requirements, and injuries all serve to deplete the available talent pool, the same way that transfer student-athletes and incoming freshmen expand it. Differences in team quality and potential from one season to the next may be subtle or broad, depending on the team's depth and the players' skills, experience, and leadership. Whatever differences exist must be accounted for in considering styles of play.

Ideally, the changes required to maximize your team's potential will be minimal. If so, the problem can be handled simply by adapting last year's scheme to this year's players, providing a smooth transition, and reducing learning time to a minimum. Such minor adjustments may take any of three forms:

1. Devising new plays for existing patterns or alignments
2. Changing individual responsibilities within a play or pattern

3. Altering a pattern or alignment to give it a different look without changing the basic offensive or defensive philosophy underlying its use

If these techniques seem rather obvious, it's because they are the kinds of things that every coach does in daily practice and in games.

Minor adjustments in playing style. Game plans are based on the notion, "We'll try this; if it works, we may not have to do anything else—or at least we'll stay focused on our basic offensive or defensive strategy, even if we throw in a few other things to keep the opponents honest. If it doesn't work, we'll do a little fine-tuning, make a few minor adjustments, and see what happens."

The same line of reasoning and approach to game preparations and strategy also applies to preparing your team in preseason practice. You begin with what the players already know and build on it. It's important to recognize your team's quality and potential from the start; if you misjudge where your team is starting out, you probably will also over- or underestimate what it is capable of accomplishing.

The start of the season is usually too late to start over with wholesale changes in playing style without massive confusion of the sort that can disrupt an entire season. (That also explains why, even for a veteran coach, the first year in a new coaching situation is often more difficult and demanding than subsequent years. The players must adjust, not only to your personality, coaching style, expectations, values, and work ethic, but also possibly to a new playing style, new alignments and patterns, and perhaps different ways of executing fundamentals, all of which may have to be learned from scratch).

Major adjustments in playing style. Because of the difficulties involved, comprehensive changes in playing style normally occur only when the team's previous style doesn't meet its needs even with adjustments, or when the team faces a sudden—and drastic—change in personnel or team composition.

Every offensive and defensive playing style depends for its success on certain team and individual characteristics (e.g., speed, strength, athleticism/fundamental soundness). It is important for the coach to select a playing style that uses his or her players' abili-

ties to best advantage, whatever they might be. It is equally important, however, to recognize changes in the team's composition that
adversely affect the team's chances of remaining successful using
that style of play.

For example, let's say that your senior-laden high school basketball team goes 27–3 one year and makes it to the state semifinals.
It's unquestionably a Very Good team, somewhat slow afoot but tall,
talented, and sound defensively. With excellent senior leadership,
good ballhandling, a strong inside game, and better-than-average
outside shooting, it's an experienced, intelligent squad that exe-
cutes your game plans with precision and makes few mistakes at
either end of the court. With better team speed and greater
depth—seven of the eight players you used most of the time were
seniors—it might have become a Great team. Still, with 27 wins and
an appearance in the state's Final Four under your belt it's hardly
necessary to debate the relative status of Very Good and Great
teams. It was a good ride all the way, exciting and rewarding for players and coaches alike.

Just as you're getting used to the idea of calling meaningless
timeouts late in games to remind the fans who is coaching this mar-
velous collection of basketball talent, the funniest thing happens:
graduation. Gone in the twinkling of an eye are your five starters and
two of your three top reserves, your senior leadership, your good
ballhandling, and good shooting. They are likely to be replaced
next season by one returning letter winner, four benchwarmers who
were used mainly in mop-up roles when the outcome of games was
already decided, and a motley crew of inexperienced freshmen and
sophomores from this year's junior high and jayvee squads.

As if that were not bad enough, the *really* bad news is that,
unless someone develops a growth enhancer between now and the
start of next season, the tallest player on next year's team will be
6'1". Your varsity team will be extremely quick—thank heaven for
small favors (pardon the pun)—but your perimeter shooters have
all graduated, your point guard is inexperienced at the varsity level,
and your 6'1" center is unlikely to overwhelm opponents at low
post. Except for full-court pressing and fast breaking, there's
absolutely nothing you can use from this year's style of play that will
give you a decent chance of winning more than a handful of your
games next year.

So what do you do, coach? Dialing a 1-900 psychic help number and scanning the newspapers' advertising sections for teaching/coaching vacancies come to mind readily. But do you really believe Madame Olga's tea leaves or crystal ball will solve your coaching problems for you? And when's the last time you heard of a coach getting a job—even a *bad* one—through the want ads? Anyway, this is home for you, and you aren't interested in pulling up stakes and moving elsewhere.

If you're not a very good coach (and have no aspirations to become one), your response to such unfortunate circumstances is likely to be throwing up your hands in defeat, cursing the Fates for treating you so unkindly just when things were going so well for you, and treating next year's collection of speedy but somewhat uncoordinated runts as if they were capable of doing the same kinds of things that this year's athletes did so beautifully. You may even blame the players when things fall apart—as they will—and your team winds up losing most of its games using a playing style that is as alien to your players as the Declaration of Independence recited in Mandarin Chinese.

If you're genuinely concerned about things like winning and program building, however, your actions will be vastly different from those of the coach who looks for quick and easy solutions and meekly gives up without a fight when none are immediately forthcoming.

The first step you should take when facing disaster is to study the situation objectively from every conceivable angle. While this might seem obvious, the key word here is *objectively*. For one thing, that means considering the possibility that *you* might need to change your way of thinking regarding styles of play, rather than trying to fit your players into your preferred way of doing things. For another, it means assessing your team's strengths, weaknesses, and potential as accurately and honestly as possible.

In the example used here, you already know (or at least you strongly suspect) that the tactics that worked so well with this year's talented seniors will fail miserably with next year's small, inexperienced speedsters. Last year's half-court zone defense won't work because your 6'1" center and 5'11" forwards won't be able to control the middle even by double-teaming at the posts. And when opponents miss perimeter shots, their taller players will play volleyball with the offensive rebounds.

Offensively, you know that opponents will attempt to counter-act your speed by sitting back in a tight zone defense, giving up the outside shot that none of your kids are likely to make with any con-sistency, and controlling the defensive boards to give you only one shot every time you have the ball.

(Here, incidentally, is where a measure of unreality can creep in: If you aren't completely honest with yourself, you might be tempted to think, "Well, I can teach them to shoot a good percent-age from the perimeter; after all, I have a whole year to do it." States are, and have been for several years, tightening up the reins where out-of-season team practice and supervised coaching is concerned, however. Unless your kids are willing to supplement what little off-season instruction you're allowed to give them with hundreds of hours of work on their own to improve their form and groove their shots, whatever gains they experience in shooting proficiency are likely to be minimal. Ideally, your players will want to pay that price for the team's sake and their own pursuit of excellence, but if you plan on it, you may be in for a major disappointment. You always hope for the best, of course—but if you're smart you also plan for the worst.)

Finding the answers. Probably the greatest obstacles to be over-come, whether in coaching or in life, are *inflexibility* and *wasted time.* Flexibility involves your willingness to do whatever it takes to improve your team; wasted time is whatever you might do (or fail to do) that does not carry your team and your program forward. If you've analyzed the overall pluses and minuses of the coming year's team thoroughly and objectively, you'll know whether major changes in the team's playing style are necessary. At this point, it's not necessary to have all the answers, or even any of them; all you need is the willingness to find the answers.

Seek, and ye shall find.

—Matthew 7:7

If the answers you're looking for aren't readily apparent to you from your own knowledge of the game, your assessment of the team's strengths and weaknesses offers important clues as to what may or may not work. Thinking about the problem and possible solutions is important, but there's another, possibly better, way to do it: *Consult other coaches, especially those who are knowledgeable or have experienced problems similar to yours.* Talk to your high school or college coach about your problem, or discuss it with a coaching friend or acquaintance, or with anyone else whose expertise is greater than yours. Attend coaching clinics. If you haven't collected an extensive personal coaching library in your sport, visit a state university that offers a major in physical education and look in the library for coaching books that might offer answers to your problem. You can check them out through your local library if your state has an interlibrary loan system. While you're there, scan the indexes of the coaching journals—*Scholastic Coach, Coaching Clinic, Women's Coaching Clinic*—for articles relevant to your problem.

If you already know what style of play best suits your players, but you don't know much about that style, read up on it and talk to coaches who have used it successfully. Be advised, though, that their use of the offense or defense may not exactly coincide with your own needs, since their personnel may be vastly different from yours.

I found the answers I needed to a similar problem at a basketball coaching clinic in Birmingham. The list of guest speakers was impressive, including Dean Smith, Denny Crum, Lefty Driesell, and Gene Bartow, but it was Jerry Tarkanian's presentation that showed me how to focus on speed to the exclusion of practically everything else.

Since we had no effective half-court offense, I decided to scrap it entirely and depend on our pressure man-to-man defense, fast breaking, and taking the first available shot if the fast break layup wasn't available. I didn't particularly care if we made the outside shot or not, since if we didn't get the layup I preferred our being on defense and trying to steal the ball. The important thing was for us to keep the game moving at the fastest tempo imaginable in order to outrun our opponents and wear them down physically. We *didn't* want the opponents to rest in a lazy zone defense where their superior size could negate our speed advantage.

Similarly, we went to full-court man-to-man pressure defense so opponents couldn't stand around resting in a lazy zone offense. We dogged their ballhandlers relentlessly, fronted the posts, played the passing lanes, and tried to steal every pass. In daily practice, we worked on conditioning, defensive stance and movement, full-court pressing, half-court sideline-influence man-to-man defense, high-speed ballhandling and fast breaking, and free-throw shooting.

Admittedly, it was a risky and somewhat scary proposition for me, since I had previously been extremely conservative in my approaches to offense and defense. I was adopting an offensive style of play in which we had no half-court offense at all beyond the simple instruction: *Look for the layup; if it's not there, take the first shot you can get.* We didn't call timeouts, because they gave our opponents a minute to rest.

I felt that our strategy, risky as it was, was no more of a gamble than *not* adopting a new playing style would have been. We never could have controlled opponents with a half-court zone defense, a pint-sized center, and no effective outside shooters. We started the next season with one win and four losses. Just as I was beginning to think that I might have made a mistake in switching styles of play, our defensive quickness and conditioning started paying off for us, producing turnovers regularly and tiring out taller opponents, who tried to run with us. We won 13 of the next 18 games to finish with a 14–9 record. We improved to 17–6 the following year, and topped it off at 20–3 the year after that, when our mighty mites were seniors themselves.

I made at least a thousand coaching mistakes with each of those teams, but one mistake I *didn't* make was trying to force my players to use a style of play that was beyond their skills. If good coaching was involved—and I like to think it was—it was that I recognized a need for change and was willing to act on it in the team's best interests.

I didn't invent the up-tempo, quick-shot style of play, nor did I perfect it—but I didn't hesitate to use it. The only way I might have added to Tark's usage was in not caring whether we made the quick shot at the end of the break when the layup wasn't there. Coach Tarkanian dismissed as frivolous my preference for us to be on defense, rather than to give the opponents time to rest while we passed the ball around looking for a good shot. Tark attracts good shooters, though; he's never had to work with kids whose perimeter shooting skills were so poor.

You may or may not find the answers you're looking for at a coaching clinic, but *the answers to every problem you have are out there somewhere, and a diligent, thorough search will find them.*

Assimilating the new playing style. When you have found your answer, your next task is to study the new style with the same diligence and thoroughness with which you approached the task of finding it. You don't have to become the world's leading authority on the subject, but you *do* have to become an expert on it *as it relates to your team and the way you hope to use it*. You must understand it well enough to answer your players' questions, and to adapt the basic pattern(s) and related techniques to fit your players' skills and hide their weaknesses.

In adopting Tark's up-tempo, quick-shot style, for example, I quickly found that none of my players could dribble left-handed—a situation that could severely disrupt the formation of our fast breaks. We practiced high-speed weak-hand dribbling in our daily practices, of course, but that skill—and the confidence to use it in game situations—is developed rather slowly. I opted for an easier, quick-fix solution that worked nicely for us in games, given our dazzling foot speed. I taught my ballhandlers to use *one* left-handed dribble to get by an overplaying defender, after which they were free to return to right-handed dribbling for the remainder of the break. It wasn't textbook coaching, but it got us through the learning period and allowed us to concentrate on other important things, like finishing fast breaks without shooting layups over the backboard.

The example given here is by no means the only kind of broad change that a coach might be forced to make, of course. Change can also result in a sudden improvement in team quality—as when two schools consolidate, or when highly skilled transfer students or athletes from the feeder program, playing varsity ball for the first time, join the team.

I chose to illustrate a sudden drop in overall team quality because it's more likely than a sudden influx of highly skilled athletes. It's also more difficult to deal with. If your Good, Very Good, or Great team is suddenly made better, you don't normally require major changes in your playing style in order to continue to be successful. All you have to do is fit the new players into your present system.

Even with a Very Good or Great team, you may want to switch from a relatively conservative playing style to a more aggressive style that entails greater risks but offers greater rewards. Most coaches wouldn't do it—not just because of the difficulty involved in installing a high-risk system that is new to the players (and possibly the coaches as well)—but also because future personnel changes might require going back to the former style of play. Changing playing styles is too important a decision to be taken lightly. It requires total commitment on the part of the coaches and players alike.

8

UNDERSTANDING STYLES OF PLAY

On the surface, sports like football, basketball, baseball, softball, soccer, hockey, and volleyball appear to have little in common. Some are played indoors, others outdoors. Scoring systems and the number of players competing at a given time vary widely, as do the uniforms, equipment, terminology, and rules. There are, however, two common threads that bind these and other team sports together: First, all of them are competitive and produce winners and losers; and second, all involve either of two general approaches to competing and playing the game—*aggressive* or *conservative*.

AGGRESSIVE STYLES OF PLAY

Perhaps a bit of clarification is necessary here. Playing aggressively doesn't mean playing to win. We all want to win, and to succeed in what we're doing. Baseball and softball players don't step into the batter's box with the intention of striking out. Playing aggressively doesn't mean playing hard, either, since everyone is expected to play hard, regardless of the sport or the situation. Playing aggressively means forcing the action, as opposed to playing it safe and waiting for favorable circumstances to arise, or waiting to be attacked. Aggressive playing styles normally entail a measure of risk, since every time the aggressive action or strategy fails, the advantage momentarily shifts—sometimes dramatically—to the other team.

The penalties for failure when playing aggressively are greater in some sports than in others. In football and baseball (or softball), giving up a touchdown or as many as four runs with a single swing of the bat dictates that coaches carefully consider the risks involved in playing aggressively. Other team sports are relatively less demanding, since a ten-point deficit in basketball, a one- or two-goal deficit in soccer or hockey, or the loss of a point in volleyball is irredeemable only at the end of games or matches.

THE STRATEGY UNDERLYING AGGRESSIVE PLAY

Winning aside, the ultimate goal of playing aggressively is *domination*, not control. Perhaps the most recognizable policy statement regarding aggressive playing styles in team sports is Nolan Richardson's "Forty Minutes of Hell" approach to basketball at the University of Arkansas. If all Coach Richardson wanted was to control opponents, the Razorbacks could use a "Thirty-eight Minutes of Normal Basketball and Two Minutes of Hell" approach, but that's not what he's after. Richardson's philosophy—and that of all aggressive approaches taken to their logical extremes—is that relentless pressure applied throughout an entire game or match will: upset the opponents' mental equilibrium; force them to make mistakes that they would not make otherwise; take them out of their preferred playing style, game tempo, and comfort zone; and challenge their physical condition—*all at the same time.* Any one of those results could win a game over forty minutes of play; attacking the opponent in all of those areas at once dramatically increases the odds that one or more of them will succeed. Richardson's "ace in the hole"—and one that coaches often overlook in evaluating the potential of aggressive playing styles—is that *when his strategy succeeds in one area, it tends to extend to others, because the results are cumulative.* For example:

■ If your up-tempo style of play succeeds in tiring out *my* players, not only will we function below par in our own offense or defense but we're even less likely to handle *your* offense or defense while we're tired. We're at your mercy until the fatigue passes—and I can tell you from my own experiences with up-tempo attacks that a ten-minute halftime, or taking two or three consecutive timeouts, won't solve the problem. As Vince

Lombardi so aptly noted, "Fatigue makes cowards of us all." Defeat becomes preferable to physical collapse.

■ If your team's constant pressure succeeds in forcing my players into a series of mistakes, the resulting pressure on my kids not to make the same mistakes is likely to cause them to make other mistakes.

Presumably, I've told my team what to expect from yours and how to deal with it. Since what we're doing isn't working, however, I'll spend most of my timeout(s) correcting the mistakes we've already made. There simply isn't enough time in one-minute timeouts for me to go over all of the possible mistakes we haven't made yet.

■ If your aggressive playing style succeeds in taking away some or all of the things we do best, or in altering the game tempo in ways that disrupt our game plan, it follows that whatever adjustments we make will move us farther along the path toward losing control of the game. Every team plays best at its own rhythm and timing; when opponents succeed in altering that rhythm and timing, the results usually are confusion, and loss of confidence and concentration.

PREREQUISITES FOR USING AN AGGRESSIVE PLAYING STYLE EFFECTIVELY

Note that each of the preceding points began with an *if*; make it a very large *IF*. Aggressive styles of play aren't for every team; they involve three prerequisites, the absence of any one of which will immediately shoot down your aggressive intentions.

1. Players must possess the physical skills to make the play work, and athletic ability sufficient to recover when they are beaten. While the same can be said for all playing styles, it is even more important when you use aggressive styles, because errors are magnified in direct proportion to the risks involved. In basketball, for example, if two of my players trap your ballhandler, your team has a four-on-three advantage every time we fail to contain the ball; that advantage will continue until you score, or until at least one of my two defenders on the ball recovers, retreats, and restores numerical equality.

In football, man-to-man defensive coverage is almost necessarily played more aggressively than zone coverage, since, if a defensive back is beaten one-on-one, no help is immediately available. The results can be disastrous, as the Atlanta Falcons discovered a few years ago when they decided to play Jerry Rice and the other 49er receivers man-to-man. Fantasy football league coaches were furious with the decision because Rice caught six touchdown passes that week. Falcons fans weren't too happy about it, either—and rightfully so. Six touchdown receptions by one receiver against man coverage constitute a coaching error.

If you're going to play aggressively, your players *must* possess whatever physical skills are required to make the strategy work as designed. They also need the athleticism to recover quickly and regain offensive or defensive control whenever things go wrong.

Great teams—and many Very Good teams as well—are capable of playing either aggressively or conservatively, as dictated by the situation or the coach's philosophy or preferences. I've always believed that the ultimate team in any sport would be stocked with outstanding players (e.g., the 1992 U.S. Olympic basketball team, "Dream Team I"), using a style of play that attacks opponents with unrelenting pressure throughout every second of every game.

You don't see many such teams or strategies. Most teams aren't Great—and of those that *are*, most tend to play aggressively only in certain situations. After all, why take unnecessary chances with a potentially Great team for the sake of being more dominating than you already are? If you're dealt four aces in poker, you don't throw them away and try for a royal flush. And you don't get extra credit for winning games by 50 points rather than by 25.

Or do you? Recent trends in high school and college indicate that more and more coaches are winning big and trampling opponents in order to impress the voters and improve their state or national rankings. Without taking sides in the controversy over whether running up astronomical scores on Weak opponents is necessary, ethical, or sportsmanlike, I offer the following for your consideration or rejection:

There are two ways to run up scores. Using a methodical, conservative approach will do the trick, but it generally requires your starters to stay in the game longer than you might prefer. Using an attacking style of play will usually do the job faster, and thus more convincingly. Even then, however, it's easier to switch from an aggressive to a conservative style than to go from playing it safe to going for broke—except when your players are unused to protecting a lead. In either case, the better your players are, compared with the opponents, the more likely your strategy is to succeed.

Some Good teams, and possibly even a few Fair teams, are capable of using an aggressive playing style effectively against teams of equal or lesser skills. The less talented a team is, however, the more likely its players are to make mistakes *regardless of the playing style they employ*. Deciding whether to use an attacking strategy or a passive, wait-and-see approach against a given opponent (and whether to use it on a full-time, part-time, or not-at-all basis) involves two important questions:

a. Who is more likely to make mistakes; are we, or are the opponents?

b. Who is more likely to profit from those mistakes?

When you have a Weak team using aggressive tactics, the opponents are more likely to profit.

Once, in my first year in a new coaching situation, I inherited a winless high school girls basketball team whose returning players had averaged only 7.8 ppg. collectively the previous year. With a leading scorer who had averaged 2.5 ppg. and a senior point guard who hadn't played since her freshman year, our attacking potential was roughly equivalent to the quick-strike capabilities of the Somalian air force.

Rather than trying to win games, we had our hands full simply trying to keep scores respectable against opponents who were used to beating our teams by 30 to 60 points. Our using aggressive tactics was out of the question—with one notable exception that was forced on us by our opponents during the first half of the season.

Aware of our many weaknesses, most opponents full-court pressed us early on with the intention of putting us away as usual in the first two and a half minutes of the game. But because our preseason priority was beating the opponents' presses,[1] we were prepared to fast break *every time we were pressed.* Our "selective aggressiveness" strat-

---

[1] To state the obvious, if you can't beat the presses, you'll never get the ball to your offensive end of the court.

egy worked, too—but not in the way we expected. By halftime, opponents usually discovered that all they had to do was quit pressing us and two-thirds of our offensive potential disappeared.

If this had been a movie (e.g., like *Wildcats*, the 1986 comedy in which Goldie Hawn takes over coaching an inner-city high school football team and miraculously transforms a bunch of losers into city champions in eight weeks, through skillful coaching) our season would have ended on a high note of triumph. This was reality, however, and real-life miracles usually take a bit longer to produce. We won fifteen games the following year (thanks largely to some capable replacements from the junior high team), but that first year, all our varsity girls had to show for their hard work and determination was six wins and fifteen losses—that, and reducing our opponents' victory margin from 33.8 to 8.6 ppg.

2. Players must act quickly and decisively in gaining control of the situation. Aggressive strategies are designed to create and exploit small, momentary advantages that—if not countered successfully—can turn into huge advantages for the attacking team. Failure to act quickly and decisively, however, and at the proper moment, tends to reduce or eliminate whatever advantages arise. Players who hesitate even momentarily will be a step or two slow in carrying out their responsibilities, and the opportunity is likely to be lost.

Bear Bryant often stated his belief that, in a close football game, a single 15-yard penalty can lose a game. Missed opportunities can lose games, too, especially in such sports as football, soccer, hockey, and baseball, in which scoring opportunities aren't as prevalent as they are in, say, basketball.

Regarding your players, it should be noted that certain personality types are more prone to aggressive styles and strategies than others; they are better equipped emotionally to deal with situations aggressively. While most athletes can be taught to play aggressively regardless of their personality type,[2] it's wise to consider players' basic aggressiveness in the player selection portion of team tryouts.

---

[2] The process involves: 1. modeling aggressiveness in your approach to coaching (think: Jerry Tarkanian or Steve Spurrier); 2. recognizing and reinforcing players' aggressive behavior *even when it results in mistakes*; 3. focusing on fundamental skills that will improve players' confidence in playing aggressively; and 4. thoroughly familiarizing players with the strategies and techniques involved in the particular system being used, especially their specific roles at every point along the way.

3. The coach must understand the system thoroughly—such underlying theory and technical points as alignments, attacking points, personnel requirements, and deployment—in order to achieve maximum results. Vince Lombardi said, "You don't do things right some of the time; you do them right all of the time." Unfortunately, the risk factor inherent in all aggressive styles dictates that mistakes will be made. Aggressive theories are based on the idea that, if *we* can dictate when, where, and how pressure is applied, our familiarity with the system and process will cause the opponents to make the mistakes, and not us. This is true, however, only if we devote sufficient practice time to rehearsing the movements and timing—and five minutes a day simply isn't enough. In most cases, the mechanics of aggressive styles of play are complex enough to require twenty minutes or more of daily practice *even after they have been learned.*

If you aren't willing to devote such a large block of daily practice time to working on, say, the triple-option play in football, you shouldn't expect it to work as designed, any more than you could reasonably expect to develop an effective passing offense with five to ten minutes of daily practice. That triple-option play might work once or twice under favorable circumstances, but you shouldn't count on it. Failure to spend enough time practicing the mechanics is bound to catch up with you.

If you aren't convinced 100 percent that aggressive play is the way to go, you shouldn't be going that way. If you're a football coach who just wants an option play in his playbook for occasional use, you ought to skip the options and use the alignment for three called plays (the dive play to the fullback, the quarterback keeper, and the pitch to the trailing back). While those plays don't begin to approach the attacking potential of the true option series, they are safer than risking fumbles when your kids haven't mastered the mechanics and techniques that make it a potent attacking style of play. If they have mastered the options, why are you using it as a complementary play, rather than as the primary focus of your offensive game plan?

The answer to that question? Because you don't trust it. There are many reasons why you might mistrust aggressive styles of play, and they are all valid, as long as you understand the nature and potential of the system involved and consider it not worth the risks involved. Aggressive strategies offer quicker dominating potential than any other approaches. Whereas power games pit strength against strength and wear down opponents physically, aggressive styles are more subtle; they attack opponents mentally and emotionally as well as physically, pressuring them constantly to make *quick* and *accurate* decisions or face being blown out of games. Don't overlook or dismiss aggressive styles of play simply because they entail a measure of risk.

Coaches who use aggressive styles of play more often than occasionally do so because forcing the action causes things to happen *now*, not at some indefinable point in the future. Nolan Richardson's approach to basketball is that, if his team's "in-your-face, no-holds-barred, take-no-prisoners" aggressiveness builds early 20-point leads, many opponents will surrender emotionally and go through the motions of playing the rest of the game. As for the rest—well, Coach Richardson probably would agree that it's easier to protect or build on a 20-point lead than it is to overcome a 20-point deficit. Dominating games early makes it easier to control them later.

Still, no one with a grain of sense adopts an aggressive style because someone else has been successful using it; the risks are too great, and the requirements for its effective use too stringent and demanding. Not every athlete or team is physically, mentally, or emotionally equipped to pursue victories aggressively, and not every coach is comfortable with the risks involved. That's why most coaches prefer situational aggressiveness to keeping relentless pressure on opponents throughout every second of every game. It's a matter of *acceptable or necessary risks*; unless your team meets the requirements for its use, you aren't likely to succeed with it, except occasionally.

CONSERVATIVE STYLES OF PLAY

Although fans almost always prefer aggressive styles of play to conservative tactics, most coaches tend to prefer the latter, and for the very best of reasons: *control*. Whereas aggressive styles involve risks that tend to hover on the edge of playing out of control, conservative approaches attempt to minimize the risks until circumstances favor attacking. After all, it's unnecessary—and often unwise—to force the action and attempt to dominate opponents when you can control them with far less risk involved. The same quick-strike potential that renders aggressive styles appealing to some coaches is regarded by many others as unnecessarily hazardous. It all depends on what your players are capable of doing, and how comfortable you are with their doing it.

A conservative style of play really is playing the percentages—weighing the alternatives in any given situation and taking chances only when the odds are in your favor. It's "playing within yourself"—controlling opponents by doing what you do best—and it's hiding or minimizing your weaknesses (e.g., by using double-teams or zone defense in football or basketball). It's "going by the book," as in employing a hit-and-run or sacrifice bunt in baseball rather than risking the baserunner's being thrown out stealing second. Sometimes, all that's necessary is to give opponents the chance to beat themselves. Many a boxing manager has, in the heat of the action, exhorted his overeager fighter to "back up and give him room to fall!"

Here's why coaches adopt conservative playing styles:

1. To Use Superior Strength to Overpower Opponents with as Little Risk as Possible

One of the defining characteristics of an aggressive playing style is that *the style of play itself is designed to create weaknesses that the attacking team can exploit.* This is a somewhat compelling notion if you over-look the risks involved, but it's also unnecessary if your players can do the same thing without the risks.

2. To Use the Individual Talents of Superior Players to Full Advantage

If you're a football coach who is fortunate enough to have a superi-or athlete with the talent of, say, a Bo Jackson, every team you play will focus on him and try to take him out of the equation; you, in effect, do the same thing yourself if you use him in a triple-option attack in which the odds of his getting the ball are only one out of three.[3] The same applies to basketball: With a dominating center in your lineup, you may want to build your offense around an inside power game, rather than emphasizing full-court pressure defense

---

[3] Actually, the odds are less than that; if he's the pitch back, the cornerback will play the pitch and make your quarterback keep the ball.

and a fast-breaking style that keeps the ball out of your center's hands more effectively than the opponents may be capable of doing.

An advantage is useful only if it's exploited. Playing styles evolve and remain with you forever—to be used whenever the need arises; the same cannot be said for outstanding players whose talents must be exploited *now*, while they are available to you. While it's true that no one player, however talented, is more important than the team, team needs dictate that superior players be used in such a manner as to maximize their skills, and thus the team's chances of winning as well.

During the 1960s and 1970s, first John MacKay and then John Robinson used a series of All-America running backs at Southern Cal to dominate the (then) Pac-8 Conference and NCAA Division I football as well. It was not at all uncommon for USC I-backs Mike Garrett, Anthony Davis, Charles White, Ricky Bell, O. J. Simpson, and Marcus Allen to carry the ball thirty to thirty-five times a game because, as MacKay thoughtfully pointed out, "The ball doesn't weigh very much." The theory behind "letting the Big Dawg run" as much as possible is this: If you give him the ball ten times, he'll probably break at least one or two plays for long gainers; if he carries the ball thirty times, he's likely to break five to six (or more) for big gains or touchdowns.

Great players have a way of making great things happen, especially late in games when lesser, weaker players are beginning to tire or feel the pressure of the situation. The difference between ten and thirty carries is found in the extra wear and tear inflicted on opponents over the course of a game in trying to contain, chase down, or tackle a big, strong, quick running back who regards being tackled as a personal affront and defensive lapses or mistakes as scoring opportunities. Keeping the ball out of the hands of such a player is a mistake that few coaches can afford to make.

3. TO CONTROL THE SCORE AGAINST SUPERIOR OPPONENTS

This is the opposite side of point 1. If you don't have the horses to make a race of it against a clearly superior opponent, your best strategy is to try to keep the ball away from them for as long as possible; they can't score while your team has the ball. This in turn requires minimizing the risks involved and stretching out the time between your scores and theirs. An aggressive, gambling approach to offense or defense simply won't work because superior teams are better equipped to take advantage of mistakes. Granted, Great teams almost always beat Weak teams anyway, but in such cases winning and losing usually are minor considerations; the more important goal is staying competitive and keeping the score down.

4. To Protect a Lead, Control the Clock, or Keep the Ball Out of Opponents' Hands

Closely allied to point 3, this strategy extends to practically *any* situation in which a team might profit from keeping the ball away from the opponents. Even the most aggressive of teams occasionally needs to abandon its attacking strategy and play conservatively; failure to do so may be heroic in the sense of refusing to admit defeat, but it's also foolhardy in the sense of fighting to preserve a lost cause. All of us have had games when our players seem to have left their minds at home, or to be playing the game with their hands in their pockets and their shoelaces tied together; in such cases, the best strategy usually is to slow things down to a controllable level and try to make the best of a sorry situation. As country singer Kenny Rogers noted, playing poker to win involves, among other things, knowing when to hold up, fold up, walk away, or run.

5. To Control Your Players' Performances as a Basis for Controlling Opponents

One of coaching's most fundamental principles is that, regardless of whether you can control what the opponents are doing, you can at least control what your own players are doing. Controlling opponents is an outgrowth of controlling your own team.

The term *control* means different things in different contexts. In game situations, controlling opponents means finding ways to limit what they can do; normally, that process involves preparing and following a game plan or strategy for success. Controlling your own team means ensuring that your players follow your guidelines as closely or as broadly as you prefer. Conservative styles of play generally permit or require more direct coaching control than aggressive styles that emphasize individual initiative or decision-making responsibilities.

6. To Provide Additional Support in Areas Where You Are Weak or Your Opponents Are Strong

Most of us probably would rather win games the macho way, by using our superior strengths to steamroller every opponent who dares to get in our way. Sadly, life doesn't always work out that way; sometimes the two teams are evenly matched, and sometimes the opponents are vastly superior. In either case, when you cannot reasonably expect to win by virtue of your strengths, your main concern should be avoiding losing by virtue of your weaknesses.

Protective strategies include such tactics as: using zone defense to intensify coverage in selected areas of the court or playing field;[4] double- (or even triple-) teaming superior athletes; playing off speedy, elusive wide receivers or running plays toward a particular defensive lineman to reduce his pursuit capability in football; and using intentional walks or infield-outfield shifts to reduce the threat posed by outstanding hitters in baseball.

7. To Protect Certain Areas of the Court or Playing Field

Offensive strategy begins with attempting to establish points of attack favorable to the offensive team. In most team sports, the preferred initial point of attack is the middle of the playing area because it offers equal attacking potential on either side, whereas shifting the ball to one side of the court or field reduces passing angles and brings zone defenders closer to each other and the ball.[5]

This is not to say that the actual attack will come from the middle, of course; the point of attack shifts with ball movement to either side of the court or field. In volleyball, for example, spikes usually occur along one sideline or the other to prevent the defensive front line from triple-teaming in the middle, but the set-ups come from the middle whenever possible because the defense cannot determine where to double-team until the pass is made. The same cannot be said for set-up passes that originate from the sideline, due to the predictability and reduction of the passing angles.

---

[4] Or to enhance rebounding effectiveness in basketball.

[5] In football, it also enables the defenders to use the nearer sideline as a twelfth player.

In basketball, getting the ball to low post against zone defense seldom involves a direct pass from the top of the circle; under normal circumstances it takes two passes—point-to-wing, wing-to-low post—to do the job, with the entry pass to low post made *while the defense is shifting toward the ball*. If the ball is brought up or established on one side of the court, the defenders can deny the entry pass by shifting toward the ball before the first pass is made. The difference between the two approaches is significant. When the point of attack shifts quickly, the defense must adjust equally quickly or risk losing control. The quickest changes in points of attack occur when the initial attack originates from the middle; that's why defensive strength up the middle is always a top priority in sports such as football, baseball, and basketball. If you can't protect the middle, opponents won't have to attack you anywhere else.

The problem becomes even more acute when the opponents' style of play is geared to attacking the middle, as in dive plays in football and low post–oriented offenses in basketball. In such cases, the defensive rule of thumb is *do whatever it takes to protect the middle.* If one person or man-to-man coverage can do it (e.g., by overplaying or fronting to deny entry passes to low post or the lane in basketball), fine; if not, double-team or play zone defense to intensify coverage in those areas.

Double-teaming is always a desperation move, since it reduces coverage elsewhere to a certain extent. But desperate situations require desperate solutions, and it doesn't get much worse than the basic inability to protect the middle.

Zone defenses also give up something in return for the added protection they provide in certain areas of the court or field; if it were otherwise, every team in the world would already be using man-to-man coverage and no one would need anything else. Still, giving up something (e.g., perimeter coverage in zone defense in return for strengthened post coverage in basketball) doesn't necessarily mean that the opponents will be able to capitalize on your "gift"; they may not be equipped, in terms of personnel, to attack whatever weaknesses your coverage produces. That is especially true if you've done your coaching homework in terms of deciding exactly what you can afford to give up once you're able to control the areas where they intend to beat you.

If I'm going to lose, I want my game plan and strategy to dictate how you beat me, rather than my simply allowing you to beat me any way you want to. For example, you may have five seven-footers in your basketball lineup, and you may beat us 100 times out of 100 tries with superior offensive rebounding and follow shots; still, I'll do everything in my power to find a way to ensure that your first shot every time downcourt doesn't come from low post or the lane. I may not be able to control much of what your combined thirty-five feet of starting lineup does, but I'll control the ball side low post if it means aligning all five defenders within hugging distance of your post player(s) and turning the game into a wrestling match. I'm exaggerating, of course, but the points remain:

- If I can find a way to control the areas where you are most likely to beat us, you'll have to find other ways to beat us.

- If I can dictate where and how you beat me, I retain a measure of coaching control over the situation that can extend to other games and other times when your team's superiority is not nearly so pronounced.

- You'll probably win anyway—and maybe even by as large a victory margin as you would have achieved under normal circumstances—but taking you out of your basic game plan is something I can point to as a measure of the progress our team is making toward becoming the kind of team we want to be.

8. TO CONTROL THE GAME TEMPO AGAINST FASTER OPPONENTS

Among the many mistakes you can make, few are likely to leave a stronger or more lasting impression than treating a vastly superior opponent as your equal by pitting *your* strengths against *their* strengths, your power vs. their power, or your speed vs. their speed. As a coach, I'll lay out the truth for you in plain and simple terms that cannot possibly be misunderstood: Aesop was a liar. Tortoises *never* outrun hares; most of the time, they don't even make it across the highway.

The *only* way to overcome the effects of superior speed is to take it out of the equation entirely and force faster opponents to find other ways to beat you. The most common approach here is to use a low-risk, ball-control offensive strategy that, if successful, keeps the ball away from the opponents for long stretches. They will counter with whatever defensive strategies they deploy to get the ball back quickly. If their offensive game plan is based primarily on speed, their defense will be *very* aggressive in trying to produce turnovers. In basketball, they may be willing to risk giving up easy scores (e.g., backdoor layups) in their efforts to get the ball back and score quickly or regain control of the tempo.

Players and coaches who don't understand the extremes that up-tempo teams will go to in order to control the tempo are likely to be fooled by a few uncontested layups into thinking that the high-speed game isn't really so difficult to master, after all. In such cases, by the time your players learn the truth about aggressive, up-tempo styles of play, they're likely to find themselves 30 points down and sinking fast, bone-weary, and out of timeouts with two and a half quarters left to play.

In the same way that speed demoralizes slower opponents, taking the speed factor away from teams that live and die with their up-tempo game can be highly frustrating for them; it can upset them to the point of their making mistakes in their high-risk offenses and defenses. More important, it takes them out of their game plan and forces them to adjust psychologically as well as physically to a style of play that emphasizes patience and technique over high-speed decision making and athleticism.

POWER VERSUS FINESSE

One of the few facts I managed to retain from my unhappy venture into high school geometry was the principle, *The shortest distance between two points is a straight line.*[6] Applying that principle to team sports reveals two basic approaches to solving the same problem:

How do I get from Point A to Point B when there's an obstacle—my opponent—in the way?

The shortest and most direct route is, of course, to follow straight line AB—to bulldoze a path straight ahead and overpower the opponent with brute strength—the *power* approach. The other

---

[6] For me, at least, those two points connected the geometry classroom and the principal's office.

way is to maneuver the opponent out of the way (e.g., by using fakes, misdirection, or other deceptive techniques) before proceeding along desired route AB—the *finesse* approach. Finesse techniques are generally "softer" than power techniques, in the sense of controlling opponents without directly confronting them.

There are, of course, other ways to get from Point A to Point B—for example, by going around the obstacle rather than through it. And because power and finesse are not mutually exclusive, elements from both approaches are often used in the same play or sequence. In football, you could use a dive play or a sweep as a pure power play by omitting any frills and retaining as many blockers as possible—or you could combine the two plays and introduce elements of finesse into the equation. The technique you use will depend primarily on the relative strengths of the two teams; if your team is stronger than the opponents', take the safer, power approach and let them worry about the finesse.

The basic elements of power and finesse should be clear by now; the use of power assumes superiority in direct confrontations—superior athleticism, superior technique, or both; finesse is used to blunt opponents' superiority by altering the circumstances under which direct confrontations arise.

Under ideal circumstances, power is always preferable to finesse because control is undiluted when applied directly to an opponent. Because ideal conditions are found more often on paper than on playing fields or courts, however, power isn't always a royal road to success. Sometimes a bit of trickery is necessary to keep opponents from loading up against what you do best. Successful coaching involves knowing when, where, and how to use power *or* finesse effectively.

USING POWER EFFECTIVELY

Power is basically conservative, not aggressive. Although it is generally applied to opponents in a highly aggressive manner, power involves relatively few risks beyond the possibility that the opponents are more powerful than your team. In addition, power techniques generally involve basic skills that every player should master, which makes power-oriented approaches popular among coaches. *Control without risk* is a deeply compelling idea—so much so, in fact, that sometimes inexperienced coaches are lured by its siren song into adopting power-oriented offenses and defenses with teams and players who possess neither the athleticism nor the skills to make them work.

There are two aspects to the use of power: the power itself—using it to overwhelm opponents or wear them down physically; and its side effects—using the threat of power to set up other options. When facing a power-oriented offense, for example, the defense absolutely *must* control the power aspects of the offense before attempting to deal with other phases of it. As has been noted repeatedly in these pages, until you find a way to stop opponents from succeeding at what they do best, you cannot reasonably expect to stop them at all. They'll take the risk-free approach of pounding away at you with their strengths (or your weaknesses) until you either regain control of that aspect of the game, or lose the game entirely.

Vince Lombardi wrote,

> Every football team eventually arrives at a lead play. It becomes the team's bread-and-butter play, the top-priority play. It's the play that the team knows it must make go, and the one opponents know they must stop. . . My no. 1 play has been the power sweep, sometimes called the Lombardi sweep. . .
>
> There is nothing spectacular about it, it's just a yard gainer. . . All (of our other) plays are successful only after the defense has been forced to respect the sweep, our no. 1 play.[7]

That is what the effective use of power is all about, regardless of what sport we're referring to. It's a matter of identifying your strengths and using them as a foundation for everything else you do. Having a play—or using a style of play—that succeeds more often than it fails gives a team confidence in ways that nothing else can do: confidence in the coach, that he or she has selected the proper path for the team to follow; confidence in the team's ability to make the play (or style of play) work as designed; and confidence in the players' ability to carry out their individual responsibilities within the team context.

Coach Lombardi used the power sweep as his no. 1 play because, in order to be successful, it required maximum effort from

---

[7] Lombardi, Vince. *Vince Lombardi on Football, Vol. I* (New York: N.Y. Graphic Society Ltd. and Wallynn, Inc., 1973), pp. 19, 62.)

all eleven players—not just three or four. When it worked—which was usually the case, given the almost religious fervor with which Lombardi's players regarded their sweep play—it was because everyone contributed equally to its success. That was Lombardi's style, and his players embraced it wholeheartedly as being in their (and the team's) best interests. Not every coach needs to emulate his style, philosophy, or coaching techniques to be a successful coach, of course, but every team must identify itself with a given playing style that everyone involved believes in and is dedicated to making work.

Confidence breeds success, and success breeds further successes. Even so, you are well advised to remember that power is a tool, nothing more or less—a tool that can be used or abused. Don't use a power-oriented style of play because it's the macho thing to do, if it doesn't suit your team. Coaches who consider *any* style of play except basic straight-ahead, smash-mouth, three-yards-and-a-cloud-of-dust power football an affront to their manhood are unlikely to consider alternatives to power. Here's what I mean:

1. Lazy coaches tend to gravitate toward power approaches because they think they are easier to teach. If you're a lazy coach—and you aren't, or else you wouldn't be reading this book to extend your understanding of coaching control[8]—using a power-oriented style of play will allow you to teach as little as possible and blame whatever shortcomings and failures arise on the kids you coach. When it works, of course, you can humbly suggest that the players had something to do with the team's success, too.

(The thoughtful reader will note that I am *not* implying that advocates of power football, power basketball, etc., are lazy. Far from it. Vince Lombardi, Bobby Knight, John Wooden, Jerry Tarkanian, Denny Crum, Woody Hayes, Bud Wilkinson, Vince Dooley, Danny Ford, John McKay, Jody Conradt, Pat Summitt, and Ed Jucker [who won back-to-back NCAA titles at the University of Cincinnati in 1961–1962 and authored a basketball coaching textbook entitled *Cincinnati Power Basketball*]—all of them and many other highly successful coaches are, or have been, advocates of the power game, and none could conceivably be called lazy.)

---

[8] If you want to find out exactly where you fit in the coaching continuum, read Chapter 2 of my book *Coaching and Winning* (Prentice Hall, 1988).

2. Power can be distracting, almost hypnotic. One of the best things that can happen to a young coach is to inherit, early in his or her career, a team that lacks the necessary strengths to dominate opponents offensively and defensively. Power approaches won't work against opponents who are clearly superior to you; they'll overwhelm your strengths with their own.

If, as an inexperienced coach, all you know is how to use superior talent to beat teams who couldn't beat you regardless of what offenses or defenses you use, you'll probably stick to a basic, power-oriented game plan and win most (or all) of your games. When the opponents have all the strength, however, you won't have the necessary knowledge to play the game. There's nothing like having a Weak or Fair team to show you exactly what you still have to learn about coaching, and to dispel any illusions you may have that power is the only way to control opponents. Experience is the best teacher, or so they say—but it's true only when it involves stretching beyond yourself and what you already know to find ways to squeeze gallons of performance from pint-sized players, or players who wouldn't know a fold block from a folded paper airplane.

> *Power never takes a back step—only in the face of more power.*
>
> —Malcolm X

If the power is there, you don't really need anything else; that's *the line of least resistance to success.* That statement is true, of course, as far as it goes—but it's also true that strength-based approaches don't adequately prepare you for occasions when strength alone is not enough to save the day. Power is hypnotic; it can lull you into thinking that nothing else is necessary. It can blind you to the need for extending your team's strengths beyond what your players are currently doing well.

3. Power is limited. During a conversation with a veteran basketball coach a number of years ago, the coach surprised me with the following statement: "There are two ways to win a state championship. One way is to have the best players. The other is to use a strategy that makes your players better than the other guys."

I had been a coach for only three years at the time, so I had no idea whether his theory might be valid. But since his teams had been to the state quarterfinals twice and the semis once and I was coaching at the junior high level, I listened carefully to what he had to say:

Only one team takes home the championship trophy every year.[9] Once you're past the region finals, all it takes is a loss in the state tournament and your season is over.

If you checked the records, I think you'd find that most teams don't make it past the first round the first time they go to state. I know it's true of teams reaching the finals; they usually lose the first time they get there. Unless your kids have been there before, they can't imagine how great the pressure is. They just don't understand that everything—the pressure, the effort required to win, the atmosphere surrounding the game—is raised a couple of notches when you reach that level of play. It's like Dorothy says in *The Wizard of Oz:* "I guess we're not in Kansas anymore, Toto."

The pressure and demands are still there the second time around, but the kids don't feel it as much when they've been there before.

Another point is that most teams have weaknesses of one kind or another. They may not be obvious, the way they are with most of the teams you play during the regular season. They may not even show up in region play or the early rounds of state. But if you have weaknesses of any kind, somebody's going to find them somewhere along the way. They aren't going to let you take home that championship trophy without a fight.

What this means for most coaches is, you try to play the game your way and not the other guy's. That means doing what you've done best all season. You stay with the one that brought you to the dance. That strategy is as basic as biscuits and gravy are to a down-home Southern breakfast. The only trouble is, a strength-against-strength strategy will work *only for the stronger of the two teams.* That's all right if your team is the stronger one, but it's not so hot the other way around.

Upsets occur, of course, but not as often at the State level as you might expect. Coaches tend to be even more conservative in the playoffs than they usually are. In my case, we lost to the same team two years in a row in the second round of state because I was too stubborn to change my game plan.

---

[9] I'm taking the liberty of presenting, as direct quotes, segments of an informal conversation that occurred nearly a quarter of a century ago. The other coach is deceased, but I don't think he'd mind my attempting to restate his views as faithfully as possible.

Don't get me wrong, it was a good game plan. Nobody in our region could touch us. But our region wasn't very strong, and my game plan wasn't good enough to beat *this* team because they matched up with us better than we did with them. They weren't a lot better than we were, but just enough to control the game in little ways.

I wanted to blame the kids for those losses, but of course I couldn't do that, so I blamed it on the pressure. After the second loss, I had to admit that I didn't prepare for those games as well as I should have. Because we were winning consistently against the folks in our region, I didn't bother to extend our basic game plan in directions that might have created greater obstacles for the stronger competition we'd face in the state playoffs.

Since then, I've used the regular season as an extended tuneup for the playoffs. It's the kind of approach that Denny Crum uses. I'm always looking for ways to expand our basic strategies to make it tougher for teams of equal or superior strength to control us. The more we can do, and the better we can do it, the better prepared we'll be for the kinds of problems we'll face when we get to state.

Ultimately, the coach was saying that *power is limited*; in any given high school classification, with the possible exception of cochampions in football, there is only one state champ per year in each sport.

Only the very best teams are capable of winning by virtue of their strengths alone. In other cases, games are decided by the extent to which one team or the other is able to supplement its strengths with strategies that opponents are unprepared to control.

USING FINESSE EFFECTIVELY

Whereas power strategies generate direct confrontations, finesse involves the use of skill or deception to avoid direct confrontations or alter the circumstances under which they arise.

On an individual basis, the difference between the two approaches is easy to compare: in baseball, Randy Johnson's overpowering 102-mph fastball vs. Greg Maddux's mediocre 90-mph fastball supplemented by his uncanny ability to paint the corners of the strike zone; in basketball, Shaquille O'Neal's raw power around the basket vs. Kareem Abdul-Jabbar's legendary sky hook; and in football, the brute force of an Earl Campbell or a Larry Csonka vs. the elusiveness of a Barry Sanders.

On a team basis, the differences between power and finesse are generally less well defined because many power-oriented plays and styles of play feature both components. Football offers at least three playing styles that are based almost entirely on finesse: the shotgun passing attack, the run-and-shoot, and the triple option.

Although widely (and sometimes *wildly*) different in many respects, pure finesse approaches have several traits in common:

■ They attempt to limit opponents' effective use of power by attacking in areas where power is unlikely to be the determining factor in the play's success.

■ They force opponents to make accurate high-speed decisions at every point or face the prospect of losing control offensively or defensively at the point of attack.

■ They entail high risks when applied aggressively as intended by their designers.

■ They require a great deal of intensified daily practice before and after their installation in order for players to master and retain the mechanics and timing involved in their execution.

The first two points explain why coaches might consider using a finesse-oriented offense or defense; the last two points explain why most coaches are understandably leery of such an approach, at least, on a wholesale basis.

In the former case, pure finesse approaches are designed to take opponents out of their game plan or preferred style of play and force them to react to what *you're* doing rather than the converse. Rigorously applied, this tactic can serve to dominate most opponents and control the rest even when the team does not possess the power to do so otherwise—assuming, of course, that the players have mastered the elements involved.

Between 1985 and 1990, Georgia Southern University's football teams won four NCAA Division I-AA national titles and finished second one year. Only once during that seven-year span did the

Eagles have the best personnel in I-AA.[10] What they *did* have was a splendidly innovative triple-option attack that consistently punished in the playoffs opponents who thought they could adequately prepare for it by bringing in a high school quarterback to run the wishbone against their defenses the week before their game with GSU.

The Danish theologian Soren Kierkegaard (1813–1855) described his belief in an unseen, all-powerful Supreme Being as a "leap of faith." Had he been a coach, he might have used the term to describe the conviction necessary to adopt a finesse-oriented style of play. It takes a lot of faith to entrust your team's chances of winning to a playing style in which your players are almost as likely to make mistakes as the opponents are. That's why you don't see many football teams using shotgun passing attacks except in third-down-and-long situations, or when they're behind and have to catch up in a hurry.

Many coaches are currently entertaining serious doubts as to whether the run-and-shoot is a valid approach to team offense, and as long ago as the early 1980s, some football coaches and critics were proclaiming that defenses had caught up with option football.

Some of the arguments against finesse-oriented styles are valid, and others are not. Invalid objections usually have arisen from a misunderstanding of what the offenses are designed to do and how they are designed to do it. Misunderstanding leads in turn to misapplication, as in using the wishbone primarily as a power-oriented attack, or using controlled fast breaking in basketball—in either case with the intention of making the strategy "safer." It can be done, of course, but not without sacrificing the qualities that render finesse effective as a means of attacking opponents—and not without making it easier for opponents to use power principles in defensing it.

---

[10] In 1989, when they went 15–0.

9

RELATING STYLE TO STRATEGY

A coach is like an auto mechanic who has all of the parts of the car laid out.
If there's a piece missing, the thing won't work.
You've got to find that piece.

—Bobby Bowden (Florida State)

With the exception of private high schools that can recruit talented athletes from the public school system, program building is normally a rather slow and lengthy process—agonizingly so, if your school has established a reputation as a doormat in your sport for the rest of the schools in your area or conference. I know; I've suffered the simultaneous resentment of: home fans who felt that I was driving their sons and daughters too hard; opposing players and fans who were angered and frustrated at our teams' refusal to roll over and play dead for them as we had done in the past; and coaches who felt that beating us by any score they wished was their God-given right and I had no business interfering. Fighting back doesn't exactly endear you to teams and coaches who believe that the function of flies is to provide meat for the flyswatter!

The process whereby coaches transform losing programs into winners is predictable. It starts with a coach with a vision and a plan for turning sour grapes into fine wine. So that's where we'll start, with Weak teams and coaches who refuse to accept that condition as permanent.

When you lose, you doubt yourself and your plans. Losing
creates doubt just like winning creates momentum.

—Danny Ford (Univ. of Arkansas)

WEAK TEAMS

I once kept stats for an incredibly weak high school football team. Playing in Class A, Georgia's lowest classification, the school (which has since consolidated with a larger school) not only lost all ten of its football games by a combined score of 560–47, but the team managed to lose in ways that belied the closeness of those scores. To wit:

- The team gave up 20 points or more *in the first quarter alone* in eight games; in seven of those games, the opponents were ahead by at least 35 points by halftime.

- In five games, opponents scored in at least six different ways, including: returns of kickoffs, punts, blocked punts, fumbles, or interceptions; plays from scrimmage; safeties; and extra point conversions.

- In two games, the opponents scored the first six times they touched the ball. (I'm not referring to offensive possessions or touchdown drives, either, but to plays, whether offensive or defensive, in which an opposing player touched the ball.)

- Of the opponents' plays from scrimmage, 113 resulted in gains of 15 yards or more; 46 of those plays went for 30 yards or more. Both totals would have been higher but for opponents' returns for TDs that denied them opportunities to play offensively.

- On numerous occasions in virtually every game, opponents ran plays in which the closest any defender came to the ball was when the two teams lined up for the snap. On sweeps, it was not at all uncommon for an entire side of the defensive line to disappear completely, leaving a gaping hole for the ball-carrier that two semis could have driven through, side-by-side, with room to spare.

Although the coach of the aforementioned team was relatively inexperienced, he was in fact a brilliant tactician with a broad understanding of his sport. In his first three years of coaching the school's fledgling varsity football program, he managed to compile a highly respectable 11–19 record, including a 5–5 mark in the school's third year of competition. With, at best, nineteen players to work with, however—and without a local recreation league, junior high, or B-team to restock the undermanned varsity program with experienced players—he and his players were fighting a battle that they couldn't win.

A very important point to remember: *The extent to which a Weak team is able to remain competitive (i.e., motivated to play hard) in games against superior opponents depends primarily on two factors*—skills *and* expectations.

Without a nucleus of skilled players who can successfully execute the fundamentals of that sport (e.g., blocking and tackling in football), a Weak team cannot reasonably expect or hope to control superior opponents for longer than it takes to fashion a white flag of surrender to run up the mast. And a team so inured to losing that it enters games either expecting to lose or waiting for things to go wrong, usually will not be disappointed in either case.

With teams who lack the skill to win, the will to win, or both, team quality may be so poor that anything less than a blowout defeat is regarded as a moral victory. Faced with such dismal prospects, what can you do to make the players and team competitive? Actually, there are several things you can, should, and *must* do:

1. Focus on One Day at a Time

Build team unity in everything you do. Teach basic skills and fundamentals. Use competitive drills and teach team patterns in small doses. Use your most important drills every day, but focus on a different aspect of the game every week. Work the players hard, but not to the limits of human endurance, or they'll quit on you. There are three things you might do in daily practices to forestall your players' rebelling en masse against your new—and probably unpopular—work ethic: (a) alternate between physically demanding activities and instructional activities; (b) remind the players *why* they are working hard, and assure them regularly that their hard work is paying off and will continue to do so; and (c) don't let your daily practices become stale or get in a rut. Give your players something to look forward to in every practice (e.g., letting them do something fun, offbeat, or unusual).[1] Be positive and upbeat, and once the season starts, use individual and team stats to show the players that they are learning and making steady progress toward team goals. And no matter how tempting the idea might be, *never* mention winning as a goal for any game; if you do, all of your other goals will suddenly become unimportant by comparison.

As anyone who has been through that first year of coaching in a hard-core losing situation can tell you, it is somewhat akin to high-rise window washing in a hurricane; there's never a time when you can sit back and enjoy the view.

2. SCHEDULE AS MANY WEAK TEAMS AS YOU CAN

Assuming that you do a creditable coaching job, there's still no guarantee that a Weak team will be competitive more often than occasionally, but there are some things you can do to increase those odds. Before you can realistically think about winning games regularly, you have to find a way to keep from being steamrollered regularly. Since Weak teams represent the bottom of the competitive food chain, the best way to keep scores respectable is to schedule other Weak teams wherever possible.

The process whereby teams progress from consistent losers to consistent winners starts with teaching the team that previously was blown out of most of its games how to keep games close. From there, the team finds ways to win the close games. Then it finds ways to win most of its games. Finally, it is capable of dominating most of its opponents. These stages correspond roughly to the five team categories we've used in this book: Weak, Fair, Good, Very Good, and Great.

A wholesale leap up the ladder of success in one year—say, from Weak to Very Good—is possible, but it is extremely unlikely without the addition of a number of highly talented transfer student-athletes or players from last year's junior high or jayvee squad. Normally, the process takes four or five years in football and three or four years in

---

[1] For a change of pace, a baseball coach occasionally uses an imaginary ball for infield practice.

basketball—the difference in the two resulting from the greater number of skilled players required to turn a losing football program around.

Last year, we couldn't win on the road. This year, we can't win at home.
I don't know where else to play.

—Harry Neale, general manager
(Vancouver Canucks)

Of course, it's not always possible to schedule Weak teams at will, since your region or subregion may be so large that virtually your entire schedule will necessarily involve teams you are required to play. If that's the case, your only realistic alternatives are to take your lumps for a year with regular scheduling, or to drop back and play a nonregion schedule for a year or two while you teach your players how to play the game.

On the positive side, the nonregion schedule will allow you to schedule anybody you want to, and thus avoid the sort of crushing defeats that playing in a tough region would bring. On the negative side, you won't be eligible for postseason tournament play (nor will any other team from your school in that sport) until you resume region scheduling. Your travel expenses are likely to be greater than they normally would be—and your athletic director or principal may not agree to your request for nonregion scheduling anyway. Too, in sports other than football, you may have trouble finding and scheduling enough Weak opponents within the allowable week-night travel limits set by your state association.

Our schedule is so tough, we could have a great year and never know it.

—Charlie McLendon
(Louisiana State University)

If, on the other hand, your region or subregion games don't completely fill your schedule, you should fill out the rest of the schedule with the weakest opponents you can find. A desirable goal might be to play at least 70 percent of your games against teams that you expect to be competitive against. You should, however, try to avoid scheduling teams from higher classifications than yours, unless you saw them play the previous year and know for sure that they won't be too great a challenge for your players. After all, what's

Weak at one level of play isn't necessarily Weak at a lower level—and big schools, having more students to choose from, are more likely than small schools to make greater improvement from one year to the next.

If all of this seems "wimpy" to you, you can follow the standard operating procedure: Schedule region teams and teams that are closest to you geographically, and take whatever lumps are in store for you. Keep in mind, however, that losing games by lopsided scores isn't necessarily the best or fastest way to turn around a losing program. Your players already know how to lose by lopsided scores; what they need to learn is how to keep games close in order to give themselves a chance to win.

GAME STRATEGIES WITH WEAK TEAMS

Pity the poor football coach. He may be the greatest offensive tactical genius since Bill Walsh or Don Coryell, but the opponents get the ball back every time his team fails to get a first down or score. That alone makes football coaching far more difficult than, say, coaching basketball, where—at the high school level at least—there is no 24-, 30-, or 45-second clock and my team can limit your team's scoring ability by holding the ball for long stretches.

There are, however, some strategies that weak teams might pursue:

1. CONTROL THE BALL ON OFFENSE

Admittedly, this is more easily said than done, but you have to start somewhere. In football, many of the mistakes Weak teams make offensively stem from poor line play.[2] A good approach here might be to use an inside belly offense and its variations or a triple-option offense featuring the fullback dive play, or a simple passing attack with the quarterback using a three-step drop or sprinting out. Regarding the first two, quick-hitting plays don't require linemen to hold their blocks as long as other types of plays do. We'll have more to say about triple-option football later, but for now we'll note that,

---

[2] A vigorous off-season and summertime weight training program will improve their play if you can persuade them to work out regularly.

despite its reputation as a high-risk offensive style, it is relatively simple to learn—always a bonus where Weak teams are concerned—because the three options constitute an offense in themselves. The bulk of your offensive practice time is devoted to one play.

Passing may prove effective because high school teams are more likely to be better at run defense than pass defense. (A five- or seven-step drop won't work, however—except possibly with screen passes—because your linemen won't be able to hold their blocks long enough to allow your quarterback time to set himself and throw.) A three-step drop and look-in, hitch, or slant pass is better, or sprint-out passes to receivers flooding a zone. Play-action passes and misdirection plays can confuse Good defenses because of their unpredictability.

In basketball, while controlling the ball with a Weak team might seem to imply freezing the ball via a four-corner spread or something similar, that strategy won't work against a Good team. They'll come out after you, pressure the ball, play the passing lanes—and because their players are better than yours, sooner or later the pressure will get to your players. They'll panic and start making bad passes, and before you know it the opponents will be ringing up scores right and left.

A better way to freeze the ball consists of teaching your players a simple continuity man-to-man pattern of some kind—say, the Shuffle, Wheel, or variation thereof—and a simple zone offensive pattern or two that feature players posting up and others moving around the perimeter. Within those contexts, you should emphasize *very* careful shot selection and instruct your players to run the pattern for longer than they might be tempted to do otherwise.

Think about it: If, twice a quarter, you're able to run your pattern for one full minute before shooting, you'll have held the other team without scoring for eight minutes—the equivalent of *one full quarter*! Only Very Good or Great teams can afford to go a whole quarter without scoring against *any* opponent.

In freezing the ball, you're basically trying to protect it—as opposed to trying to score—and allowing the defenders to play aggressively rather than trying to protect the basket. In playing a "normal" offense but severely delimiting the shots your players take, however, you retain the scoring threat and the defenders must honor it or risk surrendering easy baskets. The difference between the two approaches is greater than it might appear at first glance.

Of course, your first offensive priority is to beat the press; if you can't do that, you won't have to worry about doing anything else offensively.

Even with a Weak team of no better than average speed, it's imperative to fast break when you beat the press; if you don't, they'll stay in the press all night long and get more than their share of steals and forced turnovers. Fast breaking can take the edge out of opponents' presses by forcing them to think in terms of retreating and protecting the basket; it can even force them to abandon pressing altogether.

I once had a *very* Weak junior high girls team that showed signs of life only when we were pressed; the rest of the time, the pages on our side of the scorebook looked as if they had been filled out with disappearing ink. Our games generally were close until it gradually dawned on opposing coaches (usually in the second half) that all they had to do to beat us was call off the press and let us beat ourselves.

Our team was terrible that year—our record was 2–8—but we took pride in our ability to consistently punish teams that pressed us. When you're 2–8, you look for positives wherever you can find them!

2. DEFENSIVELY, PRIORITIZE YOUR POINTS OF ATTACK AND DICTATE HOW AND WHERE OPPONENTS WILL HAVE TO SUCCEED IN ORDER TO DEFEAT YOU

In football, this means, first of all, attempting to seal off the middle; after all, if you can't stop the opponents there, they won't have to go anywhere else to beat you. One way to do it might be to use Joe Paterno's old wide-tackle six alignment that features eight players near the line of scrimmage at the snap. If that doesn't work, you might vary your defensive alignments or shift before the snap to confuse opponents' blocking schemes—or even bring in one of the defensive backs and dare opponents to beat you passing the ball. (They probably will, but even if they throw five touchdown passes it's probably no worse than they would do if they were able to run against your eight-man alignment.) At any rate, a 4-3, 3-4, or Oklahoma (52) alignment with four defensive backs won't get the job done if you have a Weak team against a team with a strong running attack. Those seven interior players will need all the help they can get in order to prevent the opponents from opening holes in the line that a 747 jetliner could pass through untouched.

In basketball, a Weak team's first defensive priority is to seal off the low-post area. Man-to-man defense is out of the question, since your players simply aren't skilled or experienced enough to know how to play it properly. An odd-front zone defense (e.g., 1-2-2 or 1-3-1) will force the ball away from the top of the circle and make it easier to set up the double-team at low post. The 1-2-2 is preferable because it tends to keep more defenders near the basket, regardless of the ball's location along the perimeter—but you may prefer, say, a 2-3 zone.

With a double-team at low post, someone is going to be open elsewhere; thus, it becomes necessary to decide just what shot you're going to give up. The baseline shot is tempting because the absence of the backboard reduces depth perception. If, as a result of scouting, you determined where opposing shooters are more (or less) effective, you may want to steer the ball away (or toward) those areas by the way you align your other three players. Whatever plan you choose is acceptable, as long as you've considered the various alternatives.

3. DON'T TAKE CHANCES AGAINST SUPERIOR TEAMS

The only real hope you have in remaining competitive against the better teams you play lies in simplicity. Trick plays are out; your players' inability to execute will cause them to backfire on you. Dramatic changes of any kind, whether offensively or defensively, will confuse your players more than the opponents. Your best bet is to use simple offensive patterns, and work on man-to-man defensive coverage in daily practice—but don't use it in games until your players improve; use zone coverage and double-teams instead. Teach constantly in practice *and in games*; add new wrinkles to your system sparingly, and always with an eye toward your players' progress and skills development.

One other suggestion that might help against superior opponents is to treat such games as scrimmages in which you're coaching only one of the teams. Tell your players to ignore the score, and to focus instead on listening to you and thinking about what they're doing. Tell them early (and often) that neither the other team nor the score matters; all you're trying to do is teach them how to play the game the way you want it played. With a Weak team, keeping the players' attention focused in worthwhile directions is the most productive thing you can do for them; against superior opponents, it far outweighs any clever strategies you might be tempted to try out.

If all this appears negative—well, it *is*. There are no secret strategies that great coaches use with Weak teams to defeat superior teams, because there are none. In the Bible, little David defeated the giant Goliath—but David had a hidden weapon—his sling—that equalized the contest. Coaches of Weak teams have no such hidden resources, or else their teams wouldn't be Weak teams. If you choose not to use "creative scheduling" to improve your team's competitive opportunities, you should expect to get pounded regularly while your kids learn how to play the game. Under the circumstances, the best you can hope for is to dictate how and where those poundings are administered, and how your players react to them.

To defeat a weak opponent is not the problem. The problem is to win when he is as good as or better than you are.

—Gen. Bob Neyland
(Univ. of Tennessee)

FAIR TEAMS

A realistic (but unstated) goal for the coach of a team in the *Fair* category might be to: defeat all Weak opponents and achieve at least a split with the Fair teams on the schedule; and to win a quarter of the games against Good teams, an eighth of the games against Very Good Teams, and a sixteenth of the games against Great opponents. If that goal isn't realistic or achievable, it at least reveals the relationship between Fair teams and others. Assuming that a Fair baseball or basketball team plays, say, twenty games divided equally among opponents in each of the five categories and accomplishes its goals against its Weak, Fair, and Good opponents but not the others, its season mark will be 7–13. An equivalent team in football will go 3–7 or 4–6.

The ability to win 30–40 percent of its games—depending on scheduling, of course—indicates that a Fair team is not entirely devoid of talented players; there simply aren't enough of them to meet the bulk of the team's needs. Such teams tend to be short on depth, and to lose control of games when their better players are sidelined for any reason. Such problems suggest several strategies; two of them follow:

▪ With a weak bench, it is imperative that the starters be in superior shape physically, since their rest periods necessarily will be few and brief. Insufficient attention to physical conditioning is one of the two easiest ways to turn a Fair team into a Weak team.

▪ Game strategies usually revolve around finding ways to use the skills of the team's best players to best advantage—that, and finding ways to hide the team's obvious weaknesses.

Using the best athletes as fully as possible is both obvious and necessary; it is also fraught with risk, since your Fair team will become a Weak team if its better player(s) sustain injuries that take them out of the lineup. The Atlanta Falcons' Tommy Nobis was one of the finest NFL linebackers of the 1960s—but because the rest of the Falcons' defense was, let us say, somewhat less than spectacular, opponents were able to double- and triple-team Nobis at will. Today, he walks with the fragility of someone twice his age.

Because Fair teams are somewhat athletic, they can be competitive against Weak, Fair, and most Good teams; they tend to have less difficulty in using their skills and hiding their weaknesses than Weak teams do.

> *Almost all games are lost by the losers, not won by the winners.*
>
> —Gen. Bob Neyland

HIDING WEAKNESSES

At its most basic level, game strategy dictates that, before you can win games by playing to your strengths, you have to avoid losing them via your weaknesses. Hiding weaknesses does not mean eliminating them, an obvious impossibility; rather, it means structuring your offense or defense in such a manner as to make it difficult for teams to exploit whatever areas of weakness exist in your lineup.

On a team basis, hiding weaknesses can refer to such things as: putting your least-skilled players where they can do the least harm to the team (e.g., covering wide-outs against run-oriented football teams or playing the point in 1-2-2 or 1-3-1 zone defense in basketball); using zone defense to compensate for individual weaknesses in man coverage in basketball or football; or using unskilled players to set screens for your shooters in basketball, or run-off techniques with decoy wide receivers in a run-oriented football offense. In all cases, hiding weaknesses refers to sharply defining and delimiting the roles of players who are unable by virtue of their skills to take active (as opposed to passive or supportive) roles in the team's efforts to win or remain competitive.

Hiding weaknesses and playing to strengths generally go hand in hand. For example, in trying to protect a lead in basketball late in the game, you want to keep the ball in the hands of your best free-throw shooter(s) as much as possible—and, by inference, to keep it out of the hands of your poorer shooters.

Fatigue and injuries aside, the greatest threat to basketball players' playing time is foul difficulty. If you need to keep a given player in the game when he or she has picked up more fouls than you'd like, you can either move the player to a guard slot in your zone defense or switch defensive assignments in your man-to-man defense to have that player guard the opponents' least productive offensive player.

PLAYING STYLES

Power-oriented playing styles are most likely to be productive against teams of equal or lesser ability. When your Fair team is facing a Very Good or Great opponent, they are likely to smother your power with their own. Teams that are capable of winning at least 75 percent of their games don't get that way by letting themselves be pushed around by teams that are capable of winning 30–40 percent of their games.

Of course, it's possible that a vastly superior opponent will have an off night because the players are looking ahead to their next opponent, in which case you may be able to play them close or even defeat them. Even so, your best chance lies not in challenging them strength-against-strength, but in using power sparingly, and only to keep them honest—that is, to keep them from overplaying everything else you do. In football, that "everything else" might include trap plays, dives, counters, look-in or slant passes, or other plays that develop quickly and normally complement your power.

You aren't likely to defeat a clearly superior opponent at what it does best. In basketball, for example, with a relatively slow team, you may have early success in fast breaking against an up-tempo running team, but playing the game at their tempo rather than your own doesn't help your chances any. In the long run, you're better off fast breaking selectively, if at all (e.g., when you beat their full-court press), and slowing down the game to a more comfortable pace the rest of the time; otherwise, by the time your players realize that they're playing out of control and the opponents aren't, the game may be irretrievably lost.

High-scoring basketball teams usually rely on pressure defense and fast breaking for the bulk of their scoring. A truly effective up-tempo team, such as UNLV during the 1970s–1980s, can put points on the scoreboard faster than a Jerry Lewis Labor Day telethon. The only ways to defeat such a team are to play better defense than they do (which is unlikely, or else *you'd* be the team scoring 110.5 ppg), or to reduce their scoring by holding onto the ball and looking for high-percentage shots of your own.

BASEBALL STRATEGY—WEAK AND FAIR TEAMS

Michael Jordan showed the world that it takes more than pure athleticism to succeed in baseball. Football has its "skill positions," and shooting a basketball requires hand-eye coordination—but three of baseball's four major components—pitching, batting, and defense—require a high degree of neuromuscular coordination from every player. Only in baserunning is raw athleticism likely to be a major determinant of success. In that respect, baseball is in a class by itself.

Ted Williams has always contended that hitting a baseball is the single most difficult skill in sports. While that statement may be debatable, it is undeniably true that getting base hits ranks among the most difficult tasks in team sports. In what other professional sport is a lifetime failure rate of only 63 percent so difficult that no one has ever attained it?

> *Hitting is timing. Pitching is upsetting timing.*
>
> —Warren Spahn (Milwaukee Braves)

PITCHING

At the high school level, at least, excellent pitching is rare; depending on your level of play, all you generally need to go a long way in the postseason playoffs is batters who can hit their weight or better and a couple of top-notch pitchers throwing bb's. The latter is precisely what you are least likely to have with a Weak or Fair baseball team.

The key to success in pitching is, of course, *control.* Many young players mistakenly think velocity is the key, but that's true only when the velocity is controlled. Control requires mastery of the mechanics of pitching, which in turn requires much diligent, patient instruction and countless hours of practice.

Pittsburgh Pirates manager Jim Leyland considers the three keys to successful pitching to be staying ahead in the count, changing speeds, and pitching fast. To stay ahead in the count you have to throw strikes, which requires control regardless of the pitch used. Whereas a control-oriented pitcher such as Greg Maddux aims for the corners of the strike zone, an inexperienced high school sophomore is likely to aim for the center of the strike zone in order to have any hope of getting the ball over the plate. If so, your strategies are reduced to telling him either to pitch for the corners, in which case his control will be further reduced, or to aim for the strike zone and rely on changing speeds to keep the hitter off balance. In the latter case, the likelihood of the hitter's being confused will vary in direct proportion to the velocity differential between the pitcher's fastball and off-speed pitches—and to the relative movement of the ball, of course.

BATTING

Emphases in this area include improving hand quickness and bat control, and teaching the players to recognize the strike zone and be selective in what they swing at. Since these skills normally are acquired through experience and extensive drill and practice, inexperienced or unskilled hitters might be advised to use the following rule of thumb: *When in doubt, don't (swing).* Make the pitcher throw strikes. Another strategy weak hitters might employ is crowding the plate and not trying terribly hard to avoid getting hit by inside pitches (except those in the vicinity of the head, of course). To look like they're trying to avoid the pitch, specialists in this ploy duck their heads and turn their backs to the ball.

Players whose bat speed is slow can benefit considerably from a combination of instruction in the mechanics of the swing, time spent working out in the weight room, and being videotaped in batting practice and in games. They may also find it beneficial to choke up on the bat to give it better balance in their hands.

A high school coach in Florida spends the first two weeks of preseason practicing bunting rather than swinging at the ball in batting practice. He says that it not only teaches his batters to see the ball better, but it also helps to familiarize them with the strike zone.

A fast-pitch softball coach says that, along with bunting, he has his girls play pepper games to improve their bat control before letting them swing away. He also teaches his right-handed batters to drag bunt left-handed, and to slap bunt from both sides. He explains, "It's only sixty feet from home to first in girls softball, so it's almost impossible to get the batter out if she lays down a good drag bunt in fair territory. Bunting gives weak hitters a chance to get on base that they might not have in swinging away; slap bunting lets them be aggressive at the plate without overdoing it. If a girl doesn't have her timing down, I'll have her bunt every time she comes to the plate."

There are other advantages. Bunting is easier than swinging away, since the motion involved in making contact with the ball is restricted and the bat and ball are constantly in view. Bunting also is an excellent way to make use of speed, and the constant threat of bunting tends to force opponents at the corners to play closer than they normally would.

The goal is to get runners on base by any means possible. With a Weak or Fair team, coaching baserunning is likely to produce positive results faster than any other phase of your coaching.

BASERUNNING

This is one area where the axiom, *Don't take chances against a team that is better than you are,* doesn't necessarily apply. Since most high school pitchers don't have a really effective pickoff move, baserunning strategy should begin with challenging the pitcher *on every pitch*—not necessarily by trying to steal bases on every pitch but by taking the longest possible leads that will allow runners to get back safely when throws are made. As a south Georgia baseball coach explained it to me,

I don't want my baserunners ever to go back to the bag standing up when the pitcher throws over. I want them taking a big
enough lead that they'll have to dive back on their stomachs to
make it back ahead of the tag. With that kind of lead, two things
can happen: The pitcher will make the throw over, or he'll go
ahead and make the pitch.

If he makes the throw, I want my baserunner to be expecting it.
If the pitcher tries it often enough, either he or the first base-
man will make a mistake sooner or later and give us extra bases.
If he makes the pitch, the runner's lead will give him a good
shot at stealing second, or at least of beating the throw to second on a ground ball. But none of that will happen if he takes
a three-step lead off the bag.

There are two ways to steal bases, on the pitcher or the catcher. If you hadn't seen my team play, I might have my catcher throw
half-hearted lobs out to second base during infield practice to make
you think your kids can steal on him—but when's the last time you
saw that done? Scouting the catcher's arm in pregame warmups is a
reliable strategy for determining how successful your players might
be in stealing bases against today's opponent. A good high school
catcher can make an average pitcher look great. With a Weak or
even a Fair team, though, tell your players to go for it, even with a
team of no better than average speed. Most pitchers aren't very
good at holding runners on base, and the catcher still has to make
the good throw every time—and with a weak hitting team, aggressive baserunning is the best way to make up for a lack of power or
weaknesses in other areas.

There's a certain scent when you get close to winning.
You may go a long time without winning, but you never forget that scent.

—Steve Busby, pitcher
Kansas City Royals

GOOD TEAMS

With a Good team—one that is capable of winning anywhere from
half to two-thirds of its games—your top priority might be to win *all*
of the games you play against Weak opponents, *most* (or all) of your
games against Fair teams, and at least half of your games against

Good teams. Defeating Very Good or Great teams is always nice, but since to win such games you have to play up to your full potential, it's better to think in terms of simply playing well enough to stay competitive until the fourth quarter and give yourselves a chance to win if the breaks go your way.

Don't use those terms with your players, of course. It's better for them not to consider winning or losing at all, but rather to concentrate on their individual and team responsibilities. Of course, they *will* be thinking about winning and losing—why else would they be playing the game?—but emphasizing the importance of winning only increases the pressure on them.

Winning *is* important, because it breeds confidence and motivates players to work hard in order to keep on winning. As Bum Phillips (Houston Oilers) put it, "How do you win? By getting average players to play good and good players to play great. That's how you win."

WINNING THE CLOSE GAMES

The most obvious difference between Fair and Good teams lies in the ability of the latter to win close games. Much of the ability to win the close ones is due to confidence. Players who expect to win are capable of finding ways to win, or at least of finding ways not to lose. Confident players don't feel the pressure of down-to-the-final-buzzer nail biters as intensely as players who doubt themselves or their teammates; consequently, they are able to concentrate on the task at hand with minimal loss of skill. Less confident players are focusing on the situation rather than their responsibilities within it. Confidence comes, not just from being a skilled athlete, but also from having been properly prepared for the game,[3] including understanding the strategies associated with various game situations.

There's more to winning the close games than merely having confidence, however. There is also *the will to win.* Some coaches and teams have a greater will to win than others. Just as confident teams steal wins by not bowing to pressure, teams with an overpowering drive to win will give whatever effort is necessary to ensure victory.

---

[3] "There are two types of preparation—physical and mental. You can't get by with just one or the other." —Ken Stabler (Oakland Raiders).

Once, when one of Bear Bryant's Alabama teams was clinging to a slender lead late in the fourth quarter, an opposing runner broke free on a long run that would have been the winning touchdown, only to be chased down and tackled by a defensive back short of the goal line as time ran out. A reporter later asked the Alabama player how he managed to make up so much lost ground and catch the ballcarrier. "Well, sir," the young man replied, "he was just running for a touchdown; I was running for my life!"

Beyond that, there is also conditioning. As Bear noted, "You have to be willing to outcondition your opponents." Along those same lines, he also pointed out that, while you can't win all the time, *there is no excuse for not playing tough in the fourth quarter.* Toughness was a way of life for Alabama's Bear: "I don't care how much talent the team has—if the boys don't think tough, practice tough, and live tough, how can they play tough on Saturday?"

Good teams play tough—especially in the fourth quarter.

STRATEGIES AGAINST SUPERIOR OPPONENTS

Strategically speaking, there are four ways to approach must-win games against superior opponents.

First, you can pit *your* strengths against *their* strengths, mano a mano, no holds barred, no quarter asked or given. This is a common approach; it's based on the logic that your strengths are what got you to the point where this game is so important. It will work if the two teams aren't too far apart, with respect to talent. If your troops are clearly outnumbered in the talent department, you're liable to learn more than you wanted to know about humility.

Second, you can do the same thing but challenge your players to raise the level of their play to new heights. Since the opposing coach is doing likewise with his or her players, however, the best you can hope for here is that your motivation works and his or hers doesn't.[4] You're in serious trouble when your best chance of winning lies in the hope that the opponents are taking your team lightly.

---

[4] "Sometimes it's frightening when you see a 19-year-old kid running down the floor with your paycheck in his mouth." —Bob Zuffetalo (Boston College)

A third course of action is to prepare the best game plan you can for holding the opponents in check (i.e., make adjustments in your regular game plan to control the opponents' strengths and hide your weaknesses), and toss in a couple of "gimmick" plays that can turn the tide in your favor if the game is close enough to be won by either team.

Although some coaches dislike trick plays (especially when used against them), there *are* certain advantages to their use. Players love to practice them, and look forward to using them in games. Having them succeed in games offers a team the sort of emotional lift that thunderous breakaway slam dunks do in basketball. And if, like Bobby Bowden (Florida State), you're known as the sort of coach who always has a bagful of tricks up his or her sleeve, opposing coaches have to waste valuable practice time preparing their players for the kinds of trick plays that you may or may not intend to use against them.

Fourth, you can use an aggressive, high-risk playing style that, when used correctly, forces opponents into mistakes that they wouldn't make otherwise. The value of such an approach is that it *does* produce mistakes, since the style of play itself literally functions as an extra player, the way that the sideline in football, basketball, and soccer functions as an extra player for the defense. The negative side of the strategy is that, unless your players are thoroughly familiar with the style, *they* will be the ones making most of the mistakes.

Prepare your players for such a style of play. In the same way that some coaches of Weak basketball teams practice man-to-man techniques daily but use zone defense in games, you can devote a small part of every early season practice to working on various aspects of the offense or defense, with an eye toward incorporating the style in game plans later when you've put it all together and the players understand it well enough to use it.[5]

---

[5] Larry Chapman (AUM) uses a variation of this approach in preparing his basketball team for upcoming opponents: "If you know beforehand via scouting, past experience, and the like, what your league opponents like to do offensively and defensively, you can begin preparing for them early by breaking down their offenses and defenses into drill segments and incorporating them into your daily practices long before you play them. For example, you can work on down picks in the flex and how to play them, screens on the block and how to play the cutter, double-down screens and how to play them, and whatever else your league opponents might do—and later . . . when you introduce the opponents' offenses and defenses, your players already will be familiar with the techniques necessary to combat them." Chapman, Larry F., and Warren, William E. *Basketball Coach's Survival Guide*, p. 145.

PLAYING STYLES: FOOTBALL

With a Good football team, there are at least three offensive styles a coach might choose from. First, of course, there is the power-oriented attack that is primarily based on overwhelming opponents by force rather than guile (although both elements may be evident in various phases of the offense). Second, the coach might choose option football. Third, there are the "off-the-wall" offenses that some coaches prefer. Three examples from the latter category are the single wing, the Notre Dame box, and shotgun passing attack.

Because its basic requirements don't change much from one season to the next, most football coaches tend to gravitate toward power. It's a solid rock upon which to build a strong program for years to come. Its basics are generally straightforward and easily learned, and a good feeder program can keep you supplied with athletes who can make it work for you. Its only real limitation is that, in a strictly power-against-power approach, the stronger team will win every time—and if your team isn't the strongest team, you're limited in how far that style will take you.

Properly applied, triple-option football can probably take you where you want to go faster than a power-oriented approach. While the weaknesses of option football are obvious (e.g., its high-risk fumbling potential and its relative weakness as a catch-up offense), it's also true that "it is easier to learn to run the triple-option play than to learn how to defense it properly."[6] The belief that defenses have caught up with the option play is a fallacy based on misapplication of the offense, either by using it primarily as a power formation or by aligning the backs deeper than originally intended by the creators of the offense. *Any* offense is essentially a power offense when you align your running backs seven yards deep in the backfield.

The advantage of option play is that you are practicing only one play rather than an entire series of plays, especially with a Good team that is likely to lose up to one-third of its games. You can dictate where eight of the opposing players must be positioned in order to properly defense the three options. In addition, your opponents' nonoption quarterback has probably been running the option play in practice the week before your game to get their

---

[6] Warren, William, and Scarborough, Stan. *Option Football: Concepts and Techniques for Winning.* (Boston: Allyn & Bacon, 1983), p. x (Preface).

defense ready to face your option quarterback, who has spent the entire preseason and every daily practice since then learning to read defenses and run the options efficiently and accurately.

Option football is not necessarily superior to other styles; you don't have to abandon what you're currently using to become a disciple of the Wishbone, Veer, or I formation. But the triple option is, or can be, a shortcut to success because it is so difficult to defense when taught and used properly. If you don't understand it, don't use it—but on the other hand, you shouldn't reject it simply because much of what you've heard about it is negative.

I've always liked the idea of having a team that is difficult to prepare for. One way to do it is to have more good athletes than anyone you play. The other way to cause problems is to run something that no one else runs.

In the case of run-oriented offenses, there's probably a very good reason why most coaches don't use Bobby Dodd's (Georgia Tech) belly series anymore—or the aforementioned Notre Dame box or single wing, or the Lombardi sweep—as a bread-and-butter play. Bob Dylan was right: The times, they *are* a-changin', and the game has grown far more sophisticated than it was in the old days of two-platoon football.

The same cannot be said of pass-oriented offenses, however. Whether you use the shotgun or a dropback/rollout passing attack, high school defenses haven't improved to the point where passing is necessarily a low-percentage proposition, provided you have a quarterback and receiver who can find the seams and holes in the defense.

Most coaches, mindful of Darrell Royal's (University of Texas) warning that "there are only three things that can happen when you put the ball in the air, and two of them are bad," are run-oriented in their thinking. To many coaches, passing is what you do on third-and-twelve if you don't run a draw play; the rest of the time, you *run.* That most coaches prefer to run the ball unless forced to do otherwise is a convincing argument for passing more often than they would like to see you do it—provided, of course, that your quarterback's arm is somewhat more substantial than wet spaghetti.

To use passing more often, you have to believe in passing as strongly as does LaVell Edwards at Brigham Young. You also have to live with the idea that, if your star quarterback goes down and doesn't get up, you might as well have bought round-trip tickets on the Titanic.

Another way to make game preparations difficult for opposing coaches is to use a wide variety of offensive formations and include a lot of motion.

PLAYING STYLES—BASKETBALL

Because their strengths generally outnumber their weaknesses, Good teams are capable of mastering—and winning with—a playing style that is geared toward their players' strengths. While these strengths afford Good teams a certain amount of versatility, their weaknesses tend to limit that versatility to specific situations and specific opponents (i.e., teams of equal or lesser ability).

Good teams are most likely to be effective operating within a single offensive or defensive style, whether simple or complex.[7] For example, a basketball coach whose teams are always Good (or better than that) told me that, although he never varies from his 1-2-2 half-court zone defense, regardless of the situation or opponent, he uses it in a variety of ways. He may use it in its basic form—retaining the "Jug" shape regardless of ball location along the perimeter—or else by double-teaming the ballside low post or employing help-and-recover, match-up, or trapping techniques to confuse opponents or achieve other goals. This is an excellent approach to team defense with a Good basketball team: Choose a defensive style, whether zone or man-to-man, that you're comfortable with and that fits your coaching philosophy, and milk it for all it's worth—using variations of that style to provide diversity rather than trying to teach your players two vastly different playing styles. That way, at least, you're never straying far from what your players know and do best.

The same principle applies equally well to team offense, which should incorporate and emphasize whatever strengths the team possesses. For instance, having capable ballhandling immediately suggests using some kind of motion offense such as the Flex or passing game, and having one or more tall players who are effective around the basket suggests using an inside power game. Posting up tall guards against smaller defenders in man-to-man coverage is easy to do and offers broad offensive advantages, as any NBA player who

---

[7] To the opponents, that is. No playing style is complex if your players understand it thoroughly.

has ever guarded Magic Johnson, Toni Kukoc, or Danny Manning around the blocks will agree.

The important consideration here is to select a playing style that gives your best offensive player(s) opportunities to use their skills fully within the team context. How much leeway you give those players in terms of freelancing or exercising their skills creatively depends on how much you trust them; however, you may want to limit your other players' freelance opportunities in order to avoid losing control offensively. There's nothing wrong with doing so, since you are fully obligated to ensure that your players have ample opportunities to do what they do best—keeping the team's best interests in mind.

> *The key to winning in baseball is pitching, fundamentals,*
> *and three-run homers.*
>
> —Earl Weaver (Baltimore Orioles)

PLAYING STYLES—BASEBALL

Good baseball teams are sound fundamentally and defensively, and their pitching is at least adequate.

There are two ways that a baseball team might be Good: with strong pitching and adequate hitting, or with adequate pitching and strong hitting. With the former, pitchers should be encouraged to use all of the strike zone; hitters should be coached in a manner similar to that described earlier in the *Weak and Fair Teams* section. With the latter, pitchers should be coached to pitch within themselves, exercise control, and change speeds rather than trying to overpower opposing batters.

A good hitting team should be able to hit and run effectively, and to advance runners by sacrificing themselves—if, that is, you are able to build strong commitment to team goals. To lift their game to the next level, players must be willing to overcome any selfish impulses and forgo their individual stats for the team's sake whenever necessary. More than other team sports, baseball is statistics-oriented; consequently, it's not always easy for coaches to convince their players that such sacrifices are necessary or desirable. One coach explained, "I've had players fail to lay down a bunt and tell me later that they missed the sign, when both of us knew for a fact that they just wanted to swing away. And I'm supposed to recommend *those* players for a college scholarship? Forget it. If they won't play the game *my* way, they won't do it for a college coach, either. They'll end up making me *and* the school look bad."

Whether a Good team is conservative or aggressive on the basepaths depends in part on the amount of power in the lineup, and partly on the coach's philosophy and the players' speed and knowledge of baserunning. Consider this, however: It's easier to control aggressive baserunners in critical situations than it is to increase the baserunning efficiency of players who are basically passive.

VERY GOOD TEAMS

Year in and year out, no men's college basketball team plays a tougher regular-season schedule than the University of Louisville team.

With two NCAA titles to his credit, Denny Crum understands the importance of preparing his teams for postseason play. Rather than following the standard practice of scheduling a series of early-season nonconference patsies to pad his won-lost record, Coach Crum seeks out the toughest teams he can find. By doing so, he hopes to prepare his players for the broad array of challenges that NCAA tournament competition always offers. Such strategy tends to produce more regular-season losses than might otherwise be the case; it also places Crum's teams farther down in the Top 20 weekly rankings than a better won-lost mark would produce—and it tends to afford his Cardinals a more difficult road to the Final Four by denying them no. 1 or no. 2 slots in the pairings. He doesn't care, though, because (a) rankings don't win championships, (b) he still has to win the same number of tournament games to get to the Final Four regardless of his tournament seeding, and (c) it's easier to get a team up for tough opponents than to prepare for opponents that are supposed to be pushovers. Like his mentor at UCLA, John Wooden, Crum has his eyes on the prize. He likes the challenge of preparing for difficult opponents.

Also like Wooden, Coach Crum changes his offenses and defenses very little from one year to the next; after two decades at Louisville, he is still using the same high-post offense that he learned as an assistant coach under Wooden at UCLA.

EXTENDED CONTROL CAPABILITIES

Teams that are capable of winning 65–85 percent of their games seldom have to worry about hiding their weaknesses; with the possible exception of depth, they simply don't have the kinds of weaknesses, individually or as a team, that most teams are capable of exploiting. As a result, Very Good teams are free to pursue playing styles that emphasize their strengths and take advantage of opponents' weaknesses.

> *Tradition is a rich asset for any team.*
> *Tradition and success are traveling companions.*
>
> —Wallace Wade (Univ. of Alabama)

In every sport, you'll find schools with rich winning traditions. Such traditions always begin with a coach who has a dream and the ability to communicate that dream to the people who matter most—the players, the school administration, and the community.

Very Good and Great programs come and go; some of them—the ones that are based on superior athletes rather than the combination of superior athletes and effective coaching—are fleeting and transitory. Those that last—the traditional powerhouses that are always found at or near the top of conference or league standings—are due to effective coaching and community support as well as the presence of superior athletes.

In many cases, tradition is rooted in a style of play with which the team becomes identified. In that regard, the school and sport that always come to mind when I attempt to define Very Good teams is Southern Cal football during the 1960s–1970s under coaches John McKay and John Robinson. Admirers referred to the school lovingly as "Tailback U.," referring to the talents of such gifted running backs as O. J. Simpson, Marcus Allen, Ricky Bell, and Charles White—to name a few of the greats who made life miserable for USC foes during that period. Operating from an I formation, the Trojans ran their vaunted "Student Body (Left/Right)" power sweep with chilling effectiveness. It wasn't option football except in the sense that, after the quick pitch to the tailback, Simpson, Allen, Bell, etc., were free to choose which hole they attacked on the side where the play was going. The Trojans passed often enough to keep defenses honest, but running was their game, and they did it very well.

John McKay was the first major college football coach to allow his star running backs to carry the ball thirty to thirty-five times a game. It's a common strategy nowadays (at the high school and college levels, at least), but it was considered daring back in the late 1960s, despite coach McKay's argument that footballs aren't heavy. From the USC experience, coaches learned that big, strong, quick running backs who carry the ball thirty-five times a game aren't any more injury-prone than their smaller counterparts who carry the ball fifteen times a game. More important, coaches learned that: (a) big, speedy running backs positioned seven yards deep in the backfield can hit the line as quickly as slower running backs who are lined up four or five yards deep; (b) offensive linemen don't have to hold their blocks as long for big, fast I backs who hit the line quickly and power their way through arm tackles; and (c) when properly conditioned, such running backs tire far less quickly than the defenders who have to chase and tackle them thirty to thirty-five times a game.

In basketball, Dean Smith (University of North Carolina) probably epitomizes the coach associated with specific playing styles. At various times during his lengthy and highly successful tenure with the Tarheels, Coach Smith has been identified with: the Carolina Corners delay game (before the advent of the shot clock); run-and-jump full-court pressing defense; the passing game freelance offensive style of the 1980s; and man-to-man defense played a number of different ways to keep opponents off balance without switching to zone defense. Such techniques mark Smith, not merely as an innovator who is always looking for ways to improve his teams, but also as a capable tactician who takes his styles of play to the limits of what they are capable of producing.

Coaches like McKay, Robinson, and Smith may have been blessed with players of above-average talent, but they have also used that talent to their—and their teams'—best advantage. Suffice it to say that, with a Very Good team, you'll never stray far from the road to success if you use a style of play that you and your players believe in and are comfortable with. If your style emphasizes your strengths, your players will, in most cases, do the rest by taking advantage of opponents' weaknesses.

A Style to Beware of

Aside from personnel problems—which may encompass such things as satisfying players' desire for adequate playing time, keeping players academically eligible, and handling disciplinary problems—the only real problem facing coaches of Very Good teams is the tendency to play too conservatively. A conservative strategy will tend to keep the score close against stronger opponents and give you a chance to win in the fourth quarter—but against opponents of equal or lesser ability it can also serve to keep *them* in the game and give *them* a chance to win.

As we noted in Chapter 8, aggressive playing styles entail risks that many coaches prefer not to take—but it's also somewhat risky to use a playing style that treats the first three quarters of a game as a warmup for the fourth quarter. With a Good team, I'll be more than happy if your Very Good team uses a cautious playing style that limits both teams' scoring; what makes me uneasy is the idea that your team will come out and blow us away in the *first* quarter, not the fourth. Of course, with superior athletes you just might do that anyway—but the more conservatively your team plays, the less likely it is.

Weak teams play conservatively because they have to; Very Good teams that play conservatively do so because someone—usually, the coach—prefers not to take chances—and that's all right, too. But if you aspire toward Greatness, you might want to consider the words of the Greek philosopher Herodotus (485–425 B.C.): "Great deeds are usually wrought at great risk."

I've seen that glint in Eddie Robinson's eye. He's got that old feeling that you get when you're about to kill a gnat with a sledgehammer.

—Mario Casem (Alcorn State)

GREAT TEAMS

In defining a Great team as one that is capable of dominating its opponents, we're describing the kind of team that all of us would like to coach: a potential state champion, a team with no discernible weaknesses. Coaching such a team can give you delusions of

grandeur regarding your coaching skills, since practically anything
you do is likely to work with players who are better than everyone
else's. Opponents can't control the game tempo because, by definition, your players are at least as good at every tempo as they are, and
probably better. They can't overpower you or outrun you, either—
and if your players are properly conditioned, they can't outlast you.
Their only real hope of defeating you is to plan an error-free game
and hope that your players have an off night, or that your team
comes out flat and unmotivated.

Even then, however, two factors are working in your favor if
you've prepared your team properly. First, because your team is outstanding defensively, it's extremely unlikely that you'll lose control
of opponents even if you don't dominate them. (Again, by definition, you can't have a Great team that isn't outstanding defensively.
As Vince Dooley [University of Georgia] has pointed out, "You've
got to do everything well, but you've got to play defense first.")

With solid defense and players who are fundamentally sound
or highly talented offensively, your team will find ways to win on
those rare occasions when the offensive carburetors aren't carbing
and the pistons aren't working, either. You'll win because your kids
know how to win, expect to win, and play to win regardless of
whether their shots fall, their passes connect with receivers, or their
line drives find the gaps. On such nights, defense will keep you in
the game and your players' skills will do the rest.

Second, motivating your players shouldn't be a problem. In
the case of powerful opponents, your kids will be looking forward
to playing them; and in the case of weaker opponents, you have two
effective motivational approaches at your disposal.

Getting Your Team "Up" for Weaker Opponents

The first approach consists of what might be called "divide-and-conquer"
motivational tactics. It involves telling your players, "We *are* going to win the
game, so don't worry about that. What you should worry about is whether
you're going to be the one doing the winning, or someone else on the team
will be doing it while you're on the bench watching." You can pit either your
first team against your second team (and third team, etc., in football), or individual players from your depth chart against each other. Either way, the message is the same: "If you aren't ready, whether as a unit or individually, to
storm the gates and tear down the walls tonight, I'll find someone

else who is and you can watch (him/her/them) get the playing time that you should be getting."

A complementary approach that ensures high motivation in what might otherwise be meaningless games is to emphasize statistics and individual achievement rather than team goals. I call such games "average-fatteners"—opportunities to artificially inflate totals and averages in whatever statistical categories you keep.[8] Here's how it works:

Let's say that your Great (18–0) basketball team is playing my Fair (7–12) team. You beat us last time by nineteen points in my gym. Realistically, my team has little or no chance of playing you close unless your players decide that the game is already won and all they have to do is walk out on the court and we'll collapse in fear and trembling at their illustrious presence. You don't want your kids to think that way, so in your pregame talk to the team, begin by addressing the subs and benchwarmers:

"Frankly (you say), I don't think they (the starters) want to play tonight, judging from the way they practiced the last couple of days. If I'm right, that means that *this* is going to be the night when you can really shine if you want to."

From there you go around the room, telling players one by one what you expect from them, and what the increased playing time can mean to their individual stats.

"Rodrickus, I've been telling people all season that you're gonna get a triple-double one of these days; well, tonight's the best chance you'll have this season, because it won't get any easier from here on. . . . Shedrick, time's running out if you're gonna break the school record for steals this year. They're not going to hand you the ball, though; you've gotta go out and take it from them! . . . Martin, all you need is fifteen points tonight to raise your average to ten

---

[8] Yes, this is essentially a selfish (as opposed to team-oriented) approach to winning games, but such a strategy is no more opposed to team goals than, say, letting your star running back carry the ball thirty times a game, or urging your leading scorer to look for shots every time your team has the ball.

As NBA great Bill Walton has observed, "Every great player fears something." He was referring, not to playing scared, but rather to the motivation that impels great players toward excellence and winning. The same is true of teams, of course; every Great team fears something. If the fear isn't there on a given night, for whatever reason and however deep it might be submerged in the team's collective psyche, instead of attempting to motivate the team to do what it's expected to do, you might try to motivate individual players toward peak performances in whatever statistical categories you (and they) consider important.

points a game. . . . Alvin, you haven't gotten but four rebounds in the last three games; I'm looking for a season high from you tonight. . . . That applies to you too, Joe, if Alvin decides that he'd rather watch you clean the boards than do it himself. . . . Juan and Freddie, you'll be our on-the-ball defender in our press; if either of you can generate seven steals and forced turnovers tonight, I'll name you our Outstanding Player of the Game no matter what anyone else does. . . ." And so on, and so forth, down the line until you've described individual goals that each player would like to accomplish. Then you promise them playing time sufficient to accomplish those goals if they make an honest effort to achieve them.

Now, you tell me: If you use that sort of approach in preparing your Great team to play my Fair team, how likely is it that your players will come out and play as if the game doesn't matter? Under the circumstances, I'd consider anything less than a thirty-point win by your team to be evidence that my kids played the game of their lives.

Your subs and benchwarmers will be especially receptive to such an approach, since it offers them the chance to show what they're capable of producing if given adequate playing time. (Of course, they *will* receive adequate playing time, whether because your starters put the game out of reach early or because the starters don't respond to your challenges. In either case, my team isn't likely to offer more than token resistance to your superior players.

PLAYING STYLES

With Great players who are extremely gifted athletically, fundamentally sound, intelligent, experienced, and capable of dominating opponents in a variety of ways, virtually anything you do offensively and defensively is likely to work. Still, you have to select a style of play for your players to use, probably from one of the four broad categories named below:

- A simple, basically conservative style that features high-percentage play and forces opponents to play the game your way, toward your strengths and at your tempo

- A complex playing style that generates confusion and indecision as opponents try to figure out (and keep up with) what you're doing

■ A creative or freelance offensive style that permits your players to use the full range of their skills

■ An aggressive style that attacks opponents in order to take the ball away from them or force them into making mistakes

Regarding these styles, in his autobiographical *Hey, Wait a Minute (I Wrote a Book!)*, John Madden said that he never liked the idea of using simple offenses that were easy to defend against, or simple defenses that were easy to attack. Still, how complicated do you have to make a Dream Team III basketball offense or defense to ensure its effectiveness? How big a sledgehammer does it take to kill a gnat?

Complex styles require intelligent, experienced players—but that's not generally a problem with Great teams. One of Tom Landry's players once compared learning the Dallas Cowboys' offensive playbook, with its multiple sets and shifts, to memorizing the Greater Fort Worth-Dallas phone book—but, as many Cowboy opponents of that era would attest, defensing it successfully was similarly challenging and equally frustrating. Dean Smith runs pretty complicated offenses and defenses at UNC, too—but you don't hear anyone complaining about it except Tarheel opponents.

If you're a fan of freelancing (and not using it as an excuse for lazy coaching) it can be highly effective with athletic players. Basketball's passing game offense is essentially freelance, and triple-option football combines elements of freelancing (e.g., the quarterback's option reads) with aggressive tactics designed to attack specific areas of the defense.

Regarding aggressive approaches, we might harken to Darrell Royal's (University of Texas) warning: "You can't be aggressive and confused at the same time." This isn't normally a problem with intelligent players, except while they're learning the offense or defense. From that point on, though, it's likely to be extremely rough going for opponents, since the combination of Great players and an aggressive playing style is incredibly potent.

But if that's so—and it is, as fans of the 1996 Kentucky Wildcats national championship team will agree—*why don't more Great teams do it that way?* Some do, of course (e.g., UNLV in 1991 and the University of Arkansas in 1994), but there's always the risk factor to consider. In basketball, at least, an aggressive playing style can get your players in foul trouble in a hurry. If your depth doesn't go to at least ten players, your aggressive strategy may be more of a gamble than you need to take.

(Incidentally, the fact that more and more college football teams are winning regularly by incredible margins indicates that coaches are becoming more aggressive offensively with each passing year. The same holds true at the high school level in football *and* basketball; the culprit here is the desire to attain a higher state or national ranking, with its attendant publicity for your program. When national championship games are won by 62–14 scores, as Nebraska's Cornhuskers dismantled the Florida Gators in the 1996 Fiesta Bowl, it's evident that Woody Hayes' [Ohio State] "three-yards-and-a-cloud-of-dust" theory of offensive football is largely a thing of the past.)

COACHING HINTS FOR GREAT TEAMS: THREE FOR THE ROAD

To win it all, a team has to be obsessive about the fundamentals and the little things.

—Joe Gibbs (Washington Redskins)

1. DON'T DWELL ON THE FUNDAMENTALS—BUT DON'T FORGET ABOUT THEM

How much practice time you devote to individual fundamentals depends on two factors, namely, the skills involved and how well your players execute them. Some skills—especially those that involve precise training and coordination, such as hitting, pitching, and fielding in baseball; shooting, dribbling, and passing in basketball; and passing and receiving in football—are so complex as to merit work in those areas every day. Other skills, such as those involving strength, may not require regular work except when timing is also involved. The best indicator that fundamentals work is needed is that what you're currently doing isn't working.

Stripped to their lowest common denominators, plays and patterns are nothing more than action sequences involving timing and the execution of fundamental skills. When the timing is wrong, practice the play; when the execution is wrong, go back to the basics and work on the fundamentals.

The price of victory is high, but so are the rewards.

—Bear Bryant (Univ. of Alabama)

2. YOU CAN—AND SHOULD—WORK GREAT TEAMS HARD IN YOUR DAILY PRACTICES

You *can* do it because, unlike players on Weak teams, players on Great teams won't quit on you if you work them hard.

You *should* do it because no individual or team can achieve its full potential with less than a total effort in daily practice as well as in games. Thinking otherwise inevitably leads to falling short of one's goals, regardless of how high (or how low) those aspirations might be. Psychologically, the difference between Weak and Great players is that, while Weak players focus on the effort involved and its attendant physical discomfort, Great players focus on the rewards.

Perhaps Vince Lombardi said it even better: "Each Sunday, after the battle, one group savors victory; another lives on the bitterness of defeat. The practice and the hard work of the season seem a small price for having won. But there are no reasons that are adequate for having lost."[9]

Your players understand that; you should, too.

Any athlete with pride wants to compete against the best.

—Lance Alworth,
San Diego Chargers receiver

3. GREAT TEAMS RESPOND TO GREAT CHALLENGES

Great teams need, first of all, a challenging schedule. Challenges are the life's blood of Great teams and Great players; without sufficient challenges, they grow stale and listless in their performances, and their attitude toward playing suffers accordingly. Worse, they cease to grow and develop, and they lose the competitive sharpness that otherwise characterizes their play.

---

[9] Lombardi, Vince, *Vince Lombardi on Football*, Vol. 1, p. 16.

From a coaching standpoint, the thrill of watching the way Great players respond to great challenges cannot be matched. They may not always win, but even when they don't, the level of competitiveness is likely to produce individual and team performances that linger in the memory long after the game itself has ended.

Great players don't have to be externally motivated (i.e., inspired by their coach) to get "up" for big games; all they need to know is that the game is important, and how they should play it. Supplied with that information, they'll do the rest. You just sit back and enjoy the ride.

10

THE UNCONTROLLABLES

THE LUCK FACTOR

Are you superstitious?[1]
Do you believe in luck?[2]

Most coaches probably hold beliefs similar to those of Bill Watterson's comic strip character Calvin (of "Calvin and Hobbes"). Like Calvin, who plays the odds in case Santa Claus exists, some coaches won't allow their "game" clothes (including underwear) to be washed as long as the team is winning; some male coaches don't shave during a winning streak; and—possibly the strangest superstition of all—one high school basketball coach swears that the secret of his team's success one season was his finding money on campus.

"We started out 18–0," the coach said in his slow, south Georgia drawl, "and I found money before every one of those games. Sometimes it was a nickel, or maybe a dime or a quarter, but mostly it was pennies. I'd find them in the parking lot, or in the hallway or out on the p. e. field. Mostly, though, I found them in the gym. Students sitting in the bleachers at the beginning and end of p. e. class liked to toss pennies across the gym floor when nobody was

---

[1] "I don't believe in a jinx or a hex. Winning (in football) depends on how well you block and tackle." —Ralph (Shug) Jordan, Auburn University

[2] "If you think you're lucky, you are." —Bobby Dodd (Georgia Tech)

looking. Sometimes I found money when we pushed the bleachers back and swept the floor the morning after games.

"All I know is, the first game we lost came when I didn't find any pennies. We were 19–4 that year—but we were 19–0 in games where I found money beforehand."

"Had that ever happened to you before?" I asked. "And has it ever happened again?"

"Naw," he said. "I'm not usually superstitious like that. But it just kept building up as we kept on winning until all of us, the players and managers too, started believing it."

"Maybe they were leaving pennies where they knew you'd find them," I suggested.

He nodded. "Yeah, I thought of that, too. But they swore that they weren't the ones doing it. It didn't really matter, though, because they were playing like they believed luck was on their side."

And therein, perhaps, lies the answer. If you believe that you're going to win, whether by luck, skill, or anything else—or that you *deserve* to win, for whatever reason—you'll *play* to win. The line that separates winning and losing can be exceedingly fine; when teams are evenly matched physically, the winning edge may be found in the psychological advantages.

> *Sure, luck means a lot in football.*
> *Not having a good quarterback is bad luck.*
>
> —Don Shula (Miami Dolphins)

THE TWO SIDES OF LUCK

Unfortunate circumstances are the breaks of the game; their only redeeming feature is that, in the long run, they tend to equalize. Today, it's *our* All-State player who goes down, or *our* player whose desperation play succeeds and wins the game; next time, the agony or the ecstasy may be the opponents'. Nobody has a corner on good *or* bad luck, but the pessimist tends to believe that a glass of water is half empty, while the optimist sees the same glass as half full.[3] What we think of as "getting the breaks"—whether they fall our way or the opponents'—often isn't a matter of good or bad luck; it's due to other factors.

---

[3] "An optimist," one coach told me, "is a coach whose team hasn't played its first game yet."

We've all seen enough last-second desperation plays succeed to know that sometimes they win games (except when *our* team tries them, of course). But do they *really* win games? It's often difficult to believe otherwise—but unless both teams played perfectly up to the point where a desperation play is attempted, one team or the other (and probably *both* teams) squandered opportunities earlier in the game that would have rendered the final scoring attempt meaningless.

Many coaches believe that games are won or lost, not by good or bad luck, but by the degree of offensive and defensive control that our teams are able to exert over our opponents. We'll take wins any way we can get them—good, bad, or ugly—but unless we've managed to control the opponents (whether throughout a game or in sections where we really needed to), we don't feel in our heart of hearts that we deserved to win. And if we've played hard and given it our best shot, we've earned the victory, regardless of the final score. Winning can also be an attitude and a state of mind.

I'm as superstitious as the next coach; it shows most clearly in my belief that *teams are given only a certain number of chances to affect the final outcomes of games, and when enough of them are squandered (however many chances there might be), losing is inevitable.*

That is, in fact, the basis for many coaches' philosophy and style: to prepare their players in terms of (a) the skills necessary to win games, and (b) being ready to take advantage of chances to affect the final outcome of games—whenever and wherever they arise.

> *Chance favors the prepared mind.*
>
> Louis Pasteur (*The Life of Pasteur*, 1927)

Like the late New York Yankees slugger Roger Maris, many coaches believe that games are won, not by chance, but by preparation.[4] If your kids are ready to take advantage of opportunities when they arise; and if they're looking for—and are prepared to deal with—the unexpected as well as the expected, they will get more than their share of the breaks along the way, courtesy of opponents who aren't so well prepared. To make a difference, lucky breaks have to be capitalized on.

---

[4] "Luck is what happens when preparation meets opportunity." —Darrell Royal

LOOKING FOR THE BREAKS

Every sport has its drills for preparing players to expect the unexpected. Football has its defensive tip drills and fumble recovery drills; in basketball, Bobby Knight practices bad pass drills, loose ball drills, and others to accustom his players to finding the ball in unexpected places. You can find such drills and others for your sport in the various coaching drills books—or you can devise drills of your own. In either case, you are stacking the deck in your favor when you teach your players to anticipate the breaks of the game and turn them in your team's favor.

Luck is what you make of it—and the less you make of it, the better off you probably are. Harking back to the coach who found pennies, you can use the idea that your team has Lady Luck in its corner to provide an occasional psychological boost—but you should be aware that that strategy can backfire, too, when you don't find the pennies. After all, the coach was 0–4 in his penniless games, two of which came when he needed them the most—in the playoffs.

If you bring up the luck factor at all to your players (and most coaches probably don't), it should be in this context: *We are going to make our own good luck by forcing the opponents into mistakes, and by taking advantage of their errors when they occur.* Every team suffers bad breaks in the course of every game; don't encourage your players to regard it as evidence that luck is working against them. (Coaches aren't the only pessimists in the world.) Such thinking not only offers easy excuses for losing; it increases the chances of players' giving up when the breaks are going against them.

> *Luck is what you have left over after you give 100 percent.*
>
> —Langston Coleman, football player
> (University of Nebraska)

Why should luck be considered a factor in winning at all? This question—and its answer—cuts to the very heart of the coaching mentality. Coaches want to win games, but they cannot control the unpredictable flight or fortuitous bounce of the ball. When luck— or fate, or the *chance factor,* or whatever you want to call it—kicks in, the coach is powerless to control the outcomes of games except within rather narrow limits. And within those limits, *control* is the name of the game.

CONTROLLING THE UNCONTROLLABLES

Assuming that both teams show up to play a game, the outcome will be decided in one of three ways:

1. Your team may win the game or lose it through the quality of your play.
2. The opponents may win the game or lose it through the quality of their play.
3. Other factors may affect a team's chances of winning or losing the game.

The first two outcomes relate directly to coaches' efforts to prepare their teams to win. Those efforts may encompass any or all of four overlapping strategies: taking advantage of one's strengths; hiding one's weaknesses; neutralizing opponents' strengths; and taking advantage of opponents' weakness. All of those strategies fall within the scope of what coaches can control—on paper, at least.

Some things, however, are largely beyond our control, like death, taxes, and saving the ozone layer or the Brazilian rain forests. And luck. And officials' calls, most of which are as final as Supreme Court decisions. Other factors may be equally uncontrollable—yet given our nature as control-oriented beings, it is hardly surprising that most of us try to control them. Whether such measures are feasible—or ethical—depends on their interpretation, and on the nature of the factors as well.

PLAYING CONDITIONS—OUTDOORS

Unless your cousin runs a cloud-seeding operation, you're probably not going to do much about the weather except talk about it. You can, however, prepare your players for inclement weather by practicing under muddy conditions or in the rain, if you're not put off by little things like an occasional lightning bolt. You can have your players do more stretching exercises than usual when competing outdoors in cold weather. You can alter your playing surface to accommodate your team's style of play or impede your opponents' style of play:

▪ In the 1960s when the L. A. Dodgers' Maury Wills was stealing every base that wasn't nailed down, the team's groundskeeper went to great lengths to protect the basepaths at the Chavez Ravine stadium from moisture. The result was clay surfaces that were baked so hard they could have been used for skateboarding. To combat the Dodgers' speed, opponents routinely watered down their own basepaths and infields so thoroughly when the Dodgers were in town that their pitchers' mounds looked like high ground in a flash flood.

▪ A football coach whose slow-footed squad needed all the help they could get described his theory of groundskeeping thus:

Players run faster on hard surfaces that give them better traction. That's a fact, or else you'd see them running track meets on grass. And since my kids aren't likely to outrun anybody who isn't using a walker to get around, I try to slow down the other guys every way I can find, like watering down the field all day, every day during the season. Our monthly water bill probably looks like it was supposed to go to a Las Vegas golf course, but since our kids are as slow as a one-legged tightrope walker, I want the other team to slow down a tad, too.

With a slow team like this one, I won't mow the grass either. I checked the rules, and there's nothing in there that says how often you have to cut the grass. Our field hasn't been mowed but once since late July. (The coach was speaking in late September.) Our quarterback is a little bitty guy, a freshman, and when he squats down under center all you can see is his head. It doesn't make him any harder to tackle, but if that tall grass slows down the other teams even a smidgen, it's worth it.

("*Is* it worth it?" I asked. He shrugged.)

Who knows? We haven't won a game yet, and we're getting beaten by 43 points a game—but only by 35 points a game at home. That eight points a game less isn't much, I guess, but it helps me to feel that I'm doing all I can to give our kids a chance to play against better teams. And there isn't much else I *can* do that I haven't done already, at least, not until the refs start taking MasterCard, or we get some players who run faster than a turtle with arthritis!

PLAYING CONDITIONS—INDOORS

The standard length of basketball courts is 84' × 50', but many older gyms are decidedly substandard. I recall one old gym that was so small that the court had four sidelines and two half-court lines. With bleachers crowding the regulation sidelines, the narrower sidelines were used to inbound the ball, after which the regular sidelines formed the boundaries during play. And instead of a half-court line and hash marks to mark the midcourt area, the hash marks had been replaced by solid red lines across the court that marked the overlapping half-court areas. If it sounds confusing, it was—to visiting teams. The collapsing/expanding court dimensions were, in the coach's estimation, worth six points a game for his team.

It has been said that the parquet floor of the old Boston Garden was worth several turnovers a game to the Celtics by influencing opposing dribblers toward the dead spots in the floor.

Basketball players who are used to playing on wooden floors sometimes have difficulty adjusting to quieter surfaces that absorb much of the sound of dribbles.

Lighting. I used to dread taking my basketball teams to one of the schools in our area, not because their teams were superior to ours—they weren't—but because the lighting was so atrocious in their gym. The walls were dingy gray, the backboards an opaque gray from years of use, and the paint had long since faded from the rim. Perimeter shooting was inadvisable in the dim lighting because the rim literally disappeared in a sea of grays somewhere about 10 feet out from the basket.

"In dark gyms," a basketball coach once advised me, "use set plays or a continuity pattern that gives you layups or shots inside the paint. The defense will sag on you and give you the three-point shot if you do that, but even so I think you're better off looking for the high-percentage shots inside than taking shots you can't make because the lighting is poor." I agree.

Visiting teams faced exactly the opposite problem at another gym in our region. There was a stage with bright fluorescent lights overhead at one end of the floor, and whenever the visitors had that end of the court their free-throw shooters were blinded by the lights shining through the backboard.

When I complained to the referees, they said the coach told them that the switch that controlled the stage lights also controlled some of the overhead lights. When the teams exchanged ends at halftime, the lights on the stage were off. All of the overhead lights were burning brightly.

The steps involved in handling such a problem are: (1) Complain to the referees and the head coach of the home team. If nothing is done, (2) alert your principal to the problem and ask her or him to discuss the problem with the other principal. If nothing is done, (3) take the poor lighting in the first half. If you can keep the score close, at least you'll have better lighting in the second half when most close games are decided one way or the other.[5]

We've played in old gyms in which more than half of the overhead lights were burned out, and in other gyms in which so many bulbs were defective in the scoreboard that we couldn't read the score or time remaining—and I've wondered: *Is it laziness on the part of the coaches, or are they trying to give their teams an unfair edge?* Either way, it's not the sort of thing that any self-respecting coach can be proud of.

Heating/Cooling. The coach who used fluorescent lights to his advantage had a few other tricks up his sleeve. One year, for instance, we played a road game at his place in early December. Although the gymnasium itself was stiflingly hot, there was no heat in the visitors' dressing rooms. Several window panes were missing and cold air was streaming in. The cold water faucets and showers were going full blast with the handles removed; the sinks were overflowing; the dressing room floors were flooded; and someone had placed two-by-fours on the floor for us to walk on. The coach acted surprised when I told him about it. "It must have been vandals," he said. "We've had a lot of vandalism at the school lately."

I might have believed him, except for our previous problems with the lighting—and the planks that had been carefully laid out end to end to form paths from the door to the benches where the players dressed. The coach could not imagine where they had come

---

[5] Similar thinking should guide your choice of ends of the court in old gyms where one end—the basket nearest the front door—is colder than the other end due to frigid air rushing in whenever the door is opened. In the girls game, take the colder end in the first half. In the boys game that follows, take the warmer end the first half, since the doors won't be opening to admit spectators as often in the third quarter and thereafter.

from or who had put them there, either. I noticed, though, that he didn't offer to swap dressing rooms with us.

Unheated visitors' dressing rooms in winter weather—especially in football—are, unfortunately, a rather common ploy exercised by coaches who have forgotten (if they ever knew it) that the games we play are just that—*games*. One football coach purposely gives visiting teams the wrong keys to the locker room and toilet facilities, then says that his manager must have lost the proper set of keys. Such excuses tend to ring false when you hear them every year, with variations, from the same coach.

If you anticipate such unethical coaching behavior, you can have your players suit up at home and tell the bus driver to warm up the bus prior to halftime to give the players and coaches shelter from the cold. You can also comment about such unsavory tactics to motivate your players to give your opponents the whipping they— or their coach, to be more accurate, deserve.

Another alternative, if they're neither a region or subregion opponent nor a traditional rival, is to drop them from your schedule. You can, as one coach did, arrange for someone to videotape the deplorable conditions you find. (The coach showed the tape to his principal and superintendent of schools, who promptly sent copies of the videotape to the other school's principal and the state high school association along with angry letters protesting such unethical treatment. The problem vanished, only to be replaced subsequently by other subtle but equally irritating forms of unethical behavior [e.g., no lights—or no chairs or benches—in the dressing rooms, unflushed toilets overflowing and filling the room with noxious odors, no locks on the dressing room doors, etc.])

Incidentally, the state high school association did nothing to alleviate the problem, simply because there was nothing in its bylaws that covered the sort of things we're referring to here. It's possible that, in such cases, enough letters of protest from offended schools might spark some kind of investigation or letter of condemnation at the state level—but it's equally possible that nothing will be done. A coach with an unsavory reputation for questionable treatment of visiting teams has never mended his ways in nearly three decades in the profession. His teams have been good enough over the years that he should have long since outgrown his need to play it fast and loose with the limits of ethical behavior, but he's still going strong.

Crowds. At the college level, especially, many new gyms have the first row of spectators' seats crowding the court to amplify fan noise, inspire the home team's players, and make it difficult for the visiting coach to communicate with his or her players during timeouts. One way to counter this problem is to have your fans sit directly behind your bench. Since that doesn't always work—your fans may arrive late and find most of those seats already taken—other strategies may be necessary. You can try moving your bench to an open end of the court—assuming that fans sit on both sides of the court but not behind one or the other baseline.[6] You can also move your bench to wherever your fans happen to be sitting, if they're in a group.

It's not bad strategy to educate your fans always to sit together in as large a group as possible at road games, no matter how tightly packed they may have to be to do so. Once, when a group of hecklers were being especially malicious, crude, and vulgar in their catcalls to my girls in the game and on the bench, we moved the team lock, stock, and barrel into the stands and surrounded ourselves with our fans!

Educating your players to proper road behavior is equally important. My rules of thumb, which are relaxed somewhat in non-hostile environments, are: *Never speak to an opposing player or coach. Never,* ever *speak to any fan (except ours) before, during, or after the game. And never,* ever, EVER *leave the group or go off alone.*

CONTROLLING THE GAME OFFICIALS (REFEREES AND UMPIRES)

My father-in-law, the late Joe Bell, was both a high school coach of considerable accomplishment and a philosopher. "There are," he once told me, "three things that are beyond human comprehension: God, wives, and referees."

PROBLEMS WITH REFEREES

Three inevitable problem areas tend to produce adversary relationships between coaches and officials:

---

[6] This won't work at the state tournament level, where bench locations are assigned.

1. Referees, even the very best of them, are human. They make mistakes—and when they do, one of the teams suffers the consequences.

2. Mistakes aside, referees and umpires have a vastly different perpective on games from that of coaches. Coaches are interested in winning games; since calls made against our team reduce our chances of winning, we tend to agree with those that go our way and disagree with the rest. Referees, on the other hand, don't care who wins. Their concerns are dual—ensuring that the game proceeds from start to finish in an orderly manner, and establishing consistency in their calls and noncalls.

3. Aside from the professional ranks, referees and umpires are amateurs; officiating is a second job that affords them supplemental income. Some officials are very good—conscientious, fair, and hard working—but none of them spends as much time working at the craft as a coach does. And unlike coaches, officials aren't fired when a team loses more games than school administrators, boosters, or fans will tolerate.

TRAITS TO LOOK FOR IN GOOD OFFICIALS

They know the rules and understand the game. They are consistent, fair, honest, and willing to acknowledge their mistakes. They constantly search for favorable viewing angles as the action unfolds on the court or playing field. They have a sense of humor, enjoy their association with the game, and seldom lose their self-control.

> *You can say something to popes, kings, and presidents.*
> *But you can't talk to officials. In the next war,*
> *they ought to give everybody a whistle.*
>
> —Abe Lemons (Univ. of Texas)

Referees to beware of. A few bad referees can make *all* officials look bad by doing such things as: speeding up slow games by ignoring violations that would stop the clock; overlooking minor infractions or violations by a team that is hopelessly behind in order to keep the game score respectable; trying to call an equal number of fouls against each basketball team as evidence of their impartiality;[7] letting the home crowd influence their calls; holding long-standing grudges against coaches they've had trouble with in the past; or abusing their power (e.g., by having "rabbit ears" and looking for opportunities to penalize a particular coach or team).

WHAT YOU CAN (AND CANNOT) DO ABOUT POOR OFFICIATING

You cannot correct an official's incompetence—but you *can* report instances of incompetence (e.g., ignorance of the rules) to the state high school association. You can arrange with your officials' association to have certain officials barred from calling your home games, or you can change associations altogether. (Be aware, though, that officials, like elephants, have long memories, and you're likely to face those same officials in your road games.) You can also keep files on individual referees until you get to know them—including such information as temperament, game control, mobility, consistency, fairness to visiting teams, limits of allowable incidental contact, accessibility to coaches, and so on. A good way to ensure objectivity in your assessments is to watch the officials while you're on the road scouting.

UNDERSTANDING AND USING REFEREES TO YOUR ADVANTAGE

In all team sports, officiating crews divide the playing area into smaller, individual areas of responsibilities—the most obvious example being baseball's umpire behind the plate and one or more others in the field. Those coverage zones are somewhat fluid or elastic in sports such as basketball, expanding or contracting with ball and player movement. In all cases, however—and in all team sports—the officials' primary responsibility is to watch the players in their particular coverage areas; they are free to assist in watching other areas only when their own responsibilities are concluded, however briefly.

Basketball and hockey (to name two such sports) are continuous-action, high-speed games that are played in a relatively small, confined space. With ten to twelve players constantly in motion and reacting to player and ball or puck movement, contact is both inevitable and difficult to assess—whether two referees are used, or three. When illegal

---

[7] The tip-off to such intentions can be seen when they consult the scorebook at halftime and count the fouls against each team.

contact occurs, it often arises suddenly, unexpectedly, and momentarily while players are moving around the playing area at full speed. It often becomes largely a matter of guesswork for the referees to determine who initiated contact that results in a penalty or foul. The problem may be further compounded by the presence of other players blocking the official's view when the illegal contact occurs. In such cases, referees tend to penalize the player who reacts to the contact—or else to base their calls on who they think was most likely to have initiated the contact.

A few years ago, a coach had a small, scrappy but inexperienced basketball team composed mainly of freshmen and sophomores. She worked them hard on blocking out around the basket; playing tough, hard-nosed player-to-player defense; taking the charge; and the like. "The refs never gave us a break," she said. "When we blocked out, the refs allowed taller opponents to crowd us from behind and reach over our backs to get rebounds; when we tried to take charges, they called blocking fouls on us. More than one referee suggested that I quit whining about the officiating and teach my kids how to play the game."

Two years later, when those same players were juniors and seniors, her team won twenty-four games and *she* was the one getting the breaks—not her opponents. They were still the smallest team in their neck of the woods, but while their overall skills were vastly improved, she said, they weren't nearly as good as the refs thought they were.

"We were still blocking out and taking charges," she said, "but now the referees were calling the fouls in our favor because they thought we were better than the teams we played." Perhaps they were, too, but the coach said that in one game she counted seven calls that she thought should have gone against her team but didn't; in another (home) game she apologized to the visitors' coach for a series of bad calls against his team that made it look as if the refs were homers. They weren't cheating, she said; she was too poor to have bought the refs, even if she—and they—had been so inclined.[8] "They were just giving my players the benefit of the doubt on the

---

[8] This recalls the words of ex-Georgia Southern University football coach Erkskine "Erk" Russell regarding recruiting. (Under NCAA rules, Division I-AA teams were allowed seventy football scholarships, but GSU could afford only fifty-five.) Said Erk, "We'd like to cheat, but we don't have the money."

same close calls they had given to our opponents two years earlier, because we didn't look like the same team."

The moral of this little object lesson is simple: *If you want the game officials to give you the breaks, your players must be at least as highly skilled and fundamentally sound as most of the teams they play.* In basketball, you must eliminate the obvious fouls (e.g., reaching in from behind, stepping across the dribbler's path, hand-checking, swinging at opponents' shots rather than merely blocking them, etc.) and concentrate on the fundamentals: stance (stationary and moving) and position (overplaying, blocking out, etc.).

Games are often decided by two or three crucial calls—and if your players have a solid grasp of the fundamentals, it can be worth three or four calls in your team's favor during the course of a game. If the game officials believe, consciously or unconsciously, that your team—or your star player—seldom makes mistakes, they will be inclined to give your team or player the benefit of the doubt in close calls.

Think about it: When was the last time you saw Michael Jordan called for traveling or Jerry Rice called for offensive pass interference?

Certain styles of play also affect the way officials call games. For example, hand-checking arose in basketball because players were too lazy to play defense with their feet. As more and more players hand-checked dribblers, referees chose to ignore it rather than call eighty-seven fouls on each team and risk finishing the game with the teams playing one-on-one.

The same applies to all types of physical play, and to most team sports: If a team takes its push-and-shove, bump-and-run, scratching, clawing, and holding tactics to the limit of what is acceptable under the rules, the officials may initially try to enforce a kinder, gentler approach to the game by whistling infractions. As the game wears on and the physical team shows no inclination to let up, however, the officials will begin to overlook some, and then *most* of the questionable tactics. There are at least two reasons why this is so:

1. *Time constraints.* Penalties take time to be resolved; referees are understandably leery of being involved in high school games called by curfew or lasting beyond midnight when the fault might be construed as theirs for calling the game(s) too close-

ly. They also have their own agendas (travel, work the next day) to consider. No one, least of all the referees, wants to get home from a game at 3:00 A.M.

2. *Consistency.* Every referee, from the top of the list to the bottom of the barrel, wants to be consistent in his or her calls. For example, since no football game would ever end if the refs called offensive holding every time it occurred, the officials must exercise selectivity in their calls. This in turn means setting and maintaining a standard of acceptable holding. Consistency also refers to calling infractions equally against both teams; it doesn't look good from the referees' standpoint to make seventeen holding calls and nine spearing calls against one team and none against the other team. The refs can't seem to be enforcing the rules in such a manner as to penalize one team but not the other. As a consequence, officials tend to prefer to accept a broader interpretation of holding that will affect both teams equally.

Taken together, these two aspects of referee behavior explain why we so often see basketball games in which one official makes most of the calls and the other one seems to have lost his or her whistle; they aren't consistent *with each other.* One is calling the game closely, and the other—the noncaller—is exercising a more liberal interpretation of what constitutes acceptable contact or movement. They aren't cheating, although it may look like it.

It's important for coaches to know that playing an extremely physical game—and we're not talking about playing dirty or trying to hurt an opponent—tends to force referees to accept contact that they might not consider legal in a less physical game. That is certainly true in basketball, and it probably holds true for other contact sports as well. There's not a referee in the world who would admit it, but *every call is a judgment call,* in the sense that the official has to decide whether to blow the whistle or not.

Teach your players to play solid, fundamental defense—and then teach them an ultraphysical, aggressive, in-your-face, hardnosed, scratching, clawing, bruising, did-somebody-get-the-tag-number-of-that-truck? defensive style that doesn't give the opponents an inch of space or the referees a second to catch their breath all night long. If you do *your* job of teaching your players along those lines, and if they do *their* job in dogging opponents relentlessly from the first second to the last of every game, the refs will do *their* job—and they'll do it *your* way at least nine times out of ten, provided that they think your players are fundamentally sound. Now, *that's* control!

INDEX